THE
OUT-OF-SYNC
CHILD

EXCEPTIONAL

SYMBOL
OF
EXCELLENCE

PARENT MAGAZINE

THE

OUT-OF-SYNC

CHILD

Recognizing and Coping
with Sensory Integration Dysfunction

CAROL STOCK KRANOWITZ, M.A.

A SKYLIGHT PRESS BOOK

A Perigee Book

Research about sensory integration dysfunction is ongoing and subject to interpretation. Although all reasonable efforts have been made to include the most up-to-date and accurate information in this book, there can be no guarantee that what we know about this complex subject won't change with time. Readers with concerns about the neurologoical development of their children should consult a qualified professional. Neither the publisher, the author, nor the producer take any responsibility for any possible consequences from any treatment or action by any person reading or following the information in this book.

A Perigee Book
Published by The Berkley Publishing Group
A division of Penguin Putnam Inc.
375 Hudson Street
New York, NY 10014

Copyright © 1998 by Skylight Press and Carol Stock Kranowitz
Book design by Jennifer Ann Daddio
Cover design by Charles Björklund
Cover photograph © by Tony Stone Images
Interior illustrations by T. J. Wylie

Published by arrangement with Skylight Press, 260 West 72nd Street, Suite 6-C, New York, NY 10023.

First edition: March 1998

Published simultaneously in Canada.

The Penguin Putnam Inc. World Wide Web site address is
http://www.penguinputnam.com

Library of Congress Cataloging-in-Publication Data
Kranowitz, Carol Stock.
     The out-of-sync child : recognizing and coping with sensory integration dysfunction / by Carol Stock Kranowitz ; foreword by Larry B. Silver.
         p.   cm.
     Includes bibliographical references and index.
     ISBN 0-399-52386-3
     1. Minimal brain dysfunction in children.   2. Sensorimotor integration.
3. Perceptual-motor learning.   I. Title.
RJ496.B7K72   1998
618.92′8—dc21   97-14601

Printed in the United States of America   CIP
20   19   18   17

FOR ALAN

Contents

FOREWORD

The brain and mind are beautifully interwoven. Our feelings, thoughts, and actions can only occur through the
complex actions of the brain. Any changes in the brain,
even subtle changes, can have a major impact on our feelings, thoughts, and actions. Professionals can no longer
understand the psychology of the mind without understanding the biology of the brain. What is equally true is
that parents of children and adolescents with modified or
faulty "wiring" of the brain cannot fully understand their
son or daughter without fully understanding the underlying changes in the brain and the impact these changes
have on the mind.

For me, this awakening began in the 1960s. My training in Child and Adolescent Psychiatry focused only on
the psychology of the mind. The explosion of brain
research provided understanding of many disorders found
with children and adolescents because of microscopic or
chemical changes in the brain.

As we gained new knowledge about Learning Disabilities and Language Disabilities, we learned how these
problems interfere with reading, writing, math, and organization skills. We learned that these problems interfere
not only with academic progress, but also with success in

sports, social interactions, and family life. Our growing understanding led to the fields of special education and speech-language therapy, which focus on helping individuals overcome or compensate for their disabilities.

Individuals with these changes look normal. Yet, subtle areas of their nervous systems are not functioning as they should. These changes result in behaviors that confuse, frustrate, and anger parents and teachers. They wonder why these children lack self-help skills, become aggressive or withdrawn in a group, or refuse to participate in activities or sports.

In addition to problems in learning and language, children might have problems developing the ability to process information received through their senses. These children or adolescents might have problems interpreting sights, sounds, and sensations of touch and movement. They might become unusually upset by bright lights or loud noises, or by being touched or moved unexpectedly.

They also might have problems controlling, orchestrating, and using their muscles effectively. When it is hard for them to coordinate groups of large muscles (gross motor) and/or small muscles (fine motor), they might have trouble mastering running, jumping, hopping, or climbing. They might have difficulty with buttoning, zipping, or tying, and with coloring, cutting, or writing. This difficulty getting their hands and bodies to do what their head is thinking creates problems with catching and throwing balls, with managing forks, pencils, and combs, and with many other essential life skills.

Dr. A. Jean Ayres studied these children with sensory and motor problems. She expanded our thinking to look at the whole integrative process needed for our brain to tell our body what to do. How does a child know how to do such complex and sequential tasks as jumping or climbing? How does a child acquire the complex skills to tie a shoe or write thoughts on the page? Dr. Ayres integrated our thinking about many sensory systems that must work independently and as a team to accomplish these and many other tasks. She described the essential roles our tactile and vestibular systems play in the process of coordinating sensory information with motor activity.

This understanding of sensory integration led to interventions to help these children. Sensory Integration Therapy focuses on correcting, improving, and/or compensating for sensory integration disorders, much as special education therapy focuses on Learning Disabilities, and speech-language therapy focuses on Language Disabilities.

We now have a greater level of understanding of these learning, language, and sensorimotor disabilities. Yet, all too often, the underlying problems are missed until the level of frustration experienced by the child or adolescent, the parents and family, and the school and teachers results in emotional, social, and family problems. Sadly, even more frequently, educational, health, and mental health professionals focus on the emotional, social, and family problems as if they were the primary issue, missing the fact that they are really secondary to underlying neurological problems.

Let me illustrate. Recently, I evaluated a four-year-old boy because his parents thought he needed to be on medication or in psychotherapy. They also asked for parent counseling to help them handle their son better. He was a "monster" at home and at nursery school. Clearly, they were overwhelmed.

His parents found themselves angry at his immature and explosive behavior. He would not dress himself, insisting that Mother dress him. He ate with his fingers.

He did not play well with other children, acting bossy and insisting that they do what he wanted. No child would play with him. His favorite activity was to sit in the swing in his backyard and swing "forever."

His pediatrician told his parents to set firmer limits and to expect better behavior. His teacher was angry because he was so disruptive. He never listened to instructions and never did what he was supposed to do. The parents felt guilty that the pediatrician and teacher blamed the boy's behavior on their parenting. Yet, they did not know what else to do. Father often suggested that maybe, if Mother were more strict, their son's problems would clear up.

I was struck with how nice this child appeared when seen alone. Then, I observed him in his preschool program. In school, I could see what the teacher and parents described. He rolled around on the floor, often rolling up to another child, touching or hugging. That child would pull away, and the teacher would yell at the child I was observing.

When they had circle time, he walked around the room, refusing to sit in the circle. When playing, if another child brushed against him, he pushed the child away. I noticed how poorly he walked and ran, how clumsy he was with the blocks, and how immature his drawings were. By the end of this full-day program, he seemed tired and irritable, crying at any disappointment.

Knowing of Sensory Integration Dysfunction, I arranged for an evaluation by an occupational therapist. The underlying disabilities with motor coordination, tactile sensitivity, and vestibular insecurity were documented. Occupational therapy, not medication or psychotherapy, was started.

This child did not need to "change his behaviors." We

needed to understand his behaviors and what they suggested as the probable underlying reason for the behaviors. We needed to remember that behaviors are a message, a symptom—not a diagnosis.

If professionals do not see below the surface problems and understand the underlying causes for the problems, interventions do not work. Unless the underlying problems are addressed, the emotional, social, and family problems will not improve. Our task is to not react to the behaviors with the same frustrations and feelings of failure that the child experiences. Our job is to understand the behaviors. Only with understanding can we know how to help.

As a professional who sees many children and adolescents with learning, language, and sensory integration problems, I see clearly that critical to any progress is helping parents understand the underlying neurological problems. Without their knowledge of the brain difficulties and the resulting school and life-skill problems, they cannot understand or help their son or daughter as much as they want to.

There are good books for parents on Learning Disabilities and Language Disabilities. My frustration has been that there has not been a good book for parents on Sensory Integration Dysfunction.

There is now. Carol Kranowitz has done an excellent job of taking complex material and presenting it in a way that can be understood—and used. Parents who read this book will understand motor planning problems, as well as tactile sensitivity and vestibular-proprioceptive difficulties. The format of the book goes beyond this understanding, offering creative ideas on helping the child or adolescent handle the challenges within the family, with peers, and in school. She helps parents understand what help is needed, and how to get this help.

Knowledge is empowering, and *The Out-of-Sync Child* empowers parents to be the successful and productive parents they want to be. Thank you, Carol, for writing this book. Many families and their children will benefit.

—Larry B. Silver, M.D.,
Clinical Professor of Psychiatry,
Georgetown University
Medical Center

ACKNOWLEDGMENTS

With deepest gratitude, I thank:

Lynn A. Balzer-Martin, Ph.D., O.T.R., dearest friend, mentor, and collaborator, who introduced me to sensory integration, coached and encouraged me as I labored over this book, critiqued umpteen drafts, and is always with me.

Georgia DeGangi, Ph.D., O.T.R.; Susanne Smith Roley, M.S., O.T.R.; and Trude Turnquist, Ph.D., O.T.R., who read and edited various versions and who exhorted me to keep revising until I got it right.

Patricia S. Lemer, M.Ed., N.C.C., who read every word and helped me see visual-motor development in a new light.

Elizabeth Dyson, L.L.B.; Jack Kleinmann, Ph.D.; and Donna Carter, Ph.D., who edited several versions—and then thanked me for the privilege!

Larry B. Silver, M.D., who gladly wrote the thoughtful foreword and who lends me his invaluable professional support.

T. Berry Brazelton, M.D., Stanley I. Greenspan, M.D., and Jane M. Healy, Ph.D., whose influence has been beyond measure.

Michael Castleberry, Ph.D., my advisor in The George Washington University Graduate School of Education, who helped clarify my thoughts when the book was in thesis form, and who gave me unconditional positive regard for my work, my mission, and my compulsion to uncover every rock.

Barbara Browne, Ph.D., another supportive GWU professor who gently broadened my thinking and convinced me that sensory integration is a good way, but not the only way, to look at children's development.

Chris Hughes Bridgeman, Catherine and Ron Butler, Deborah Thommasen, Linda Finkel and Vivek Talvadkar, Jacquie and Paul London, Mary Eager, and Denise McMillen, who contributed their thoughts and whose children have been my inspiration.

Sheri Present, O.T.R., and Anne Kendall, Ph.D., whose suggestions for home and school activities to strengthen sensory integration are included.

My co-teachers and young students at St. Columba's Nursery School in Washington, DC, whose work and play sparked the little stories herein.

Lynn Sonberg and Meg Schneider, of Skylight Press, who held my hand, shared their wisdom, and provided meticulous attention throughout the publishing process.

Sheila Curry, of Perigee Books, who recognized the importance of sensory integration, had the vision to buy the manuscript, and gave the book its final polish.

Ellen Stern, my sister, muse, and best friend since time began, who taught me how to write.

Herman E. Stock, my beloved late father, who taught me that problems are solvable, that persistence pays off, and that work is its own splendid reward.

My husband, Alan, my sons, Jeremy and David, and my daughter-in-law, Jenny, for tolerating my tunnel vision, patiently listening to me expound, and forgiving me for dustballs, overcooked meals, and divided attention.

INTRODUCTION

Most preschoolers love the classes I teach involving music, movement, and dramatic play. Every day, small groups of three-, four-, and five-year-olds come to my room to play, move, and learn. They happily pound on drums and xylophones, sing and clap, dance and spin. They shake beanbags, manipulate puppets, and enact fairy tales. They wave the parachute, play musical follow-the-leader games, and flow through obstacle courses. They swoop like kites, stomp like elephants, and melt like snowmen.

Most children enjoy these activities because they have effective sensory integration—the ability to organize sensory information for use in daily life. They take in sensations of touch, movement, sight, and sound coming from their bodies and the world around them, and they respond in a well-regulated way.

Some children, however, such as Andrew, Ben, and Alice, do not enjoy coming to my classroom. Faced with the challenge of sensorimotor experiences, they become tense, unhappy, and confused. They refuse to participate in the activities, or do so inappropriately, and their behavior disrupts their classmates' fun. They are the children for whom this book is written.

In my career as a teacher, since 1976, I have worked with more than one thousand young children. Outside of school, I have taught music classes for kindergartners in my home. I have choreographed children's dances for community performances. I have conducted dozens of musical birthday parties. I have been room mother, Cub Scout den leader, and team manager for my own sons' school and sports groups.

Many years of working with children have taught me that *all* children like lively, interesting activities. They all want to join the fun—yet some don't take part. Why not? Is it that they *won't*—or that they *can't*?

When I began teaching, the nonparticipants puzzled me. Why, I wondered, were these children so difficult to reach? Why did they seem to fall apart when it was time to join the fun?

Why did Andrew have to buzz around the room's perimeter while his classmates, sitting on the rug, sang "The Wheels on the Bus"?

Why did Ben tap, tap, tap his *shoulders* when the musical instructions were to tap, tap, tap his *knees*?

Why did Alice flop onto her stomach, "too tired" to sit up and strike together two rhythm sticks?

At first, these children annoyed me. They made me feel like a bad teacher. They also made me feel like a bad person when their inattention or disruptive behavior caused me to react negatively. Indeed, on one regrettable occasion, I told a child that turning away and covering his ears when I played the guitar was "just plain rude." That day I went home and wept.

Every evening, while preparing dinner or engaging with my own sons, I would muse about these students. I couldn't get a handle on them. They had no identified special needs. They weren't unloved or disadvantaged. Some seemed to misbehave on purpose, like sticking a foot out to trip a classmate, while others seemed to move without any purpose at all, in an aimless or listless manner. Little about their behavior could be classified, except for a shared inability to enjoy the activities that children traditionally relish.

I wasn't the only one who was stumped. Karen Strimple, Director of St. Columba's Nursery School, and the other teachers were equally puzzled by the same children. The children's parents were often concerned, especially when they compared their child's behavior with that of their other, more "together" offspring. And, if caring parents and teachers were frustrated, how must the children themselves feel?

They felt like failures.

And we teachers felt that we were failing them.

We knew we could do better. After all, since the 1970s, we had been mainstreaming into our regular school program a number of children with identified special needs. We were extremely successful with these children. Why were we less successful teaching certain "regular" kids with subtle, unidentified problems? We wanted an answer.

The answer came from Lynn A. Balzer-Martin, Ph.D., O.T.R., a St. Columba's parent and a pediatric occupational therapist. Since the 1970s, Lynn had been an educational consultant for our preschool mainstreaming program. Her primary work, however, was diagnosing and providing occupational therapy for young children who had academic and behavior problems stemming from a neurological inefficiency called Sensory Integration Dysfunction.

Few people recognize the term. An occupational therapist, A. Jean Ayres, Ph.D., was the pioneer who first described the problem. About 40 years ago, Dr. Ayres formulated a theory of sensory integration dysfunction and led other occupational therapists in developing intervention strategies. Her book, *Sensory Integration and the Child,* presents a thorough explanation of this misunderstood problem and is required reading for anyone interested in grasping the technicalities of the subject. *(See Recommended Reading.)*

It is important to recognize that sensory integration dysfunction, or SI Dysfunction, is not a new problem. It is a new definition of an old problem.

SI Dysfunction is often subtle and can cause a bewildering variety of symptoms. Because their central nervous systems are ineffective in processing sensory information, children with this hidden difficulty have a hard time functioning in daily life. They may look fine and have superior intelligence, but may be awkward and clumsy, fearful and withdrawn, or hostile and aggressive. SI Dysfunction can affect not only how they move and learn, but also how they behave, how they play and make friends, and especially how they feel about themselves.

Most parents, educators, doctors, and mental health professionals have difficulty in recognizing SI Dysfunction. Because they don't recognize the problem, they may mistake a child's behavior, low self-esteem, or reluctance to participate in ordinary childhood experiences for hyperactivity, learning disabilities, or emotional problems. Few people understand that bewildering behavior may stem from a poorly functioning nervous system.

Dr. Lynn Balzer-Martin, like other students of Dr. Ayres's work, was trained to recognize SI Dysfunction— and to treat it. Her growing concern was that many of her clients were not sent her for a diagnosis until well after they had run into trouble at school or at home, at the ages of six, seven, or eight. She was anxious to identify children at younger ages because the brain is most receptive to change while it is developing.

Preschoolers, whose nervous systems are still developing rapidly, stand a good chance to benefit from therapeutic intervention. Lynn knew that if SI Dysfunction could be detected in three-, four-, or five-year-olds, these children could receive individualized treatment that would prevent later social and academic impasses.

The challenge was to find a way to identify preschoolers with SI Dysfunction, because the available standardized tests are inappropriate for the "little guys." Lynn conceived of a quick, effective screening to see whether very young children had the neurological foundations necessary for developing into well-organized people. She asked us if we were interested.

Were we interested?!

Thus, everything came together at once. We wanted to learn more about our worrisome students. Lynn wanted to try out her screening idea. The Katharine P. Maddux Foundation, which already funded our flagship mainstreaming program, was urging us to develop more projects designed to improve the physical, mental, and emotional health of children and their families.

Lynn's first goal was to educate us about sensory integration and then, with our help, to devise a screening program that would be developmentally suitable for preschoolers.

The screening process would be fun for the children. It would be simple enough for many schools to duplicate. It would be short, yet thorough enough to enable educators to distinguish between basic immaturity and possible SI Dysfunction in young children.

Most important, it would provide data that would encourage parents to seek early intervention for their children with an appropriate professional (such as an occupational therapist, physical therapist, or sometimes a psychologist or speech/language pathologist). The purpose of early intervention is to help children function better—even beautifully—in their classrooms, in their homes, and in their daily lives.

In 1987, with the support of the school community and with my eager assistance, Lynn instituted a program at St. Columba's Nursery School in which all ninety students undergo an annual screening. We began to guide identified children into early intervention therapy. And we began to see immediate, positive, exhilarating results as these children's skills began to improve.

Under Lynn's guidance, I studied and learned everything I could about the subject. I learned to screen the children and to compile data gleaned from teachers, parents, and direct observations. I learned to make sense of some children's mystifying behavior.

As my knowledge increased, so did my teaching skills. I learned to help my co-teachers understand why these children marched to a different drummer. I gave workshops at other preschools and elementary schools to train educators to recognize signs of this subtle problem. I added activities in my class that promote healthy sensorimotor development for *all* children.

I rejoiced in the strides that children such as Andrew, Ben, and Alice made soon after they began occupational therapy. Incredibly, as they acquired more efficient sensorimotor skills, they relaxed, became more focused, and began to enjoy school. Now, when I went home at the end of the day, it wasn't to weep—it was to celebrate!

While my expertise grew, I learned that explaining sensory integration to parents requires time and skill. When children have been screened at school and show clear evidence of dysfunction, Karen and I ask their parents to come in to school to observe them in the classroom and on the playground. Then we sit down for a private conference to discuss our observations.

In these conferences, we describe sensory integration dysfunction and why we suspect it as a cause of their child's difficulties. We explain that the problem is treatable. We say that while older children and even adults can improve with treatment, it is early intervention that produces the most dramatic results. We try to allay parents' fears, assuring them that SI Dysfunction does not suggest that their child is mentally deficient, or that they are inadequate parents.

We understand that parents are inevitably filled with anxiety, questions, and misapprehensions. Often, they dash to their pediatrician, who, unfamiliar with SI Dysfunction, may mistakenly dismiss it as a problem that the child will outgrow.

We know that we raise more questions than it is possible to answer in a half-hour conference.

Thus, this book was conceived to explain sensory integration and its counterpart, Sensory Integration Dysfunction. I have attempted to make the explanations reader-friendly. They will introduce you to terms that early childhood professionals commonly use—terms with which you need to become familiar. The information will help you understand your child, and that is the book's most important purpose.

My hope is that once you grasp the subject, through the explanations and the examples of different types of children, you will be able to recognize the first signs of trouble in your own child. Then you will be prepared to provide the help your son or daughter needs to grow into a healthy, happy, and smoothly functioning adult.

—Carol Stock Kranowitz, M.A.
Bethesda, Maryland
February 1998

How to Use This Book

Whether or not your child has been diagnosed, this book will help you understand and cope with SI Dysfunction. The book is not just for parents. It is also for teachers, medical doctors, occupational therapists, psychologists, grandparents, baby-sitters, and others who care for the out-of-sync child.

In my daily work, I witness how SI Dysfunction plays out. I see behavior that parents, pediatricians, and even therapists don't have the chance to observe. Thus, the book, written from a teacher's perspective, offers insights that a specialist in another field of child development might overlook.

Part I includes an overview of SI Dysfunction and how it affects children's behavior; checklists and questionnaires (for you to mark) of symptoms, associated problems, and characteristics of out-of-sync children; a guide to normal neurological development; how the tactile, vestibular, and proprioceptive senses work, how they influence everyday life, and what happens when they're inefficient; anecdotes contrasting the responses of children with and without efficient SI; and the hope that a solution to your child's difficulties is at hand.

Part II includes criteria and guidance for getting a diagnosis and treatment; charts for documenting your child's behavior; tips for keeping a running record; how occupational therapy helps, and a look at other therapies; suggestions for a balanced "sensory diet" and for improving your child's skills at home; ideas to share with teachers for helping your child at school; coping techniques to handle your child's emotions and to improve family life; and encouragement and support—for you and your child are not alone!

The Out-of-Sync Child concludes with an **Appendix—The Sensory Processing Machine,** to explain the role of the central nervous system in sensory integration; **Resources** for materials and support; a **Recommended Reading** list about specific problems; a **Selected Bibliography;** and a **Glossary** and **Index.**

Read the book cover to cover to get a broad picture of SI Dysfunction. Use it as a reference to refresh yourself on a specific area of dysfunction. With pencil in hand, use it as a workbook. Keep it handy as an activity book. Use it to learn about your child—and perhaps to learn about yourself, as well.

Part I

RECOGNIZING

SENSORY

INTEGRATION

DYSFUNCTION

Chapter One

DOES YOUR CHILD HAVE SENSORY INTEGRATION DYSFUNCTION?

Sensory integration dysfunction is a common, but misunderstood, problem which affects children's behavior, influencing the way they learn, move, relate to others, and feel about themselves.

To illustrate how sensory integration problems play out, the stories of three out-of-sync children and the parents struggling to raise them are presented along with lists of common symptoms, associated problems, and possible causes. Also included are samples of questionnaires that professionals give to parents and teachers when a child is suspected of having some dysfunction.

This information will help you determine whether your own child is affected by sensory integration dysfunction. If your child has a significant problem, the information may strike you like a bolt of lightning. You may instantly recognize the signs and be relieved to have some answers, at last. Even if your child has a mild problem, you can use this information to gain new insight into his or her puzzling behavior.

Whether SI Dysfunction is major or minor, your out-of-sync child needs understanding and help, for no child can overcome the obstacles alone.

THREE OUT-OF-SYNC CHILDREN
AT HOME AND SCHOOL

Tommy is the only son of two adoring parents. They waited a long time before having a child and rejoiced in his arrival. But when they finally got him, they realized that they got a handful.

The day after he was born, his parents were told that he could not stay in the hospital nursery because his wailing disturbed the other infants. Once he arrived home, he rarely slept through the night. Although he nursed well and grew rapidly, he adamantly rejected the introduction of solid food and vigorously resisted being weaned. He was a very fussy baby.

Today, Tommy is a fussy three-year-old. He is crying because his shoes are too tight, his socks are too lumpy. He yanks them off and hurls them away.

To prevent a tantrum, his mother lets him wear bedroom slippers to school. She has learned that if it isn't shoes and socks that bother him, it's inevitably something else that will trip him up during the day.

His parents bend over backwards, but pleasing their healthy, attractive child is a challenge. Everything makes him miserable. He hates the playground, the beach, and the bathtub. He refuses to wear hats or mittens, even on the coldest days. Getting him to eat is a trial.

Arranging play dates with other children is a nightmare. Going to the barber shop is a disaster. Wherever they go, people turn away—or stare.

His teacher reports that he avoids finger painting and other messy activities. He fidgets at story time and doesn't pay attention. He lashes out at his classmates for no apparent reason. He is, however, the world's best block builder—as long as he isn't crowded.

Tommy's pediatrician tells his parents nothing is wrong with him, so they should stop worrying and just let him grow. His grandparents say he's spoiled and needs stricter discipline. Friends suggest going on a vacation without him.

Tommy's parents wonder if yielding to his whims is wise, but it's the only method that works. They are exhausted, frustrated, and stressed. They can't understand what makes him tick.

Vicki, a first-grader, is not a graceful little girl. She moves awkwardly, has poor balance, and falls frequently. She also fatigues easily and sighs, "I'm too pooped to do anything." A family outing or trip to the playground quickly wears her out.

However, she wants to be a ballerina when she grows up. Almost every day, she lies in front of the TV to watch her favorite video, "The Nutcracker." She was excited about taking ballet lessons and loved her purple tutu, but once she got to dancing school, she wouldn't leave her mother's side.

Because of her poor coordination and lethargy, her parents find that getting her out of bed, asking her to put on her coat, or maneuvering her into the car is an ordeal.

She takes a long time to carry out simple, familiar movements.

Vicki's father and mother disagree on the best way to handle her. Her father tends to pick her up and put her places—in bed, in the car, on a chair. He also dresses her, because she has trouble orienting her limbs to get into her clothes. He refers to her as his "little noodle."

Vicki's mother, on the other hand, believes Vicki will never learn to move with confidence, much less become a ballerina, if she doesn't learn independence. Her mother says, "I think she'd stay in one spot all day if I let her."

Although Vicki lacks "oomph," she constantly fidgets. Even when she's pooped, her knees bounce, her feet tap, her eyes dart, her fingers fiddle with her hair. She seems to crave certain kinds of movement, tilting to and fro in a rocking chair, swinging upside down, shaking her head from side to side, and bumping into furniture.

Her teacher says, "Vicki has difficulty socializing and getting involved in classroom activities. It's like her batteries are low. She needs a jump start just to get going. Then she loses interest and gives up easily."

Vicki's behavior mystifies her parents. Their experiences with their two other children have not prepared them to deal with her unusual behavior.

Peter is an extremely shy nine-year-old who dislikes school. Sometimes he asks to stay home, and his parents let him. He says he doesn't want to go to school because he's no good at anything, and everyone laughs at him.

Peter's teacher notes that he has a long attention span and an above-average reading ability. She wonders why a child with so much information to share becomes paralyzed when he has to write a paper. She says he needs to get organized so he can pay more attention to his assignments and do neater work.

His parents wonder why he is a misfit at school, because he has always fit right into their sedate life-style. Peter is a modest child, rarely seeking attention. He can spend hours studying his baseball cards, completely self-absorbed.

Peter's parents think he is the perfect child. They observe that he is unlike other kids, who are loud and mischievous. He never makes trouble, although he is somewhat clumsy, often dropping dishes and breaking toys that require simple manipulation. But then, his parents are somewhat clumsy, too, and have come to believe that physical prowess is unimportant. They are glad that their son is quiet, well mannered and bookish, just like them.

Something, however, is getting in his way. His parents have no idea what.

Why are Tommy, Vicki, and Peter out of sync? Their parents, teachers, and pediatricians don't know what to do.

The children have no identified disabilities, such as cerebral palsy or impaired vision. They seem to have everything going for them: they're healthy, intelligent, and dearly loved. Yet they struggle with the basic skills of tolerating ordinary sensations; of planning and organizing their actions; and of regulating their attention and activity levels.

Their common problem is Sensory Integration Dysfunction.

SENSORY INTEGRATION DYSFUNCTION:
A BRIEF DEFINITION

Sensory Integration Dysfunction is the inability to process information received through the senses. It is also called sensory integration disorder, sensory integrative dysfunction, or SI Dysfunction, for short.

The late A. Jean Ayres, Ph.D., an occupational therapist, was the first to describe the problem as the result of inefficient neurological processing. In the 1950s and '60s, she developed a theory of Sensory Integration Dysfunction and taught other occupational therapists how to assess it.

Dysfunction happens in the central nervous system, at the "head" of which is the brain. When a glitch occurs, the brain cannot analyze, organize, and connect—or integrate—sensory messages. The result of SI Dysfunction is that the child cannot respond to sensory information to behave in a meaningful, consistent way. He may also have difficulty using sensory information to plan and organize what he needs to do. Thus, he may not learn easily.

Learning is a broad term. One kind of learning is called "adaptive behavior," which is the ability to respond actively and purposefully to new circumstances, such as learning to meet different teachers' expectations.

Another kind of learning is motor learning, which is the ability to develop increasingly complex movement skills after one has mastered simpler ones. Examples are learning to use a pencil after having learned to use a crayon, or learning to catch a ball after having learned to throw one.

A third kind of learning is academic learning. This is the ability to acquire conceptual skills, such as reading, computing, and applying what one learns today to what one learned yesterday.

HOW INEFFICIENT SENSORY INTEGRATION LEADS TO INEFFICIENT LEARNING

Your child yanks the cat's tail, and the cat hisses, arches its back, and spits. Normally, through experience, a child will learn not to repeat such a scary experience. He learns to be cautious with the cat. In the future, his behavior will be more adaptive.

The child with SI Dysfunction, however, may have difficulty "reading cues," verbal or nonverbal, from the environment. He may not decode the auditory message of the cat's hostile hissing, the visual message of the cat's arched back, or the tactile message of spit on his cheek. He misses the "big picture" and may not learn appropriate caution.

Another possibility is that the child can read the cat's reaction but is unable to change his behavior and stop himself. He receives the sensory information, but can't organize it to produce an efficient response.

A third possibility is that the child sometimes can take in sensations, organize them, and respond appropriately—but not today. This may be one of his "off" days.

Possible results:

• The child may never learn and may get repeatedly scratched. Thus, he may continue this risky behavior until someone removes the cat, or the cat learns to avoid the child. The child loses a chance to learn how to relate positively to other living creatures.

• The child becomes fearful of the cat. He may not understand cause and effect and may be bewildered by what seems to be unpredictable cat behavior. He may become afraid of other animals, too.

• Eventually, the child may learn about cause and effect, may learn to control his impulses, may learn to treat animals gently, and may grow up to love cats—but this will happen only with much conscious effort, after much time and many, many scratches.

The brain-behavior connection is very strong. Because the child with SI Dysfunction has a disorganized brain, many aspects of his behavior are disorganized. His overall development is disorderly and his participation in childhood experiences is spotty, reluctant, or inept. For the out-of-sync child, performing ordinary tasks and responding to everyday events can be enormously challenging.

The inability to function smoothly is not because the child won't, but because he can't.

CHECKLISTS OF COMMON SYMPTOMS

Below are two lists of common symptoms of SI Dysfunction. The first list, "Sensory Processing Problems," pertains to issues that are the crux of SI Dysfunction. Some children are primarily oversensitive; some are primarily undersensitive; and some are oversensitive to some sensations but undersensitive to others.

The second list, "Behavior Problems," pertains to issues that can result from inefficient sensory processing but can also result from other developmental problems. The child with behavior problems does not necessarily have SI Dysfunction.

As you check the symptoms that you recognize, please understand that they will vary from child to child, because every brain is unique (just as every fingerprint is unique). No child will exhibit all the symptoms. Still, if several descriptions of the oversensitive or undersensitive child fit your own son or daughter, chances are that he or she may have some degree of SI Dysfunction.

The child with severe SI Dysfunction shows many symptoms. Interacting with other people, functioning in daily life, and doing the "job" of being a child are greatly impaired. The child with mild dysfunction is slightly impaired and may find ways to compensate—but the problem is frequently overlooked. The child with moderate dysfunction is somewhere in between.

Whether the child has severe, moderate, or mild dysfunction, he or she needs understanding and help. Ignoring problems won't make them disappear.

Sensory Processing Problems

Sensory integration dysfunction is suspected when the child exhibits one or more of these common symptoms with *frequency, intensity,* and *duration.* Frequency means several times a day. Intensity means that the child adamantly avoids sensory stimulation, or throws his whole body and soul into getting the stimulation he needs. Duration means that he persists in his unusual behavior for several minutes or longer.

The Oversensitive Child Seeks Less Stimulation	Sensations	The Undersensitive Child Seeks More Stimulation
☐ The child avoids touching or being touched by objects and people. She may react with a fight-or-flight response to getting dirty, to certain textures of clothing and food, and to another person's unexpected light touch.	Touch	☐ The child may be unaware of pain, temperature, or how objects feel. She may wallow in the mud, paw through toys purposelessly, chew on inedible objects like shirt cuffs, rub against walls and furniture, and bump into people.
☐ The child avoids moving or being unexpectedly moved. Insecure in regard to gravity, he may be anxious when tipped off balance. He may be earthbound and avoid running, climbing, sliding, or swinging. He may feel seasick in cars or elevators.	Movement	☐ The child may crave fast and spinning movement, such as swinging, rocking, twirling, and riding merry-go-rounds—without getting dizzy. The child may move constantly, fidget, enjoy getting into upside-down positions, and be a daredevil.
☐ The child may be rigid, tense, stiff, and uncoordinated. She may avoid playground activities that require good body awareness.	Body Position	☐ The child may slump and slouch. His actions may be clumsy and inaccurate. He may bump into objects, stamp his feet, and twiddle his fingers.

While difficulties with touch, movement, and body position are the telling symptoms of SI Dysfunction, the child may also exhibit associated sensory problems:

The Oversensitive Child Seeks Less Stimulation	Sensations	The Undersensitive Child Seeks More Stimulation
☐ The child may become overexcited when there is too much to look at—words, toys, or other children. He may often cover his eyes, have poor eye contact, be inattentive when drawing or doing desk work, or overreact to bright light. He may be hyper-vigilant—on the alert and ever watchful.	Sights	☐ Although able to see, the child may touch everything to learn about it, because her vision is not sufficiently coordinated. She may miss important visual cues such as another person's facial expressions and gestures, as well as signposts and written directions.
☐ The child may cover his ears to close out sounds or voices. He may complain about noises, such as vacuum cleaners and blenders, that don't bother others.	Sounds	☐ The child may ignore voices and have difficulty following verbal directions. He may not listen well to himself and speak in a booming voice. He may want the TV and radio to be loud.
☐ The child may object to odors, such as a ripe banana, that other children do not notice.	Smells	☐ The child may ignore unpleasant odors like dirty diapers. She may sniff food, people, and objects.

| ☐ The child may strongly object to certain textures and temperatures of foods. He may often gag when he eats. | *Tastes* | ☐ The child may lick or taste inedible objects, like playdough and toys. He may prefer very spicy or very hot foods. |

Behavior Problems

Sensory Integration Dysfunction may contribute to or exacerbate other problems, as well. Please be aware that the symptoms listed below may possibly have an SI component—or they may be caused by some other developmental problem.

☐ Unusually high activity level. The child may be always on the go, move with short and nervous gestures, play or work aimlessly, be quick-tempered and easily excited, and find it impossible to stay seated.

☐ Unusually low activity level. The child may move slowly and in a daze, fatigue easily, lack initiative and "stick-to-it-tiveness," and show little interest in the world.

☐ Impulsivity. The child may lack self-control and be unable to stop after starting an activity. She may pour juice until it spills, squeeze the glue bottle until empty, run pell-mell into trees and people, and talk out of turn.

☐ Distractibility. The child may have a short attention span, even for activities he enjoys. The child may pay attention to everything except the task at hand. The child may be disorganized and forgetful.

☐ Problems with muscle tone and motor coordination. The child's body may be either tense or "loose and floppy." The child may be awkward, clumsy, apparently careless, and accident-prone.

☐ Problems with motor planning, which is the ability to conceive of, organize, sequence, and carry out complex movements in a meaningful way. He may have trouble climbing stairs, negotiating obstacle courses and playground equipment, riding bikes, dressing, getting in and out of the car, and using eating and writing utensils. His ability to learn new motor skills, such as clapping out rhythms and skipping, may develop noticeably later than other children's.

☐ Lack of a definite hand preference by the age of four or five. The child may not use one hand consistently when handling tools such as pens and forks. She may use either hand to reach for an object. She may switch the object from right to left when handling it, eat with one hand but draw with the other, or use both hands to manipulate scissors.

☐ Poor eye-hand coordination. The child may have trouble using markers and crayons, creating art projects, building with blocks, doing puzzles, eating neatly, or tying shoes. This child's handwriting may be sloppy and uneven.

☐ Resistance to novel situations. The child may object to leaving the house, meeting new people, trying new games or toys, or tasting different foods. The child may be panicky for no obvious reason.

☐ Difficulty making transitions from one situation to another. The child may seem stubborn and uncooperative when it is time to come for dinner, get into (or out of) the bathtub, or change from a reading to a math activity. Minor changes in routine will upset this child who does not "go with the flow."

☐ High level of frustration. Struggling to accomplish tasks that peers do easily, the child may give up quickly. He may be a perfectionist and become upset when art projects or dramatic play don't meet his expectations. Insisting on being the winner, the best, or the first, he may be a poor game-player.

☐ Self-regulation problems. The child may be unable to "rev up," or to calm down once aroused. The child may perform unevenly: "with it" one day, "out of it" the next.

☐ Academic problems. The child may have difficulty learning new skills and concepts. Although bright, the child may be perceived as an underachiever.

☐ Social problems. The child may be hard to get along with and have difficulty making friends, playing with other children, and communicating. She may need to control her surrounding territory and have trouble sharing toys.

☐ Emotional problems. He may be overly sensitive to change, stress, and hurt feelings, and be disorganized, inflexible, and irrational. He may be demanding and needy, seeking attention in negative ways. He may be unhappy, believing and saying that he is crazy, no good, a dummy, a loser, and a failure. *Low self-esteem is one of the most telling symptoms of poor sensory integration.*

Please note: While many children with SI Dysfunction have behavior problems, many children with behavior problems do not have SI Dysfunction! Every child is occasionally out of sync to some degree. Careful diagnosis is imperative to determine which symptoms are related to sensory processing problems, and which are not.

WHAT SI DYSFUNCTION IS NOT: "LOOK-ALIKE" SYMPTOMS

Many symptoms of SI Dysfunction look like symptoms of other common disabilities. Indeed, Patricia S. Lemer, M.Ed., N.C.C., maintains that so many symptoms overlap that it may be difficult to differentiate one difficulty from another.

For example, if a child is inattentive and often has difficulty sustaining attention in tasks or play activities, the child may have SI Dysfunction. Similarly, if the child is hyperactive and impulsive, often fidgeting or squirming, the child may have SI Dysfunction.

But—might something else be going on? Yes, indeed. Alternative diagnoses are that the child:

- has attention deficit disorder (ADD) or attention-deficit hyperactivity disorder (ADHD),
- has learning-related visual problems,
- has allergies,

• has nutritional or vitamin deficiencies, OR . . .

• is behaving just like a normal child!

So, how can one tell the difference between SI Dysfunction, ADD (or ADHD), and learning disabilities?

The red flags of SI Dysfunction are a child's unusual responses to touching and being touched, and/or to moving and being moved.

Some children have only SI Dysfunction; some have SI Dysfunction and ADD/ADHD; some have SI Dysfunction and learning disabilities; some have a combination of all three. The overlapping circles below illustrate the relationship of these three common problems that can affect children's behavior.

How Three Common Problems May Overlap

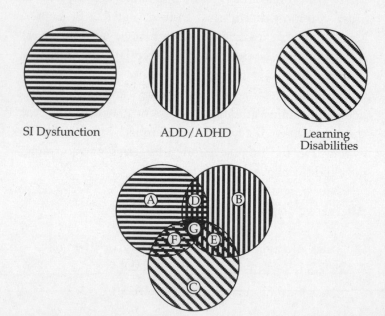

SI Dysfunction   ADD/ADHD   Learning Disabilities

A. A child with SI Dysfunction.

B. A child with ADD/ADHD.

C. A child with learning disabilities.

D. A child with SI Dysfunction and ADD/ADHD.

E. A child with ADD/ADHD and learning disabilities.

F. A child with SI Dysfunction and learning disabilities.

G. A child with SI Dysfunction, ADD/ADHD, and learning disabilities.

Unfortunately, symptoms of SI Dysfunction are often misinterpreted as psychological problems. Indeed, these may develop if the underlying cause of SI Dysfunction is neither recognized nor addressed early. *The inability to cope with emotional, physical, and social challenges is often present by the age of three or four if intervention has not yet begun.*

ASSOCIATED PROBLEMS

Attention Deficit Disorder (ADD) and Attention-Deficit Hyperactivity Disorder (ADHD)

While SI Dysfunction is not the same as its "look-alike" ADD (or ADHD), these two problems may simultaneously affect the out-of-sync child. The reason is that neurological problems are on a continuum: the more difficulty a child has in one area, the more difficulty he is likely to have in others.

Careful analysis of the child's behavior is necessary to determine that the child has SI Dysfunction and not ADD, because treatment for the two problems differs. Treatment for ADD often involves behavior management and other psychological approaches, as well as psycho-stimulants such as Ritalin, which make the child's brain available for learning.

Medicine can help the child with ADD, but medicine does not make SI Dysfunction go away. Occupational therapy that focuses on sensory integration and recreational activities that strengthen basic sensory and motor skills help the child with SI Dysfunction.

Learning Disability

A learning disability is defined in The Individuals with Disabilities Education Act (IDEA) as "a disorder in one or more of the basic psychological processes involved in understanding or in using language, spoken or written, which may manifest itself in an imperfect ability to listen, speak, read, write, spell, or do mathematical calculations."

According to this definition, SI Dysfunction is not a learning disability. However, it can lead to learning disabilities when it affects the child's auditory-language skills, visual-spatial skills, and ability to process and sequence information. The child with SI Dysfunction is a child at risk for future learning disabilities.

Auditory-Language Problems

The child may have difficulty processing what he hears. This problem is common if he has vestibular dysfunction, because the auditory and vestibular systems are closely linked. The child may have problems with listening skills, auditory perception, and language processing. He may seem noncompliant or may not follow directions well, because he cannot decode what was said.

Speech/Articulation Difficulties

The child may have trouble pronouncing words clearly enough to be understood. He may lack awareness of how his mouth, lips, and tongue feel and work together. He may say "tool" instead of "school," or "dese" instead of "these," because of difficulty positioning the muscles necessary for articulation.

Vision Problems

The child may have problems coordinating vision, especially if he has vestibular dysfunction, which influences eye movements. He may not use both eyes together as a team (binocularity). He may have trouble learning because he can't focus on faces, chalkboards, books, checkerboards, or basketball hoops.

Even if he has adequate eyesight, poor binocular vision may cause difficulty in perceiving what he sees. Instead of linking visual information with auditory, touch, and movement sensations, his brain scrambles the messages. For instance, if connecting sights with sounds is a problem, he may not know where to look when he hears the teacher's voice. If connecting sights with touch sensations is a problem, he may not know—just by looking—that a nail is sharp and a hammer is heavy. If connecting sights with movement sensations is a problem, he may not swerve around the furniture to avoid bumping into it.

Thus, he may have difficulty with eye-hand coordination, visual perception, and spatial awareness. If all the sensory pieces don't come together in his brain into a unified whole, it becomes very challenging to respond appropriately to the sights his eyes record.

Eating Problems

The child may not chew carefully and may be a messy eater. He may have unusual food preferences, or a limited food repertoire. He may eat only crispy foods, like bacon and crackers, or only soft foods, like soup and yogurt, or only cold or only hot foods. As a result, the child may have nutritional deficits affecting his behavior and development.

Digestion and Elimination Problems

SI Dysfunction may affect digestion because the child may not recognize signals of hunger and satiety (fullness). He may have poor bladder and bowel control because he may not perceive wetness, or may have insufficient muscle tone to "hold it." He may be a chronic bed-wetter or be frequently constipated.

Problems with Sleep Regulation

The child may need a long afternoon nap, or may never nap even when she's tired. Because a sleep disorder is often caused by a separation problem, she may want to sleep with her parents. She may have trouble comforting herself to sleep, or may constantly awaken during the night.

Sleep problems are often associated with a high need for movement. If the child hasn't had her quota of movement during the day, her arousal levels may fluctuate erratically, and she may become overaroused at night. Tactile defensiveness also may cause the child to feel uncomfortable in bed.

Allergies

SI Dysfunction often coexists with allergies. The child may suffer from allergic reactions to foods, dust, pollen, grass, fur, or medicines.

POSSIBLE CAUSES OF SI DYSFUNCTION

Nobody knows for sure what causes Sensory Integration Dysfunction, but current research suggests several possible factors:

1) A genetic or hereditary predisposition, often the case if the child's parent, sibling, or other close relative has some SI Dysfunction

2) Prenatal circumstances, including chemicals, medications, or toxins like lead poisoning that the fetus absorbs; the mother's drug or alcohol abuse; and pregnancy complications, such as a virus, a chronic illness, or great stress

3) Prematurity

4) Birth trauma, perhaps due to an emergency cesarean section, a lack of oxygen, or surgery soon after birth

5) Postnatal circumstances, such as environmental pollutants (although these have not been definitely proven to be a factor) and excessive or insufficient

sensory stimulation after birth; a lengthy hospital-
ization or institutionalization, or the lack of normal
sensory experiences may interfere with neurological
development

  6) Unknown reasons

So many hypotheses—so little proof! At this writing, we
are unable to point a finger at a particular cause. Sometimes,
SI dysfunction just happens, with no identifiable root.

This much we know: whatever the cause, the symptoms are similar; the treatment is the same; and many
children can be helped to overcome early problems.

WHO HAS SI DYSFUNCTION?

On a bell-shaped curve of humanity, some people have a
poorly integrated neurological system, some have an excellent one, and the rest of us fall somewhere in the middle.

Think about people who are graceful and popular, like
ballerinas, athletes, charismatic politicians, and delightful
children. These people may be blessed with exceptionally
efficient sensory integration.

Now, think about people you know who have problems functioning in certain aspects of their lives. They
may be clumsy, have few friends, or show neither common
sense nor self-control. They may have SI Dysfunction.

Who does have SI Dysfunction? We know specific
populations whom it affects. We know that it intensifies
the bigger problems of children with autism, pervasive
developmental disorder, and serious language difficulty. It
usually is a considerable, though secondary, problem for
children with fetal alcohol syndrome, fragile X syndrome,

and severe mental retardation. It often interferes with the development of children who have been adopted after institutionalization in orphanages. It frequently co-exists in children with learning disabilities and/or attention deficits. For all these children, remediating their sensory issues through occupational therapy has an overall, positive effect.

We also know that some "normal" children, who are not regarded as having any significant or diagnosable problems, have SI Dysfunction. These children, whom intervention also helps, are the focus of this book.

What percentage of "normal" children are challenged by inefficient sensory integration? The more we learn, the higher the estimates become. In 1979, Dr. Ayres estimated that 5 to 10 percent of children have SI problems significant enough to warrant intervention. Today, estimates range from 12 to 30 percent, depending upon the criteria being used.

Occupational therapists commonly note that approximately 80 percent of these children are boys, but this statistic is open to dispute. Many professionals believe that girls are just as likely to have neurological disorders, including SI Dysfunction, ADD, and learning disabilities. Girls, however, frequently do not display the same behavior problems that attract attention, so they tend to go unnoticed—and to fall through the cracks.

Should we be alarmed by the increasing numbers of children identified as having SI Dysfunction? Are we indiscriminately sticking labels on children? Are we just "looking for something wrong"?

No, no, no!

In fact, identifying children with SI Dysfunction is a cause for celebration. As we learn more about the mechanics of the human brain, we are finally understanding why some children are out of sync. And now—we can do something to help!

Don't We All Experience Some SI Problems?

From time to time, we all experience some problems processing sensations. Too much or too little sensory stimulation confuses the brain and can cause temporary discomfort. Illness, fatigue and stress can also interfere with smooth functioning.

For example, attending a noisy, crowded party can be overwhelming. Taking a bumpy airplane ride can overload your brain with rapid movement sensations. Lingering in bed with the flu can prevent you from receiving sufficient movement experiences and make you feel weak. Walking from a well-lit room into a dark closet can deprive your eyes of light and therefore your brain of visual sensations.

Not being in control of oneself is very unpleasant, but an occasional disorganizing experience is normal. *It is when the brain is so disorganized that a person has difficulty functioning in daily life that the person is diagnosed as having Sensory Integration Dysfunction.*

Two Sample Sensorimotor History Questionnaires

Below are samples of questionnaires that parents or teachers complete when a child begins to be evaluated by an occupational therapist. The questionnaires help the therapist learn about the child's sensorimotor history. After analyzing them, the therapist determines whether the child needs treatment and, if so, uses them to design an individualized program.

The first questionnaire, for parents of preschoolers, is used in the annual screening program that Lynn A. Balzer-Martin, Ph.D., O.T.R., designed for St. Columba's Nursery School in Washington, DC. The second is Dr. Balzer-Martin's questionnaire for teachers of elementary-school-age children. The abbreviated questionnaires are printed here with her gracious permission.

Take some time to study the questions. They will help you understand how sensory integration affects your child's overall development. Some questions pertain to the child's responses to sensations, including touch, movement, body position and body awareness, sight, sound, and the pull of gravity. Other questions pertain to the child's developmental skills, coordination, attention, self-regulation, and behavior, all of which are strongly influenced by sensory integration.

Check "yes" or "no" after each item on the parents' questionnaire. Copy the second questionnaire, if you wish, for your child's teacher to check and return to you. (Most of the questions are applicable both to preschoolers and to elementary-age children.) Many "yeses" suggest that SI Dysfunction affects your child, and that a professional diagnosis is in order.

SENSORIMOTOR HISTORY QUESTIONNAIRE FOR PARENTS OF PRESCHOOL CHILDREN

Prepared by Lynn A. Balzer-Martin, Ph.D., O.T.R.

1. Is your child particularly sensitive to touch?   Yes____ No____

2. Does your child particularly enjoy fast-moving or spinning activities at the playground or at home, perhaps with little or no dizziness?   Yes____ No____

3. Does your child show particular caution in approaching activities involving fast movement or movement of the body through space?   Yes____ No____

4. Does your child have unusual sensitivities to smell?   Yes____ No____

5. Is your child particularly sensitive to noise, e.g., putting hands over ears when others are not bothered by sounds?   Yes____ No____

6. Have you ever had concerns about your child's hearing, either in general or in conjunction with ear infections?   Yes____ No____

7. Have you ever had concerns about your child's speech and/or language skills?   Yes____ No____

8. Have you ever had concerns about your child's vision?   Yes____ No____

9. Does your child have a more "loose" or "floppy" body build than others?   Yes____ No____

10. Does your child have difficulty orienting his/her body effectively for dressing activities, such as putting arms in sleeves, putting fingers in mittens, or putting toes in socks?   Yes____ No____

11. Do you feel that your child has not yet established a definite hand preference when using a spoon, crayon, marker, pencil, etc.?   Yes____ No____

12. Does your child avoid active physical games involving running, jumping, and use of large play equipment?   Yes____ No____

13. Does your child avoid manipulation of small objects?   Yes____ No____

14. Does your child avoid activities involving the use of "tools" such as crayons, pencils, markers, and scissors?   Yes____ No____

15. Do you feel that your child has a short attention span, even for *things that she/he enjoys?*   Yes____ No____

16. Do you feel that your child tends to be restless or "fidgety" during times when quiet concentration is required?   Yes____ No____

17. Has your child had difficulty regulating his/her sleep patterns?   Yes____ No____

SENSORIMOTOR HISTORY QUESTIONNAIRE FOR TEACHERS OF ELEMENTARY-SCHOOL-AGE CHILDREN

Compiled by Lynn A. Balzer-Martin, Ph.D., O.T.R.

I. *Touch* (Tactile)

    1. Overreacts to physically painful experiences.   Yes____ No____

    2. Underreacts to physically painful experiences.   Yes____ No____

3. Avoids messy activities.   Yes____ No____

4. Craves messy activities.   Yes____ No____

5. Dislikes being touched, especially unexpectedly; becomes irritated when crowded and isolates self from others.   Yes____ No____

6. Craves being touched.   Yes____ No____

7. Seeks out physically aggressive contact (roughhousing, crashing into walls or people).   Yes____ No____

8. Is excessively ticklish.   Yes____ No____

9. Avoids using hands for prolonged periods of time or for examining objects thoroughly. Yes____ No____

II. *Balance and Movement* (Vestibular/Proprioceptive)

1. Has poor balance.   Yes____ No____

2. Has difficulty going up and down stairs or hills.   Yes____ No____

3. Often rocks in chair or assumes an upside-down position.   Yes____ No____

4. Often props head in hands while reading or writing.   Yes____ No____

5. Seems fearful in space (e.g., swing, seesaw, heights).   Yes____ No____

6. Is afraid of, or avoids, vigorous, fast-moving activities at the playground (bouncing, swinging, balancing, or spinning).   Yes____ No____

7. Seems sensitive to movement, getting dizzy or seasick.   Yes____ No____

8. Prefers fast-moving or spinning activities, perhaps not getting dizzy or seeming less sensitive than most children to the effects.   Yes____ No____

III. *Coordination*

    1. Has difficulty with manual skills (scissors, crayons, pencils, buttons) and/or with handwriting.   Yes____ No____

    2. Seems clumsy and accident-prone, frequently falling and tripping, perhaps not catching self easily.   Yes____ No____

    3. Has difficulty learning new movement activities and/or dislikes trying them.   Yes____ No____

    4. Was slow to show a clear hand preference or is not yet clearly right- or left-handed.   Yes____ No____

    5. Must be reminded to hold paper while writing.   Yes____ No____

    6. Uses extraneous movements during physical activity (e.g., sticks out tongue, moves jaw, clenches fists).   Yes____ No____

IV. *Muscle Tone*

    1. Appears stiff and rigid.   Yes____ No____

    2. Appears loose and floppy.   Yes____ No____

    3. Has poor standing and/or sitting posture.   Yes____ No____

    4. Grasps objects too tightly.   Yes____ No____

    5. Grasps objects too loosely.   Yes____ No____

    6. Tires easily.   Yes____ No____

V. *Hearing* (Auditory)

    1. Is frightened or irritated by loud noises.   Yes____ No____

    2. Is very sensitive to background sounds.   Yes____ No____

3. Has difficulty paying attention amid surrounding
   noise.   Yes_____ No_____

4. Often shouts or speaks in a loud
   voice.   Yes_____ No_____

5. Frequently makes repetitive noises or
   sounds.   Yes_____ No_____

6. Fails to follow through on verbal
   requests.   Yes_____ No_____

7. Needs directions repeated.   Yes_____ No_____

8. Confuses spoken words
   (e.g., *bear/hair*).   Yes_____ No_____

9. Misses some sounds.   Yes_____ No_____

VI. *Sight* (Visual)

1. Appears sensitive to light, preferring dark or dim
   lighting.   Yes_____ No_____

2. Has difficulty discriminating shapes or
   colors.   Yes_____ No_____

3. Has difficulty keeping eyes on
   objects.   Yes_____ No_____

4. Cannot follow a moving object or line of print
   smoothly with eyes; loses place.   Yes_____ No_____

5. Often squints, rubs eyes, gets headaches or watery
   eyes after reading.   Yes_____ No_____

6. Becomes excited with a lot of visual
   stimuli.   Yes_____ No_____

7. Resists having vision blocked.   Yes_____ No_____

8. Reverses or confuses numbers, letters, or whole
   words.   Yes_____ No_____

    9. Has difficulty with written
       instructions.   Yes____ No____

    10. Has difficulty copying from blackboard or
        books.   Yes____ No____

VII. *Smell* (Olfactory)

    1. Is overly sensitive to certain
       smells.   Yes____ No____

    2. Ignores noxious odors.   Yes____ No____

    3. Has difficulty discriminating
       odors.   Yes____ No____

VIII. *Attention and Behavior*

    1. Is restless or fidgety   Yes____ No____

    2. Is impulsive, often jumping up before instructions
       are given.   Yes____ No____

    3. Has difficulty organizing or structuring
       activities.   Yes____ No____

Hope Is at Hand

Having looked at the questionnaires, you should be getting a feel for how SI Dysfunction can get in a child's way. If you (and the teacher) checked many "yeses," you may believe you have an out-of-sync child. You may be asking: Is my child's development out of my hands? Will my child become an out-of-sync adult?

Not necessarily. Your child has a good chance of developing into a competent, self-regulating, smoothly functioning grown-up, if he or she receives understanding, support, and early intervention.

Early intervention involves treatment designed to correct or prevent the young child's developmental delays or disabilities. Treatment for SI Dysfunction usually comes in the form of occupational therapy (*discussed in chapter 6*). With treatment, the child can become as competent as possible—physically, intellectually, and emotionally.

Young children respond well to early intervention, because their central nervous systems are still flexible, or "plastic." Plasticity means that children's brain functioning is not fixed; it can change or be changed.

As children grow, it becomes more difficult to improve their neurological functioning because their brains become less malleable and their unusual reactions to sensations become more established. If your child is older than a preschooler, however, don't give up hope! Older children and even adults benefit from therapy, too.

For the child with severe dysfunction, treatment is crucial. For the child with moderate or even mild dysfunction, treatment can make a wonderful difference.

How does treatment help?

• Treatment helps the child process all the senses, so they can work together. When the child *actively* engages in meaningful activities that provide the intensity, duration, and quality of sensation his central nervous system craves, his adaptive behavior improves. Adaptive behavior leads to better sensory integration. As a result, perceptions, learning, competence, and self-confidence improve. The child becomes able to plan, organize, and carry out what he needs and wants to do. Without treatment, SI Dysfunction may hamper his life in countless ways.

• Treatment helps the child now, when he needs assistance to function smoothly. Treatment now helps him build a strong foundation for the future, when life becomes more demanding and complex. Without treatment, SI Dysfunction persists as a life-long problem. Indeed, the child will not grow out of SI Dysfunction but will grow into it.

• Treatment helps the child develop skills to interact successfully in social situations. The out-of-sync child often lacks the skills to play—and play is every child's primary occupation. Without treatment, SI Dysfunction interferes with the child's friendships.

• Treatment gives the child the tools to become a more efficient learner. Without treatment, SI Dysfunction interferes with the child's ability to learn, at home, at school, and out in the world.

• Treatment improves the child's emotional well-being. Without treatment, the child who believes she is incompetent may develop into an adult with low self-esteem.

• Treatment improves family relationships. As the child responds to sensory challenges with growing self-control, home life becomes more pleasant. With professional support, parents learn to provide consistent discipline and to enjoy their child. In-laws become more empathetic and less critical, and siblings resent the out-of-sync child less. Without treatment, SI Dysfunction interferes with the inter-actions and coping skills of everyone in the family.

Johnny is an example of a child who greatly benefited from early intervention. When he was a preschooler, SI Dysfunction affected his ability to move, play, learn, and relate to others. It affected his posture and balance, hearing and vision, food preferences and sleep patterns. He was fearful, angry, inflexible, and lonely.

Johnny's feet never left the ground because movement made him uncomfortable. He would stand and watch but not join his schoolmates in playground activities. He always carried a stick, as a buffer against the world. When someone approached him, he would brandish the stick and holler, "You're fired!" His sole pleasure was curling up in the quiet corner, peering at a book.

Johnny was one of the first children we screened at St. Columba's Nursery School for SI Dysfunction. We shared our findings with his parents and suggested occupational therapy, mentioning that early intervention could prevent later problems.

Listening to us, his father folded his arms, scowled, and shook his head. His mother wept and said, "This is all a bad dream."

Although skeptical, his parents decided to take our advice. They took Johnny to a pediatric occupational therapist twice a week. Working with the therapist and his teachers, they devised activities at home and school to help him become as competent as he could be.

Gradually, Johnny began to participate in some school activities. He didn't learn to relish messy play or a rowdy game of tag, but he did learn to paint at the easel and pump on the swing. He stopped carrying his stick in self-defense. He started to use his "indoor" voice instead of bellowing. He found a friend, and then two. He was becoming a real kid.

Today, Johnny is a dream-come-true. As a fifth-grader, he plays soccer and basketball. He's a Boy Scout who enjoys camping and climbing rocks. He reads a book every week, for pleasure. Everyone wants to be his friend, because he is reliable and sensitive—in all the right ways.

His teacher says, "I wish I had twenty-four other Johnnys in my classroom."

Johnny's story is true. His dysfunction, once severe, is now mild. He still eats carefully, feels uncomfortable in crowds, avoids escalators, and tends to be a perfectionist.

Not every out-of-sync child will have Johnny's success. Most children do improve, however, when their parents take action. Here are some suggestions:

• Get information and share it with pediatricians, teachers, and other caregivers, when appropriate.

• Although it's difficult to do, accept that the child doesn't fit your mental image of the perfect child; acknowledge that it's okay to have differing abilities.

• Provide the child with a well-balanced sensory diet (*chapter 7*).

• Be patient, consistent, and supportive.

• Help the child take control of his or her body and life.

The journey may be long. It may be expensive. It will certainly be frustrating at times. But the journey will also be wonderful and exciting as you learn to help free your child from the prison of SI Dysfunction.

Hope is at hand.

Chapter Two

UNDERSTANDING SENSORY INTEGRATION—AND WHAT CAN GO WRONG

It is important to understand basic information about SI and Sensory Integration Dysfunction. You need to know about the senses, the developmental stages of SI through which a young child normally progresses, and what happens when SI does not go according to Mother Nature's plan.

THE SENSES

Before you can understand sensory integration, you need to understand the senses.

Our senses give us the information we need to function in the world. The senses receive information from stimuli both outside and inside our bodies. Every move we make, every bite we eat, every object we touch produces sensations.

Sometimes our senses inform us that something in our environment doesn't feel right; we sense that we are in danger and so we respond defensively. For instance, should we feel a tarantula creeping down our neck, we would protect ourselves with a fight-or-flight response. It's natural to withdraw from too much stimulation, or from stimulation of the wrong kind.

Sometimes our senses inform us that all is well; we feel safe and satisfied, and seek more of the same stimuli. For example, we are so pleased with the taste of one chocolate-covered raisin that we eat a handful.

Sometimes, when we get bored, we go looking for more stimulation. For example, when we have mastered a skill, like ice skating in a straight line, we attempt a more complicated move, like a figure eight.

To do their job well—so that we respond appropriately—*the senses must work together*. Together, they provide a well-balanced diet for the brain. A brain that is nourished with many sensations operates well, and when our brain operates smoothly, so do we.

The Far Senses

We have many senses—more than many people know! Most people are familiar with the five senses of hearing, seeing, taste, smell, and touch. These are sometimes called the "far senses" because they respond to external stimuli that come from outside our bodies.

We are conscious of our far senses, and we have some control over them. We can scan a photograph of the third-grade class to pick out our child's face, or shut our eyes to avoid looking at an unpleasant scene. We can distinguish between a telephone ring and a doorbell, or cover our ears to screen out the dissonance of an untuned violin. We can

The Far Senses

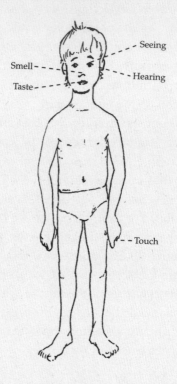

touch a keyboard letter with one fingertip, or keep our hands jammed in our pockets. As we mature, our brains refine our far senses so that we can respond to the world around us.

The Near Senses

When we think about sensory channels, the far senses come first to mind. Less familiar are the "near" senses—sometimes called the "hidden" senses, because we are not aware of them, cannot control them, and cannot directly observe them.

The Near Senses

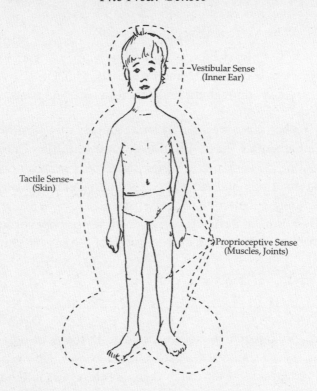

Essential for survival, the near senses respond to what is happening in our own bodies. With a "mind" of their own, they keep our bodies humming. Interoception, for one, is the sensory system of the internal organs. It regulates functions such as heart rate, hunger, thirst, digestion, body temperature, sleep, mood, and state of arousal.

Dr. Ayres highlighted the importance of three other body-centered sensory systems that provide the sense of oneself in the world. These are the topic of this book:

- The tactile sense, processing information about touch, which it receives primarily through the skin,

• The vestibular sense, processing information about movement, gravity, and balance, which it receives through the inner ear, and

• The proprioceptive sense, processing information about body position and body parts, which it receives through the muscles, ligaments, and joints.

The tactile, vestibular, and proprioceptive senses are fundamental. They lay the groundwork for a child's healthy development. When these near senses operate automatically and efficiently, the child can turn his eyes, ears, and attention to the external world.

Normally, a child is born with all his sensory apparatus intact, ready to begin his lifelong work of sensory integration.

WHAT IS SENSORY INTEGRATION?

Sensory integration is the neurological process of organizing the information we get from our bodies and from the world around us for use in daily life. It occurs in the central nervous system, which consists of countless neurons, a spinal cord, and—at the "head"—a brain.

The main task of our central nervous system is to integrate the senses. According to Dr. Ayres, "Over 80 percent of the nervous system is involved in processing or organizing sensory input, and thus the brain is primarily a *sensory processing machine.*"

When our brain efficiently processes sensory information, we respond appropriately and automatically. We do this because our brain is equipped to modulate sensory messages. Modulation is the term used to describe the brain's regulation of its own activity—and, therefore, of our activity level.

Activity level refers to mental, physical, and emotional behavior. Activity level can be high, low, or somewhere in between. For instance, mental activity is high when a child concentrates on an interesting science lesson, or low when she thinks the history lecture is dull. Physical activity is high when she leaps and low when she sleeps. Emotional activity is high when she feels threatened or exhilarated, and low when she has no special investment in routine events of the day, like running errands with Mom.

Modulation balances the flow of sensory information coming into the central nervous system. The brain turns on, or turns off, the neural switches of all the sensory systems, so that they work in tandem to keep us in sync.

Every minute of every day, we receive millions of sensations. Most of these are irrelevant to our current situation. Therefore, our brains inhibit them.

Inhibition is the neurological process that reduces connections between sensory intake and behavioral output. Inhibition is a good and healthy thing; without it, we would be giving full attention to every sensation, useful or not. For instance, it is unnecessary to respond to the sensation of air on our skin or of a shift in balance when we take a step, so we learn to ignore the messages.

Some messages are meaningless now, although they grabbed our attention at one time, such as the tautness of a seat belt. When we have become accustomed to familiar messages, our brain automatically tunes them out because they are no longer extraordinary. This process is called habituation.

But we must—and do—pay attention to meaningful sensory messages. Some of these are positive sensations, such as moving rhythmically in a rocking chair. Others are negative, such as spinning until we feel sick. These messages are facilitatory.

Facilitation is the neurological process that promotes connections between sensory intake and behavioral output. If we are doing something meaningful and beneficial, our brain gives us the go-ahead to continue.

When inhibition and facilitation are balanced, we can make smooth transitions from one state to another. A "state" refers to our degree of attentiveness, mood, or motor (movement) response. Thus, we can switch gears from inattention to attention, from sulks to smiles, from drowsiness to alertness, and from relaxation to readiness for action. Modulation determines how efficiently we self-regulate, in every aspect of our lives.

Here's an illustration of how sensory integration works for you. Suppose you are sitting on the couch, leafing through the newspaper. You pay no attention to the upholstery touching your skin, or the car passing by outside, or the position of your hands. These sensory messages are irrelevant, and you don't need to respond to them.

Then your child plops down beside you and says, "I love you." Your senses of sight, hearing, touch, movement, and body position (and maybe smell, too) are simultaneously stimulated. Sensory receptors throughout your body take in all this information. Via sensory neurons within your central nervous system, the information zooms to your brain.

Now, these sensory messages are relevant. In a swift neurological process, your brain analyzes, organizes, and connects—i.e., integrates—them.

Then, through motor neurons, your brain sends messages back out to your body, so you can produce a sensorimotor response.

You respond with language: "I love you, too."

You respond with emotion: a gush of affection.

And, because you know where you are and where your

child is, you know how much time it will take to get to her. Anticipating how much force to use for a "feel good" hug, you respond with movement. You drop the newspaper, lean over, open your arms, and embrace your child.

HOW MODULATION AFFECTS A CHILD'S BEHAVIOR

A Child with Normal SI	A Child with SI Dysfunction
During recess, Susan, seven, plays jacks. She ignores the cold pavement because the game interests her. However, her hands are cold, too, so she doesn't play well. The first time she fails to scoop up the jacks, she's disappointed. The second time, she's annoyed. The third time, she's thoroughly frustrated. She stands up and says, "I'm going to jump rope." Jumping for a few minutes warms her up and calms her. After recess, Susan returns to her classroom and is attentive until lunchtime.	Beth, seven, is playing jacks. She can't concentrate because the cold pavement distracts her. On her first two turns, she has trouble scooping up the jacks. Beth tries again, but her hands are too stiff. Suddenly, she explodes and screams, "I hate jacks!" She jumps to her feet, kicks the jacks into the grass, and leans against the building, crying uncontrollably. Unhappy for the rest of the morning, she can't calm down to attend to the reading lesson, and she refuses to eat lunch.

No one part of the central nervous system works alone. Messages must go back and forth from one part to another, so that touch can aid vision, vision can aid balance, balance can aid body awareness, body awareness can aid movement, movement can aid learning, and so forth. When sensory messages come in, and motor messages go out, in a synchronized way, we can do what we need to do.

The more efficient our brain is at processing sensory intake, the more effective our behavioral output will be. The more effective our output, the more feedback we receive to help us take in new sensory information and continue the never-ending process of sensory integration.

THREE EXAMPLES OF SYNCHRONIZED SENSORIMOTOR RESPONSES

The Blaring Horn

Sensory Intake: Walking to work, you hum along to a song playing on your Walkman. At an intersection, you look both ways, decide it's safe to cross, and step off the curb. Then you hear a blaring horn. Your auditory (hearing) sense receives the stimulus of the sound and sends the message to your brain.

Neurological Processing: Suddenly, you stop hearing the music. Your brain has a more urgent task: to filter out all irrelevant sounds, analyze the new message, interpret the sound as a danger signal, and organize the information for use.

Motor Output: Your brain tells you how to react with an appropriate motor response. You do what you need to do and jump back.

The Sour Plum

Sensory Intake: You see a plum that looks juicy, ripe, and sweet. You bite into it and discover that your expectation was wrong; it's sour. Your gustatory (taste) sense sends the message to your brain.

Neurological Processing: Your brain interprets "sour" as harmful and organizes the sensory message for use.

Motor Output: Your brain tells the muscles in your mouth how to respond. You spit out the morsel and tell yourself to check more carefully the next time.

The Changing Viewpoint

Sensory Intake: While raking, you stop to admire the growing leaf pile. Your child, catching falling leaves, comes into view. Your visual sense receives the message and sends it to your brain.

Neurological Processing: Your brain receives the information about the change in the point of focus, from the leaves under your feet to a more distant scene.

Motor Output: Your brain instructs your eye muscles to refocus on your child across the lawn.

Usually, by the time a child is ready for school, efficient sensory integration is well developed. But the development of sensory integration doesn't happen all at once. It goes through stages, as the maturing child builds his sense of self.

THE NORMAL DEVELOPMENT OF SENSORY INTEGRATION IN INFANTS AND CHILDREN

The development of sensory integration may be compared to a child's block construction. At first, the little child pushes blocks around on one level. Eventually, he figures out how to add a second level to the first. Then he adds a third level, and a fourth.

The Four Levels of Sensory Integration

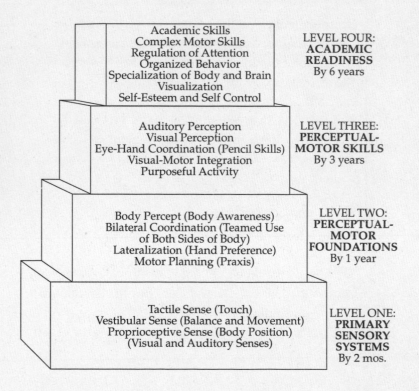

Academic Skills
Complex Motor Skills
Regulation of Attention
Organized Behavior
Specialization of Body and Brain
Visualization
Self-Esteem and Self Control

LEVEL FOUR:
ACADEMIC READINESS
By 6 years

Auditory Perception
Visual Perception
Eye-Hand Coordination (Pencil Skills)
Visual-Motor Integration
Purposeful Activity

LEVEL THREE:
PERCEPTUAL-MOTOR SKILLS
By 3 years

Body Percept (Body Awareness)
Bilateral Coordination (Teamed Use of Both Sides of Body)
Lateralization (Hand Preference)
Motor Planning (Praxis)

LEVEL TWO:
PERCEPTUAL-MOTOR FOUNDATIONS
By 1 year

Tactile Sense (Touch)
Vestibular Sense (Balance and Movement)
Proprioceptive Sense (Body Position)
(Visual and Auditory Senses)

LEVEL ONE:
PRIMARY SENSORY SYSTEMS
By 2 mos.

Sensory integration builds the same way. Each level rests on the building blocks laid down before. Just as the top level of the child's wooden block building needs support, so his readiness for complex skills rests on the foundation of the hidden, near senses.

By the time a child is ready for preschool, the building blocks for complex skill development should be in place. What are these building blocks?

- Ability to modulate touch sensations through the skin, especially unexpected, light touch, and to discriminate among the physical properties of objects by touching them (tactile sense),

- Ability to adjust one's body to changes in gravity and body position, and to feel comfortable moving through space (vestibular sense),

- Ability to be aware of one's body parts, and to move one's muscles and limbs in a coordinated way (proprioceptive sense),

- Ability to use the two sides of the body in a cooperative manner (bilateral coordination), and

- Ability to interact successfully with the physical environment; to plan, organize, and carry out a sequence of unfamiliar actions; and to do what one needs and wants to do (praxis). Praxis (Greek for "doing, action, practice") is a broad term denoting voluntary and coordinated action. The term *motor planning* is often used as a synonym for praxis.

Every child has an appetite for sensory nourishment. Inner drive, or self-motivation, urges him to participate actively in experiences that promote sensory integration. In daily life, he explores the environment, tries new activities, and strives to meet increasingly complex challenges. Mastering each new challenge makes him feel successful, and success gives him the confidence to forge ahead.

The developmental process of sensory integration takes place on a continuum. Dr. Ayres described this process as "Four Levels of Integration."

LEVEL ONE (PRIMARY SENSORY SYSTEMS)

By the age of two months, the infant is already busily integrating sensory information, thus establishing the foundation for all future learning. While all senses are operating, the primary "teachers" are skin (the tactile sense), gravity and movement (the vestibular sense), and muscles, joints, and ligaments (the proprioceptive sense).

Touch stimulation feels good on his skin and around his mouth (an extremely sensitive tactile receptor). He sucks with pleasure and enjoys being held and rocked. A strong feeling of attachment develops as a result of this sensory connection between mother and child. The baby learns that eating, cuddling, and being friendly provide positive feedback.

The baby receives information about movement through his vestibular and proprioceptive senses. With his budding visual sense, he anticipates and imitates his mother's facial expressions. He begins to regulate his movements, including his eye movements. He can see motionless objects nearby, as well as people moving around him. He learns to rely on the comings and goings of the people near him.

Vestibular and proprioceptive senses also affect his posture and muscle tone so that his responses are automatic and appropriate. He tries new movements and, after some effort, succeeds. Moving in response to the environment is effective. The more he moves, the more confident he becomes.

Vestibular sensations about gravity, coming through his inner ear and muscles and joints, give him gravitational security. He learns that he is connected to the earth. He feels safe.

LEVEL TWO
(PERCEPTUAL-MOTOR FOUNDATIONS)

Having integrated basic senses at Level One, the one-year-old begins to develop a body percept, or body awareness. A body percept is a mental picture of where body parts are, how they interrelate, and how they move. Visual feedback helps give him a sense of self.

Along with body awareness comes bilateral (two-sided) integration. This is the process that enables the child to use both sides of his body symmetrically, in a smooth, simultaneous, and coordinated way.

Bilateral integration, a neurological process, is the foundation for bilateral coordination, a behavioral skill. Bilateral coordination is necessary for such interesting work as passing a rattle back and forth from hand to hand.

A function of bilateral integration is lateralization, the process of establishing preference of one side of the brain for directing efficient movement on the opposite side of the body. As lateralization matures, the child begins to demonstrate a hand preference, uses his hands separately, and crosses the midline. He can use one hand to shake his rattle, the other to twiddle his toes.

Postural responses improve. Postural responses are automatic movements that extend the trunk, neck, and head upward, against the pull of gravity. He develops neck stability, raising his head and torso to look around.

Neck stability helps the eyes hold steady so the baby can gaze at whatever interests him. In turn, stabilization of the eyes helps the baby improve motor control, for the more he uses his eyes to observe his surroundings, the more he coordinates his movements. With developing binocularity, or eye-teaming, he looks where he's going and goes where he's looking.

He begins to crawl, then creep. As he alternates his hands and legs, he uses both sides of his brain and stimulates bilateral coordination.

His maturing tactile, vestibular, and proprioceptive senses promote praxis. He can figure out how to do something he has never done before, and then do it again without thinking much about it. Rolling over, for example, requires motor planning the first few times, until the child has practiced it so often that he can roll over effortlessly.

The child's activity level becomes better regulated, and his attention span and emotional security increase because his sensations are becoming well organized. He can sit in his car seat for a ride to the grocery store. He can bang on the piano keys for a few minutes. He can tell the difference between a parent and a stranger. He can fall asleep peacefully at the end of his busy day.

LEVEL THREE (PERCEPTUAL-MOTOR SKILLS)

As the child develops, so does his perception—the cognitive understanding of the information that his senses take in. As sensory perception and discrimination improve, his ability to interact with the external world broadens.

Hearing (the auditory sense) becomes more refined. He understands language and communicates through speech.

Sight becomes more precise. He can interpret visual data more accurately. He understands spatial relationships and can judge where he is in regard to people and objects.

Eye-hand coordination develops. Now the child can hold a crayon, draw a simple picture, catch a ball, and pour juice. Eye-hand coordination contributes to visual-motor integration, necessary for stringing pop beads or fitting a jigsaw puzzle piece into place.

Indeed, the child can do a jigsaw puzzle now—just for the fun of it—with purposeful, playful activity. When he picks up a jigsaw piece, it is his developing sensory integration that lets him see it, handle it, understand it, and fit it into the puzzle.

At the age of three, the child is continuing to develop and strengthen basic skills. Now he is ready for the "top floor" of his block building—the end products of sensory integration, on Level Four.

LEVEL FOUR (ACADEMIC READINESS)

The end products of sensory integration are academic skills (including abstract thought and reasoning), complex motor skills, regulation of attention, organization of behavior, specialization of each side of the body and the brain, visualization, self-esteem, and self-control.

These abilities become increasingly sophisticated. By the age of six, the child's brain is mature enough to specialize. Specialization (the process whereby one brain part becomes most efficient at a particular function) means that the child becomes more efficient and purposeful in his actions. His eyes and ears are prepared to take over as the primary "teachers."

His tactile discrimination improves; he can suppress reflexive responses to touch sensations. On a wintry day, he can ignore the minor discomfort of an itchy wool hat and concentrate on making a snowball. He can tell the difference between a friendly pat and an aggressive punch.

His proprioceptive sense, in tandem with his vestibular and tactile senses, strengthens his motor coordination. His gross motor skills are smooth: he can jump and run and play with his pals.

His fine motor skills are good: he can button, zip, and spin a top. He consistently prefers to use one hand more than the other for tool use. He controls a pencil or crayon to make recognizable shapes and symbols.

He can visualize past and future situations: yesterday's ball game and tonight's bath. Visualization helps him picture pretend and real images: make-believe monsters and Mommy's reassuring face.

He is socially competent, able to share ideas and toys, to be flexible when things don't go his way, to empathize with others when things don't go their way, to play by the rules, to be a reliable friend.

The child will continue to improve his sensory integration "building" throughout his life. As he encounters different situations and new challenges, he learns to make adaptations in meaningful ways. Feeling good about himself, he is ready for school.

WHEN SENSORY INTEGRATION
IS INEFFICIENT

Sensory Integration Dysfunction is the brain's inability to process sensations efficiently. Having SI Dysfunction does *not* imply brain damage but rather what Dr. Ayres called "indigestion of the brain," or a "traffic jam in the brain."

Dysfunction occurs when the open-ended, reciprocal process of intake/organization/output is disrupted. Here is what may happen:

FIRST: INEFFICIENT SENSORY INTAKE

When our brains take in too little or too much sensory information, we can't react in a meaningful way.

Taking in too much information is called hypersensitivity, or hyper-responsiveness. Our brain-computer is on overload. The result is that we avoid sensory stimuli that excessively arouse us.

Taking in too little information is called hyposensitivity or hyporesponsiveness. The result is that we seek extra stimuli to arouse ourselves.

SECOND: NEUROLOGICAL DISORGANIZATION

A. The brain may *not receive* sensory data because of a "disconnect," or

B. The brain may receive sensory messages, but *inconsistently,* or

C. The brain may receive sensory messages consistently but *not connect* them properly with other sensory messages to produce a meaningful response.

THIRD: INEFFICIENT MOTOR, LANGUAGE, OR EMOTIONAL OUTPUT

The brain is inefficient at processing the sensory messages, thus depriving us of the feedback we must have in order to behave in a purposeful way.

The brain of a child with inefficient sensory integration does not operate smoothly. A computer model of the out-of-sync child's brain may look like the one below.

*How Dysfunction May Occur
in the Sensory Processing Machine*

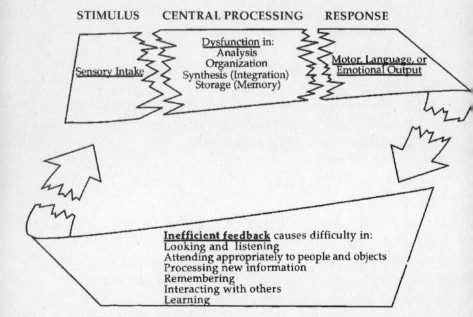

STIMULUS   CENTRAL PROCESSING   RESPONSE

Sensory Intake

Dysfunction in:
Analysis
Organization
Synthesis (Integration)
Storage (Memory)

Motor, Language, or
Emotional Output

Inefficient feedback causes difficulty in:
Looking and listening
Attending appropriately to people and objects
Processing new information
Remembering
Interacting with others
Learning

A "Short in the Circuitry"

For the out-of-sync child, sensory integration does not go according to Nature's plan. Somewhere in the circuitry of his sensory processing machine, there is a "short." For some reason, the circuitry is inefficient.

Therefore, the child will not respond in an ordinary way to ordinary sensations. The child may be hypersensitive, hyposensitive, or be "on and off" and have a combination of these extremes.

1) HYPERSENSITIVITY

One possible result of a short in the circuitry is hypersensitivity to sensory intake. ("Hyper" is Greek for "over.") Other terms are hyper-responsiveness, hyper-reactivity, over-responsiveness, and oversensitivity.

The brain of the hypersensitive child registers sensations too intensely. Overaroused by sensations, he may react as if they were irritating, annoying, or even threatening. Thus, the child may be quite distractible because he is paying attention to all stimuli, even if the stimuli are not useful.

Unable to screen the irrelevant from the relevant, he seeks to defend himself from most sensations. He may be negative and defiant, lashing out, or he may be fearful and cautious, shutting down.

The hypersensitive child may misinterpret a casual touch as a life-threatening blow, may feel that he will fall off the face of the earth if he is nudged, or may withdraw from unfamiliar people or situations. He may be distressed by changes in routine, loud noises, and crowded settings.

The child may have difficulty understanding gestural communication, too. He may overreact to nonverbal cues and respond with anxiety or hostility. He may be extremely sensitive to someone else's displeasure, even if the displeasure is not directed at him.

The child may avoid touch and movement experiences, because he can't tolerate them. He needs guidance to engage in active, meaningful play.

2) HYPOSENSITIVITY

Hyposensitivity to sensory intake is another possible result. ("Hypo" is Greek for "under.") Other terms are hyporesponsiveness, hyporeactivity, under-responsiveness, and undersensitivity.

The brain of the hyposensitive child registers sensations less intensely than normal. The child is not getting enough sensory information. Thus, he needs a lot of stimulation just to achieve ordinary arousal or alertness.

The child may be a "toucher and feeler," and a "bumper and crasher." He may collide with walls or people because he seeks extra stimulation . . . or because he doesn't perceive them in time to move aside . . . or because he lacks good motor control. His brain and body are telling him that he must act, but he acts in an incoordinated and disorganized way.

On the other hand, he may be withdrawn and difficult to engage, or self-absorbed and preoccupied with his own inner world. He may tire easily and seem sleepy. He may be a passive type who lacks initiative and just can't seem to get going. He may appear to be a "space cadet" or "out to lunch."

The hyposensitive child may miss cues that other children catch easily. He may hurt himself because he doesn't register "hot" or "sharp" as painful sensations. He may chew on inedible objects, like shirt cuffs and toys, to get sensory information through his mouth.

The hyposensitive child may have trouble understanding gestural communication. He may misinterpret
nonverbal cues and respond slowly to unspoken messages.
He may not "read" other people's facial expressions and
body language. The child may not laugh at a clown's
antics, may not comprehend that the teacher is beckoning
the children to go indoors, and may not respond to a person's frown or an animal's growl.

The child needs help to find safe, appropriate activities that will encourage more organized and purposeful
behavior.

3) A COMBINATION OF
HYPER- AND HYPOSENSITIVITY

The third possible result is a combination of hypersensitivity and hyposensitivity. The child with this problem
may be oversensitive in some ways and undersensitive in
others. His brain can't modulate sensations. For some reason, the switches are jammed.

The child may seek intense sensory experiences—
such as spinning on playground equipment—but be
unable to tolerate them. Or, he may seek intense experiences some days but avoid them on other days. His over-
or underreaction may depend on the time of day, the
place, and the stimulus.

His sometimes-on-sometimes-off processing is especially bewildering to the adults who care for him. Sometimes he will seem to be in sync, and sometimes he won't.
This child is particularly challenging to raise and to teach,
because it's so hard to know how and when to help him.
He is a child at risk.

His distractibility, impulsivity, and activity level may
be high, making people think he has ADHD, when in fact,
he fidgets both to protect himself and to make sense of his

world. Indeed, his attention span for things he enjoys may be excellent, as long as sensory processing problems don't get in his way.

The child has great difficulty functioning in daily life. He is not on an even keel and becomes easily upset. Once upset, he may have difficulty recovering.

He may be well regulated at home but have problems at school, or vice versa. He may feel safe and in control in one place but uncertain and out of control in another. The need to feel in control of people, objects, and experiences is a major issue for the child who does not feel in control of himself.

This child requires assistance to find activities that will suit his on-again-off-again needs.

A short in the circuitry means that the child lacks some of the basic building blocks for functioning in daily life. He may have difficulty interacting with others. He may have problems paying attention because of his inability to look, listen, conceptualize, and remember. He struggles mightily to feel in sync with the world.

FIVE IMPORTANT CAVEATS

In this book, you will find many checklists of characteristics of children with SI Dysfunction. You will also find numerous examples of out-of-sync behavior that illustrate the various ways SI Dysfunction plays out at home and school. You may say, "Eureka! This is my child, to a tee!" On the other hand, you may say, "This is definitely not my child, because my child doesn't have all these symptoms." Perhaps your child is somewhere in between.

As you read along, please remember the following caveats:

1. The child with sensory dysfunction does not necessarily exhibit every characteristic. Thus, the child with vestibular dysfunction may have poor balance but good muscle tone.

2. Sometimes the child will show characteristics of a dysfunction one day but not the next. For instance, the child with proprioceptive problems may trip over every bump in the pavement on Friday yet score every soccer goal on Saturday. *Inconsistency is a hallmark of neurological dysfunction.*

3. The child may exhibit characteristics of a particular dysfunction yet not have that dysfunction. For example, the child who typically withdraws from being touched may seem to be hypersensitive to tactile stimulation but may, instead, have an emotional problem.

4. The child may be both hypersensitive and hyposensitive. For instance, the child may be extremely sensitive to light touch, jerking away from a soft pat on the shoulder, while being rather indifferent to the deep pain of an inoculation.

5. Everyone has some sensory integration problems now and then, because no one is well regulated all the time. All kinds of stimuli can temporarily disrupt normal functioning of the brain, either by overloading it with, or by depriving it of, sensory stimulation.

Comparison of SI and SI Dysfunction

	Sensory Integration (SI)	SI Dysfunction
What:	The ability to take in sensory information from one's body and from the environment, to organize this information, and to use it to function in daily life.	The inefficient processing of information from the tactile, vestibular, and/or proprioceptive senses. The person may have difficulty with other basic senses, as well.
Where:	Occurs in the central nervous system (nerves, spinal cord, and brain), in a well-balanced, reciprocal process.	Occurs in the central nervous system, where the flow between sensory intake and motor output is disrupted.
Why:	To enable a person to survive, to make sense of the world, and to interact with the environment in meaningful ways.	Neuronal connections in the central nervous system are inefficient.
How:	Happens automatically as the person takes in sensations through sensory receptors, including the skin, the inner ear, and the muscles and joints.	Sensory neurons don't send efficient messages into the central nervous system, and/or motor neurons don't send efficient messages out to the body for correct behavioral responses.
When:	Begins in utero and continues developing throughout childhood, with most functions established by adolescence.	Occurs before, during, or shortly after birth.

Chapter Three

How to Tell If Your Child Has a Problem with the Tactile Sense

Three Kindergartners at Circle Time

The kindergartners are gathering for circle time. In the center of the rug, Miss Baker has arranged a variety of squashes: acorn, butternut, pattypan, pumpkin, summer, and zucchini.

Most of the children sit down on their individual carpet squares. Robert, however, stands aside and waits until the others are seated. Then he gingerly picks up his carpet square and moves it toward the wall. He pulls two plastic dinosaurs from his pocket and grips one in each hand. Finally, he sits down, as far as possible from Leah, his nearest neighbor.

Patrick finds his carpet square, but, instead of sitting, he makes a crash landing, sprawling facedown on the rug. He spreads his arms and legs and swishes them on the rug, shouting "Look! I'm a windshield wiper!"

Miss Baker says, "Please sit up in your own space, Patrick."

He sits up and begins to wrestle with another boy until Miss Baker says, "Please keep your hands to yourself, Patrick."

Eventually, circle time begins. Miss Baker passes each squash around the circle, so the children can get a feel for them.

Patrick squeezes every squash when he gets his hands on it. He rolls the summer squash between his hands and rubs it down his legs. He licks the acorn squash and bites the zucchini.

Miss Baker reminds him, "Just use your hands, not your mouth. And please pass the squash to Leah. It's her turn."

Leah, however, is not paying attention. She gazes out the window. When Patrick flings each squash into her lap, she looks down in surprise. Without examining the squashes, she passes them quickly to Robert.

But Robert refuses to touch the vegetables. When Leah offers him the first squash, he jabs his dinosaurs toward her face.

Leah recoils and drops the squash. Having figured that Robert isn't receptive, she places the subsequent samples in front of him.

Using his dinosaurs, Robert pushes each squash away.

Miss Baker lines up the squashes in the center of the rug. She says, "Now, look at the squashes. What can you tell me about them?"

Several children volunteer their observations: "The pumpkin is heavy." "The zucchini is smooth." "The pattypan has a bumpy edge."

Miss Baker says, "You are good observers! What about you, Leah? Do you have something to add?"

Leah hesitates. Then she says, "I see six."

"True!"says Miss Baker. "Anything else?"

"Nothing," Leah says.

Miss Baker turns to Robert and says, "How about you?"

Robert says, "This is boring."

"This isn't boring!" Patrick bellows. He lunges forward, scoops all the squashes into a pile, and rolls on top of them. "This is fun!"

Miss Baker extricates the squashes from Patrick and says, "Let's put the squashes away now and sing a song. Then it's time for free play in the classroom."

Circle time comes to a close.

Atypical Patterns of Behavior

To the casual observer, Robert, Patrick, and Leah may seem like typical preschoolers. It's easy to look at their behavior and say, "That's just the way they are." But if we look closer, we may notice atypical patterns of behavior.

Touching and being touched distress Robert. He avoids being near the other children and defends himself with his dinosaurs. Handling his carpet square is unpleasant. He refuses to touch the squashes with his hands.

Touching and being touched delight Patrick. He uses his whole body to feel the rug. He tackles another child. He manhandles, mouths, and rolls on the squashes.

Touching objects to learn about them is not Leah's forte. Giving scant attention to the squashes, she doesn't perceive whether they are heavy or light, big or small, bumpy or smooth. Her only observation is about their quantity, not their quality.

These children may appear to be very different, but they have something in common: an identifiable problem with the tactile sense.

On the next pages you will learn how the tactile sense is supposed to function, followed by an explanation of the types of dysfunction that overrun Robert, Patrick, and Leah.

THE SMOOTHLY FUNCTIONING
TACTILE SENSE

The tactile system plays a major part in determining physical, mental, and emotional human behavior. Every one of us, from infancy onward, needs constant tactile stimulation to keep us organized and functioning.

We get tactile information through sensory receiving cells, called receptors, in our skin, from head to toe. Touch sensations of pressure, vibration, movement, temperature, and pain activate tactile receptors.

We are always actively touching or passively being touched by something—other people, furniture, clothes, spoons. Even if we are stark naked, our feet still touch the ground, and the air touches our skin.

Therefore, the tactile sense, or sense of touch, is a huge sensory system that gives us information needed not only for visual perception, motor planning, and body awareness, but also for academic learning, emotional security, and social skills.

Two components make up the tactile sense. First is the protective (or defensive) system; second is the discriminative system.

1. The Protective/Defensive System: "Uh, Oh!"

Whether we call it protective or defensive, it's the same: the "uh, oh!" system. All creatures are born with a protective/defensive system. Its purpose is to alert us to potentially harmful stimuli. We need it to survive.

The receptors for the protective system are in the skin, especially hairy skin on the head and the genitals. Light touch is the stimulus that causes the receptors to respond.

Sometimes light touch is alarming, such as a mosquito alighting on our skin. We respond negatively, for self-preservation. Sometimes light touch is charming, such as a lover's gentle caress. We respond positively, for preservation of the species!

Ordinarily, we become less conscious of this system as we mature. We learn to tolerate trifling tactile sensations that would have irritated us in infancy.

Of course, we can always revert to operating on our defensive system when a true threat occurs. For example, when a stranger gets too close, we shrink; when a lash gets in our eye, we blink. But usually, we ignore light touch sensations because they don't grab our attention the way deep pain or extremes in temperature do.

2. The Discriminative System: "Aha!"

The second component of the tactile sense is the discriminative system: the "aha!" system. It tells us:

- that we are touching something or that something is touching us,
- where on our body the touch occurs,
- whether the touch is light or deep, and
- how to perceive the attributes of the object, such as its size, shape, temperature, density, and texture.

It develops as neurological maturation suppresses the defensive system. (The defensive system diminishes but doesn't disappear. Indeed, messages between the two systems must continue to flow back and forth all our lives so we can interpret tactile information appropriately.)

The receptors for this system are in the skin, especially on the hands and fingers, the soles of the feet, and the mouth and tongue. Deep touch, or "touch pressure," is the stimulus that causes the receptors to respond.

The baby is born with the defensive sense, which he needs for survival. He is also born with the discriminative sense, but it is not highly effective at first. For example, an infant who has a blood sample drawn from a finger arches and howls as if his whole body were being assaulted. Even if he could talk, he couldn't say where he is being touched or what is touching him. A more discriminating preschooler, however, knows precisely which finger has been mistreated and just whom or what to blame.

As a child matures, it becomes less necessary to react to touch sensations with self-protective responses, and more necessary to learn about the environment through the more refined discriminative system. Thus, the discriminative sense should take precedence in everyday situations. The chart on the next page shows how this shift in importance occurs, as the child develops.

As you read on, you will understand why a smoothly functioning tactile system is necessary to function normally, and how an out-of-sync tactile system is disruptive. Tactile dysfunction is a major problem.

How the Discriminative System Takes Precedence
Over the Defensive System as Children Mature

Child's Age	Growing Importance of Discriminative System
INFANT: Defensive system is most important.	Defensive ⟶ Discriminative
TODDLER: Defensive and discriminative systems are equally important.	Defensive ⟵⟶ Discriminative
KINDERGARTNER: Discriminative system is most important.	Discriminative Defensive ⟶

THE OUT-OF-SYNC TACTILE SENSE

Tactile dysfunction is the inefficient processing in the central nervous system of sensations perceived through the skin.

The child with tactile dysfunction has difficulty with touching, and being touched by, objects and people. The child may be unable to distinguish between dangerous and benign tactile sensations and may misinterpret a friendly touch as a life-endangering attack. He may also be unable to discriminate physical properties of objects like apples, buttons, and pencils.

The child with an inefficient tactile system may have one or more problems with the integration of touch sensations. The child may:

1. Be defensive to touch (hypersensitive), like Robert, or

2. Be under-responsive to touch (hyposensitive), like Patrick, and/or

3. Have poor tactile discrimination, like Leah.

1. Tactile Defensiveness (Hypersensitivity): "Oh, No!"

The child who is hypersensitive to touch has tactile defensiveness, the tendency to react negatively and emotionally to unexpected, light touch sensations. The child will react not only to actual touch but also to the anticipation of being touched. Instead of responding with an appropriate "Uh, oh" to light touch, the child responds with "Oh, no! Get away! Don't touch me!" Perceiving most touch sensations to be uncomfortable or scary, he overreacts with a fight-or-flight response.

FIGHT-OR-FLIGHT FROM TOUCH SENSATIONS

If "fight" is his modus operandi, he responds with vigorous resistance or hostility. He may wrestle in your arms as you try to dress or lift him. He may wriggle out of his clothes or car seat. He may kick, punch, or scream at other children who come too close for comfort.

If "flight" is his manner, he reacts with an aversive response. An aversive response is a feeling of revulsion and repugnance toward a sensation, accompanied by an intense desire to avoid or turn away from it. The child may actively withdraw, fleeing from contact with finger paints, pets, and people. He may find the touch of unfamiliar people to be intolerable.

Or, he may withdraw passively, by simply avoiding the objects and people that distress him. He never gets close to them, or he walks away. This child often falls through the cracks; parents and teachers think he avoids petting the dog and playing in mud because "those just aren't his thing," when in fact, he avoids tactile sensations to defend himself.

SEEKING TOUCH SENSATIONS

All children need touch information to learn about the world. So how does the child with tactile defensiveness get this information? By touching!

Parents are often mystified when they learn that their child has a tactile dysfunction. They protest, "But he is forever asking for hugs and back rubs. He is always touching everything, and he usually carries something in his hands. How can you say he has a problem with touch?"

The answer to this question is the type of touch that the child avoids or seeks. The child typically avoids unexpected, light touch, such as a gentle kiss. A kiss is irritating, and the child may try to rub it off.

While the child avoids light touch, he not only accepts but also craves deep touch, like a bear hug. A hug provides firm touch and deep pressure. Deep touch feels good and actually helps suppress sensitivity to light touch.

This child needs touch information more than a child with a well-regulated tactile sense. To get the stimulation his brain needs, he may touch repeatedly those surfaces and textures that provide soothing and comforting tactile experiences. He may touch and feel everything in sight, bumping and touching others, running his hands over furniture and walls, and handling items that other children understand are "no-no's."

The child may also hold objects such as a stick or a toy in his hand. Perhaps these objects help him defend himself from the unexpected touch sensations abounding in the environment.

HOW TACTILE DEFENSIVENESS
AFFECTS A CHILD'S BEHAVIOR

A Child with Normal SI	*A Child with SI Dysfunction*
Getting ready for school, Daniel, three, tolerates having his father brush his hair and wash his face. He doesn't enjoy this experience, but he can adapt to it and can recover immediately. His maturing neurological system allows him to suppress a fight-or-flight reaction.	Getting ready for school, Will, three, flinches when his father tries to brush his hair and wash his face. He pushes his father away and cries, "You're hurting me!" His protective/ defensive system still rules his reactions to touch, so he reacts with an infantile fight-or-flight response. He's upset all during breakfast.

2. Under-Responsiveness to Touch (Hyposensitivity): "Ho, Hum"

The child who is hyposensitive to touch tends to underreact to tactile experiences. Needing extra stimulation, he may constantly touch objects and people. He may be under-responsive to touch, whether the touch is soothing or painful.

Instead of murmuring, "Mmm!" when his mother cradles him, he seems to say, "Ho, hum. This TLC has no effect on me." Instead of crying, "Ouch!" when he stubs his toe, he seems to say, "Ho, hum. I didn't notice."

Unlike the hypersensitive child, who overreacts to protect himself, the hyposensitive child may not react to touch effectively enough to do a good job of self-protection. In fact, he may seem unaware of touch altogether, unless the touch is very intense.

It is important to understand that the out-of-sync child may be both hypersensitive and hyposensitive. For instance, he may jump when someone grazes his elbow, yet be indifferent to a broken collarbone.

HOW HYPOSENSITIVITY AFFECTS A CHILD'S BEHAVIOR

A Child with Normal SI	*A Child with SI Dysfunction*
Randy, six, falls off his bicycle, scraping his knees. He runs inside and tearfully tells his baby-sitter that he had a bad accident. She bandages his wounds and soothes him. Eventually, he stops crying, although he hobbles around the house and complains for a little while. As soon as his friend comes to play, he forgets about his discomfort.	Georgie, six, falls off his bicycle. He scrapes both knees but pays little attention to his injuries. He remounts his bike and continues to ride. When his baby-sitter notices his wounds and tries to clean them, he brushes her off. "It doesn't hurt," he says.

3. Poor Tactile Discrimination: "Huh?"

If the defensive system isn't integrated by the time a child is three or four, then the discriminative system can't arise to "take charge." With inefficient or immature discrimination, the child will have difficulty using his tactile sense for increasingly complex purposes—like learning at school.

The child's brain doesn't register information about how things feel. Even when he has met Legos or soda cans before, he needs to touch and handle them repeatedly to learn about their weight, texture, and shape. "Huh?" he seems to say. "What's this?"

The child may seem out of touch with his hands, using them as if they were unfamiliar appendages. He may be unable to point a finger or button a coat without looking. He has trouble learning new manual skills, exploring the environment, using classroom tools, and performing ordinary tasks.

(The child with poor tactile discrimination may also have tactile defensiveness, but this is not always the case. Sometimes, the defensive system has matured sufficiently, but a "short in the circuit" prevents the discriminative system from developing properly.)

HOW TACTILE DISCRIMINATION
AFFECTS A CHILD'S BEHAVIOR

A Child with Normal SI	A Child with SI Dysfunction
Before Back-to-School Night, Katie's second-grade teacher asks the children to draw large self-portraits to tape to their chairs. Katie likes the idea that her parents will be able to find her seat. Patting her hair ribbons, earlobes, neck, and blouse buttons, she crayons a detailed picture. She cuts out the drawing and tapes it to her chair.	Tina, seven, works hard to draw a self-portrait. Awkwardly holding a crayon, she draws a circle, two dots for eyes, and a line for a mouth. Cutting with scissors is difficult, so she skips that step and tapes the whole sheet of paper, as is, to her chair.

How the Tactile Sense Affects Everyday Skills

In addition to helping us to protect ourselves and to discriminate among objects, the tactile sense gives us information that is necessary for many kinds of everyday skills:

- Tactile perception
- Body awareness (body percept)
- Motor planning
- Visual perception
- Academic learning
- Emotional security
- Social skills

Tactile Perception

Normally, a child's tactile discrimination teaches him to make sense of the feel of things. Feeling the warmth of Mommy's skin, the roughness of Daddy's stubble, the crunchiness of gravel underfoot, and the roundness of an orange, he learns about his world.

The out-of-sync child, however, has difficulty paying attention to the physical attributes of objects and people. He is otherwise occupied. If he avoids touch, his hands may "live" in his pockets, or he may keep his fingers curled to protect his sensitive palms. If he craves touch information, he may handle (or mishandle) everything in sight, without discrimination. Thus, his tactile perception doesn't develop well because he can't practice it properly.

Movement and touch are the child's first teachers. If the child has tactile dysfunction, he can't learn through his sense of touch. At school, where children's tactile perception is assumed, he will be at a disadvantage. Even his language will suffer, for language is built on many types of sensory experiences, and his meaningful tactile experiences are limited, indeed.

HOW TACTILE PERCEPTION
AFFECTS A CHILD'S BEHAVIOR

A Child with Normal SI	A Child with SI Dysfunction
Kindergartner Ellen, five, is making a "guitar" by pulling rubber bands over a cigar box. She chooses several with various attributes: big and small, fat and skinny, tight and loose. She stretches them over the box and arranges them carefully so they don't overlap. By strumming or plucking, she produces a variety of pleasing sounds.	Kindergartner Patty grabs a handful of rubber bands, but she has trouble detecting which ones are more or less flexible than others. They all seem the same to her, because her tactile perception is inefficient. She struggles to stretch one rubber band around the cigar box and then gives up.

Body Awareness

The tactile sense, along with the proprioceptive sense, affects a person's unconscious awareness of individual body parts, and how the body parts relate to one another and to the surrounding environment. With good tactile perception, a child develops body awareness (body percept), which is like a map of the body, and can then move purposefully and easily. The child has a sense of where he is and what he is doing.

The child with tactile dysfunction lacks good body awareness. He is uncomfortable using his body in his environment because moving means touching. He has difficulty orienting his limbs in order to get dressed. He would rather stand in a corner than risk mingling with an unpredictable group. Shifting his position may even make him conscious of how uncomfortable he is in his clothes. Better to stand very, very still, his central nervous system tells him, and avoid it all.

HOW BODY AWARENESS AFFECTS A CHILD'S BEHAVIOR

A Child with Normal SI	*A Child with SI Dysfunction*
In his third-grade music class, Tyler is enjoying the song "Head and Shoulders, Knees and Toes." He likes it when the tempo speeds up, so that tapping the right body parts at the right time gets harder. Recess is after music, and Tyler slips into his jacket, zips it up, pulls on his gloves, and heads outdoors.	Roger slumps in the back row, scowling. He hates the "Head and Shoulders" song. He always gets his body parts mixed up, and he's embarrassed. When it's time for recess, he concentrates on getting into his coat, which is still a difficult task for him. Gloves are too much trouble, so he shuffles outdoors with his hands stuck in his pockets.

Motor Planning

Each new sequence of movements requires motor planning. Certainly, the first time a child climbs a jungle gym, threads a belt through loops, or says "Lollapalooza," he must plan his movements with conscious effort. With practice, he can do these actions successfully because he has integrated tactile sensations, such as the feel of jungle gym rungs under his feet and hands.

HOW MOTOR PLANNING AFFECTS A CHILD'S BEHAVIOR

A Child with Normal SI	A Child with SI Dysfunction
Charley, four, arises and puts on blue jeans and a new belt, managing to buckle it all by himself. He runs downstairs. He steadies his grapefruit with one hand and spoons out sections of it with the other. Ready for school, he climbs into the car and fastens his seat belt. Arriving at school, he unsnaps his seat belt and jumps out. On the blacktop, he spots a new tricycle. It is larger than trikes he has ridden before, but he figures out how to mount it. He stretches his feet and arms to reach the pedals and handles. He takes it for a test drive, getting a feel for its new requirements.	Matt, four, arises slowly. He ignores the blue jeans and belt his mother has set out; they're too hard to put on. He struggles into his favorite sweatpants with the elasticized waist. He goes downstairs carefully: right foot first, then left, on each step. He jabs a spoon at his grapefruit, and the dish skitters across the table. When it's time to go to school, he maneuvers himself into the car and waits for his mother to buckle him in. Arriving at school, he needs a teacher to unbuckle the seat belt. Then he inches out of the car. On the blacktop, Matt heads for an old, familiar tricycle. He sits there, dangling his feet, while the other kids ride around him.

The more a child touches and explores objects, and the more he learns to move his body in different ways, the better his motor planning and motor skills become. Mastering one motor skill leads to trying another that is more challenging. For instance, after gaining confidence on a jungle gym, a child may use his skills to climb a tree or hang upside down from a monkey bar. This is an example of adaptive behavior.

The child who feels uncomfortable in his own skin may have poor motor planning, or dyspraxia. (Dyspraxia is a common type of sensory processing problem that interferes with the ability to perform coordinated actions.) The child may not move smoothly or may have trouble planning and organizing his movements. Thus, he may avoid the very activities that would improve his motor planning.

For instance, if he dislikes how the monkey bars feel, he won't try to hang from them or practice the skill of traveling beneath them, one hand after the other. If touching a dandelion makes him uneasy, he won't want to pick it. The less he does, the less he can do. In a world where "use it or lose it" is a fact of life, this child loses.

Gross Motor Control

Motor planning is necessary for two broad categories of movement, one of which is gross motor control. This is the smooth coordination of the large muscles, which allows a child to bend and stretch, to move his body from one place to another by creeping or running, and to move his hands or feet to manipulate objects.

The child with tactile dysfunction is out of touch with his body and with objects in his world. His gross motor skills may be delayed, making it very difficult to learn, move, and play in meaningful ways.

HOW GROSS MOTOR CONTROL
AFFECTS A CHILD'S BEHAVIOR

A Child with Normal SI	A Child with SI Dysfunction
Lynn, ten, enjoys the fast-moving "Over and Under" game. One person holds a ball over her head and passes it to the next person, who takes the ball, bends forward, thrusts it through her legs, and passes it to the next. Moving is fun!	For Kim, ten, playing "Over and Under" is hard. Her movements are slow and awkward. The ball feels uncomfortable in her hands, and sometimes she drops it. When she interrupts or slows down the game, the other kids get angry. Movement games are no fun at all.

Fine Motor Control

Motor planning is necessary for another category of movement: fine motor control, which a child develops after establishing gross motor control. Fine motor activities require the precise use of small muscles in the fingers and hands, in the toes, and in the tongue, lips, and muscles of the mouth.

Because the child with tactile dysfunction often curls his hands in loose fists or jams them in his pockets to avoid touch sensations, he has difficulty manipulating ordinary tools like scissors, crayons, and eating utensils.

This child frequently has poor self-help skills, is a messy eater, and may also have poor articulation and immature language skills. He may use more gestures than words to communicate because the fine motor control of his tongue and lips is inadequate.

HOW FINE MOTOR CONTROL
AFFECTS A CHILD'S BEHAVIOR

A Child with Normal SI	*A Child with SI Dysfunction*
Today is woodworking day for Alex's first-grade class. Alex sorts through the wood bin, chooses two pieces, and hammers them together to make an airplane. At recess, he takes it outside and experiments with different ways to hold and throw it. At dinner, he explains in detail how he constructed his lovely airplane, and how well it flies. Alex has good praxis.	Josh, six, wants to construct an airplane, too. He isn't sure how to begin, so the teacher hands him two wood pieces. Josh drops them and scrambles to pick them up. He has trouble holding and using the hammer, so the teacher helps him. His airplane looks pretty good. On the playground, he throws it a couple of times to see if it will fly. It falls at his feet. Then he stands and holds it until it is time to go home. At dinner, his father asks him what he did at school. Unable to express his thoughts, Josh holds up his lovely airplane for his father to see. Josh is dyspraxic.

Visual Perception

The tactile system plays an important part in the development of visual perception—the way the brain interprets what the eyes see. By touching objects, a child stores memories of their characteristics and relationships to one another. Looking at a rain puddle, for instance, he perceives that it is wet, cool, and fun to splash in, even without touching it, because he has touched puddles before. (The vestibular system is also crucial for the development of vision. *See chapter 4.*)

Normally, a young child touches what he looks at and looks at what he touches. Many experiences touching objects and people are the basis for visual perception.

When a child withdraws from touch stimuli, however, he can't nourish his brain with basic information about how things feel. Thus, he has difficulty analyzing, interpreting, and storing memories of tactile sensations.

HOW VISUAL PERCEPTION
AFFECTS A CHILD'S BEHAVIOR

A Child with Normal SI	*A Child with SI Dysfunction*
The kindergarten teacher hands each child a block. Each block has different attributes. It is either big or small; red, yellow, or blue; round, square, or rectangular. Then the teacher lays a series of similar blocks on the rug and asks the children to tell her which block on the floor matches the one in their hands. Bonnie knows the answer right away because she has handled many objects in her five years. She places her small red square next to its mate.	Chrissy, five, holds a big, yellow, rectangular block. The teacher asks her to match it with one on the floor. Chrissy isn't sure about sizes and shapes, but she knows her colors. She makes a guess and puts her block next to a small yellow square. A classmate points out her error, and the teacher asks him to show Chrissy how to make a correct match.

Academic Learning

Tactile integration has a big impact on a child's ability to learn at school. Many objects require hands-on manipulation: art materials, science equipment, rhythm instruments, basketballs, chalk, pencils, and paper. Taking pleasure in tactile experiences leads to exploring new materials and building a base of knowledge that will continue throughout a child's life.

Tactile dysfunction prevents a child from learning easily because touch sensations distract him. He may fidget when quiet is expected, complain that others are annoying him, and have trouble settling down for academic tasks.

The child misses out on learning skills requiring the purposeful use of tools such as pencils, forks, and hammers. He misses out on learning about nature, because getting dirty is intolerable or because he can't discriminate between an acorn and a chestnut. He misses out on learning problem-solving, communication, and "people" skills.

HOW THE TACTILE SENSE AFFECTS A CHILD'S ACADEMIC LEARNING

A Child with Normal SI	*A Child with SI Dysfunction*
Juan, six, likes science. Today, the teacher brings several caterpillars in a glass jar. Juan knows how it feels to handle caterpillars and asks, "May I hold the one that looks soft and fuzzy?" The teacher offers him the jar. He picks out the fuzzy caterpillar and puts it on his arm. "It tickles!"	Ricardo, six, dislikes science. While the other first-graders talk about the caterpillars, Ricardo averts his gaze. He rejects the teacher's invitation to hold the jar. He squirms in his chair and sits on his hands. He hates creepy bugs.

Emotional Security

With a well-regulated nervous system, we first learn to welcome the touch of the person (usually our mother) who takes care of our basic, infantile needs. Cuddling makes us feel warm and safe.

A close physical attachment to one or two primary caregivers sets the stage for all future relationships. If we feel cared for and loved, our emotional base is secure, and we learn to reciprocate warm feelings. Furthermore, if we are "in touch" with our own emotions, we develop empathy for other human beings. Even if we don't like a person, we know he feels pain when he gets a splinter and pleasure when he takes a warm bath.

Establishing strong attachments can be very difficult for the child with tactile dysfunction. The hypersensitive child may withdraw from ordinary affection, while the hyposensitive child may be under-responsive.

Feeling empathy can also be hard. The hypersensitive child feels pain or discomfort where others don't; the hyposensitive child feels no pain or discomfort where others do. He can't relate well to another person's feelings.

The child may have difficulty experiencing pleasure, enthusiasm, and joy in his relationships because of his responses to touch. While he needs even more love than others, he invites less. His insecurity in the world puts his emotional well-being at risk, as a child and as an adult.

Indeed, many adult relationships flounder when one partner's tactile dysfunction interferes with emotional intimacy. Too little touching makes the other person feel rejected; too much makes the other feel disrespected.

Tactile dysfunction also limits a child's imagination. If he lacks a rich variety of touch experiences, he can't visualize how objects and people feel. Fantasy and make-believe may be beyond his scope, and the differences between real and pretend may be vague. He may be a rigid, inflexible thinker.

HOW THE TACTILE SENSE
AFFECTS A CHILD'S EMOTIONAL SECURITY

A Child with Normal SI	*A Child with SI Dysfunction*
At nine, Mike takes pleasure in going away to Boy Scout camp. He is comfortable in novel settings and likes making new friends. One night the scouts play a creative thinking game: "What Would You Need on a Desert Isle?" Mike suggests a bucket to catch rainwater, a sleeping bag, and binoculars—familiar objects that he has handled—as well as someone to talk to. Mike's well-regulated tactile sense gives him emotional security.	James, nine, is unhappy at camp. He misses his mother. He depends on her totally and exclusively for emotional support and always wants her nearby. Forming attachments to anyone else is hard because everyone else seems unreliable. When the scouts play the Desert Isle game, he has no suggestions; all he can think is that he hates the idea of being deserted, hates being a Boy Scout, and hates being away from home.

Social Skills

A well-regulated tactile sense is fundamental for getting along well with others. Building on the primary mother-child bond, we begin to reach out to others, gladly and comfortably touching and being touched. *When we enjoy being near people, we learn how to play, one of the unique characteristics of being human.* Thus it becomes possible to develop meaningful human relationships.

When the child with dysfunction responds to physical contact in inappropriate ways, he may turn most people away. Both the "bad boy," who tackles others as he seeks deep-touch pressure, and the "sissy," who withdraws from touch, have trouble in social situations.

The child with tactile defensiveness has particular problems with socialization. Standoffish behavior sends signals that he is unfriendly and prefers to be left alone. Seeming to reject others, he is rejected in turn. He has difficulty dealing with the give-and-take, rough-and-tumble world of what child psychiatrist Stanley I. Greenspan, M.D., calls "playground politics."

HOW THE TACTILE SENSE
AFFECTS A CHILD'S SOCIAL SKILLS

A Child with Normal SI	A Child with SI Dysfunction
Standing in line to go to the lunchroom, Jake, eight, playfully bumps into Lewis. Lewis bumps him back. Laughing, they collide a few more times until all the third-graders are lined up and ready to go. When the teacher turns her attention to them and raises her eyebrows, the boys regain control and walk peacefully down the hall. Jake's positive reaction to tactile sensations is the foundation of his good social skills.	Whenever it is time to line up, Curtis, eight, tries to be last. He doesn't want anyone behind him. But today, Eli brings up the rear and brushes against him as they go down the hall. Overreacting to this unexpected touch, Curtis punches Eli. Eli punches back. The boys begin to argue, and the teacher pulls them apart. Curtis complains, "Eli started it." Eli says, "I just touched him accidentally! He's a crybaby." Establishing relationships is hard because Curtis is uncomfortable when his peers get near.

Children with tactile defensiveness frequently mature into adults who are "cool characters." They may be cautious, controlled, and often inflexible people. They may seem distrustful or judgmental. Their behavior may be considered "touchy"—a funny word for people who avoid touch! Of course, they can develop social relationships with a select group, but the relationships are often built on shared interests that do not involve physical interaction.

CHARACTERISTICS OF TACTILE DYSFUNCTION

The following checklists will help you gauge whether your child has tactile dysfunction. As you check recognizable characteristics, you'll begin to see emerging patterns that help to explain your child's out-of-sync behavior.

The child with **hypersensitivity (tactile defensiveness)** may:

☐ React negatively and emotionally to light touch sensations, exhibiting anxiety, hostility, or aggression. He may withdraw from light touch, scratching or rubbing the place that has been touched. As an infant, he may have rejected cuddling as a source of pleasure or calming.

☐ React negatively and emotionally to the *possibility* of light touch. He may appear irritable or fearful when others are close, as when lining up.

☐ React negatively and emotionally when approached from the rear, or when touch is out of his field of vision, such as when someone's foot grazes his under a blanket or table.

☐ Rebuff friendly or affectionate pats and caresses, especially if the person touching is not a parent or familiar person. The child may reject touch altogether from anyone except his mother (or primary caregiver).

☐ Prefer receiving a hug to a kiss. He may crave the deep-touch pressure of a hug but try to rub off the irritating light touch of a kiss.

☐ Overreact to physically painful experiences, making a "big deal" over a minor scrape or a splinter. The child may remember and talk about such experiences for days. He may be a hypochondriac.

☐ React similarly to dissimilar touch sensations. A raindrop on his skin may cause as adverse a reaction as a thorn.

☐ Avoid touching certain textures or surfaces, like some fabrics, blankets, rugs, or stuffed animals.

☐ Fuss about clothing, such as stiff new clothes, rough textures, shirt collars, turtlenecks, belts, elasticized waists, hats, and scarves.

☐ Fuss about footwear, particularly sock seams. He may refuse to wear socks. He may complain about shoelaces. He may insist upon wearing beach sandals on cold, wet, winter days, or heavy boots on hot summer days.

☐ Prefer short sleeves and shorts and refuse to wear hats and mittens, even in winter, to avoid the sensation of clothes rubbing on his skin.

☐ Prefer long sleeves and pants and insist on wearing hats and mittens, even in summer, to avoid having his skin exposed.

☐ Dislike being touched on the face or head, such as having his face washed.

☐ Dislike baths, or insist that bath water be extremely hot or cold.

☐ Dislike having his fingernails trimmed.

☐ Avoid messy play, such as sand, finger paint, paste, glue, mud, and clay.

☐ Be unusually fastidious, hurrying to wash a tiny bit of dirt off his hands.

☐ Avoid walking barefoot on grass or sand, or wading in water.

☐ Walk on tiptoe to minimize contact with the ground.

☐ Be excessively ticklish.

☐ Avoid giving kisses.

☐ Resist brushing his teeth and strongly resist going to the dentist.

☐ Be a picky eater, preferring certain textures such as crispy or mushy foods. The child may dislike foods with unpredictable lumps, such as tomato sauce or vegetable soup, as well as sticky foods like rice and cake icing.

☐ Refuse to eat hot or cold food.

☐ Show "fight-or-flight" response to hair displacement, such as having his hair brushed, or receiving a haircut, shampoo, or pat on the head.

☐ React negatively when hairs on his body (arms, legs, neck, face, back, etc.) are displaced and "rubbed the wrong way." A high wind or even a breeze can raise his hairs (literally "ruffling his feathers") and cause irritability, aggression, or anxiety.

For **self-protection,** the child with tactile defensiveness may:

☐ Withdraw from a group and resist playing at other children's homes.

☐ Treat pets roughly, or avoid pets.

☐ Arm himself at all times with a stick, toy, rope or other hand-held weapon.

☐ Stand still or move against the traffic in group activities such as obstacle courses or movement games, keeping constant visual tabs on others.

☐ Rationalize verbally, in socially acceptable terms, why he avoids touch sensations, e.g., "My mother told me not to get my hands dirty," or "I'm allergic to mashed potatoes."

The child with **hyposensitivity (under-responsiveness to touch)** may:

☐ Seem unaware of touch unless it is very intense.

☐ Be unaware of messiness on his face, especially around his mouth and nose, not noticing a crumby face or a runny nose.

☐ Show little or no reaction to pain from scrapes, bruises, cuts, or shots.

☐ Hurt other children or pets during play, seemingly without remorse, but actually not comprehending the pain that others feel.

☐ Fail to realize that he has dropped something.

The child with **poor tactile discrimination** may:

☐ Seem out of touch with his hands, as if they are unfamiliar appendages.

☐ Be unable to identify which body parts have been touched without looking.

☐ Be fearful in the dark.

☐ Be unable to perform certain motor tasks without visual cues, such as zipping, buttoning and unbuttoning clothes.

☐ Be a messy dresser, with shoes untied and waistband twisted.

☐ Put on gloves or socks in unusual ways.

☐ Have difficulty holding and using tools, such as crayons, scissors, and forks.

☐ Avoid initiating tactile experiences, such as picking up toys and tools that are attractive to others.

For **stimulation,** the child with tactile dysfunction may:

☐ Need to touch repeatedly those surfaces and textures that provide soothing and comforting tactile experiences, such as a favorite blanket.

☐ Seem compelled to touch certain surfaces and textures that cause other people discomfort, in order to receive strong tactile information.

☐ Need to touch and feel everything in sight, e.g., bumping and touching others, running hands over furniture and walls, and handling items that other children understand are not to be touched.

☐ Seek certain messy experiences, often for long durations.

☐ Rub or even bite his own skin excessively.

☐ Enjoy vibration or movement that provides strong sensory feedback.

☐ Prefer extra-spicy or excessively sweet foods.

☐ Use his mouth to investigate objects, even after the age of two. (The mouth provides more intense information than hands.)

The child with poor **tactile perception** may:

☐ Have trouble perceiving the physical properties of objects, such as their texture, shape, size, temperature, or density.

☐ Be unable to identify familiar objects solely through touch, needing the additional help of vision, e.g., when reaching for objects in a pocket, box, or desk.

☐ Prefer standing to sitting, in order to ensure visual control of his surroundings.

The child with poor **body awareness** may:

☐ Not know where his body parts are or how they relate to one another.

☐ Have trouble orienting his arms and hands, legs and feet to get dressed.

☐ Withdraw from movement experiences, to avoid touch sensations.

The child with **poor motor planning (dyspraxia)** may:

☐ Have trouble conceiving of, organizing, and performing activities that involve a sequence of body movements, such as cutting or bike riding. Novel experiences as well as familiar activities may be difficult.

☐ Have poor self-help skills and not be a "self-starter," requiring another person's help to get going.

☐ Have poor gross motor control for running, climbing, and jumping.

☐ Have poor fine motor control of his fingers for precise manual tasks, of his toes for gripping sandals or walking barefoot, and of his mouth muscles for chewing and speaking.

☐ Be a messy eater.

☐ Have poor eye-hand coordination.

The child with inadequate **visual perception** may:

☐ Be unable to interpret how objects feel, just by looking at them.

☐ Have trouble comparing and contrasting similar objects.

When **academic learning** is a problem, the child may:

☐ Be distracted, inattentive, and fidgety when quiet concentration is expected.

☐ Have a limited vocabulary because of inexperience with touch sensations.

☐ Withdraw from art, science, music, and physical activities.

The child who is **emotionally insecure** and has **poor social skills** may:

☐ Exhibit behavior that seems willful or "difficult," when it is actually an averse response to tactile stimuli.

☐ Be aggressive, hostile, or "pushy," verbally or physically, for no apparent reason.

☐ Act silly in the classroom, playing the role of "class clown."

☐ Appear very stubborn, rigid, and inflexible.

☐ Dislike surprises.

☐ Have a limited imagination.

☐ Have trouble forming warm attachments with others. Experiencing difficulty in social situations, he may be a loner, with few close friends.

While your child's primary problem may be with the tactile sense, perhaps the vestibular and proprioceptive senses cause problems, too.

Chapter Four

How to Tell If Your Child Has a Problem with the Vestibular Sense

Two First-Graders at the Amusement Park

Jason Green is in perpetual motion but is not much of a conversationalist. He is a "high-motor, low-verbal" kid. When he began to talk at three, his few words included "choo, choo" and "toot, toot," for his passion is trains. Jason loves trains so much that his father calls him "our little locomotive."

Kevin Brown, Jason's best buddy, loves trains, too. Kevin behaves not like a train, however, but like a conductor. He is a "low-motor, high-verbal" child. His mother jokingly calls him "NATO," for "No Action, Talk Only."

When the boys play, Kevin bosses Jason around, and Jason cheerfully obeys. Once, Kevin proposed making a train by hitching together a little red wagon, a big wheel, and an old tricycle. Jason nodded agreement. All thumbs, the boys fumbled with rope and finally managed to connect the vehicles. Then Kevin instructed Jason to push the train down his steep driveway so they could watch it plummet into the garage.

Instead of pushing the train, however, Jason clambered into the wagon. "Toot, toot!" he yelled as he plunged down the driveway. While Kevin watched, helpless and horrified, the train careened out of control.

Jason landed in a heap. He heaved himself up and said, "That was awesome! Totally fantastic! Want to try, Kevin?"

For once, Kevin was speechless.

Today is Jason's sixth birthday, and his parents are taking the boys to the amusement park. Jason loves the Ferris wheel, the merry-go-round, and especially the roller coaster. His idea of heaven is being twirled and tilted in the huge "Teacup." He never even gets dizzy.

Kevin is less enthusiastic. He has never found amusement parks amusing, because the thought of moving fast, high, and around in circles frightens him. He likes only the little train that slowly circles the park.

The first attraction the group approaches is the "Greased Toboggan." At the top of a slick ramp, riders sit in padded sacks and then slide down. Jason eagerly pulls on his father's sleeve to get his attention and permission.

Mr. Brown and Jason mount the stairs to the top. Jason ascends as fast as he can in his "marking time" fashion. He puts both feet on each step: right first, then left. In his haste, he stumbles twice.

Kevin lingers below with Mrs. Brown, watching. He doesn't want to slide; he wants to conduct. He raises his arm and shouts, "GO!" each time someone begins to descend.

Mrs. Brown asks Kevin if he would like to get into a sack with Jason. She points out that lots of people are coming down together in the same sack.

"Oh, no, thank you very much," Kevin says. "You see, I can't slide down the ramp because I have to tell everyone when to go. I have to make sure that everyone is doing it just right."

Jason and Mr. Brown swoop to the bottom. "That was so awesome!" Jason says. "Now let's go to the roller coaster. That's the most fun of all."

Kevin says, "No, let's go to the train. That's entertaining, and it isn't dangerous for children."

Jason is disappointed but agrees to do whatever his friend wants.

Toot, toot! Chug, chug! Off they go.

Atypical Patterns of Behavior

Kevin and Jason approach movement experiences very differently. They both show atypical patterns of behavior.

Moving and being moved dismay Kevin. He is uncomfortable on slides and rides that move fast or spin around. He is afraid of heights and prefers to keep his feet on the ground. He relies on his precocious verbal skills to maintain control. Hypersensitive to most vestibular sensations, Kevin is intolerant of movement and has gravitational insecurity.

In contrast, moving and being moved thrill Jason. Constantly and impulsively, he seeks fast-moving and spinning activities, but he does not get dizzy. Hyposensitive to vestibular sensations, Jason craves movement, but his movements are disorganized. His hands and feet don't work well together because of poor bilateral coordination.

Jason also has language problems. To communicate, he often uses gestures such as nodding his head or tugging on his father. He tends to be more talkative, however, after intense vestibular experiences such as sliding down the driveway and the Greased Toboggan.

On the next pages you will learn how the vestibular sense is supposed to function, followed by an explanation of the types of dysfunction that derail Kevin and Jason.

THE SMOOTHLY FUNCTIONING
VESTIBULAR SENSE

The vestibular system tells us where our heads and bodies are in relation to the surface of the earth. This system takes in sensory messages about balance and movement from the neck, eyes, and body; sends these messages to the central nervous system for processing; and then helps generate muscle tone that allows us to move smoothly and efficiently.

The vestibular system tells us whether we are moving or standing still, and whether objects are moving or motionless in relation to our body. It also informs us what direction we are going in, and how fast we are going.

The receptors for vestibular sensations are in the inner ear—a "vestibule" through which sensory messages pass. The inner ear receptors work something like a carpenter's level. They register every movement we make and every change in head position—even the most subtle.

What stimulates these receptors? Movement and . . . GRAVITY!

According to Dr. Ayres, gravity is "the most constant and universal force in our lives." It rules every move we make.

Throughout evolution, we have been refining our responses to gravitational pull. Our ancient ancestors, the first fish, developed gravity receptors, on either side of their heads, for three purposes:

1. to keep upright,

2. to provide a sense of their own motions so they could move efficiently, and

3. to detect potentially threatening movements of other creatures through the vibrations of ripples in the water.

Millions of years later, we still have gravity receptors to serve the same purposes—except now vibrations come through air rather than water.

In addition to the inner ear, we humans also have outer ears as well as a cerebral cortex, which processes precise vestibular and auditory sensations. These sensations are the vibrations of movement and of sound.*

Nature designed our vestibular receptors to be extremely sensitive. *Indeed, our need to know where we are in relation to the earth is more compelling than our need for food, for tactile comfort, or even for a mother-child bond.*

In her book, *Sensory Integration and the Child*, Dr. Ayres explains:

The vestibular system is the unifying system. It forms the basic relationship of a person to gravity and the physical world. All other types of sensation are processed in reference to this basic vestibular information. The activity in the vestibular system provides

---

*Vibrations stir up all kinds of responses. One day in my music class, I introduced a movement activity by beating a large drum. "Oooo," said a three-year-old girl, "I can feel that in my bones!" "Me, too," responded a little boy, "and I can even feel it in my penis!"

a "framework" for the other aspects of our experience. Vestibular input seems to "prime" the entire nervous system to function effectively. When the vestibular system does not function in a consistent and accurate way, the interpretation of other sensations will be inconsistent and inaccurate, and the nervous system will have trouble "getting started."

Whew! What a heavy load! Isn't it astonishing how something you may never have heard of before has such a profound and pervasive influence? As the background for all the other senses, the vestibular system gives us a sense of where we stand in the world.

Two Components: Defensive ("Uh, Oh!") and Discriminative ("Aha!")

Just as the tactile system has defensive and discriminative components, so does the vestibular system.

The defensive component functions to help us survive. When an infant feels herself falling, she reacts to this vestibular sensation as if saying, "Uh, oh!" She extends her arms and legs, as if reaching for something to grab. Her whole body responds in this automatic reflex.

As a child grows, her brain integrates reflexive responses in a process called reflex maturation. She learns to discriminate vestibular sensations. She seems to say, "Aha! I can sense the difference! I'm not a baby anymore; I can react with more sophisticated motor responses when I feel myself move."

Now, when movement sensations tell her she is off-center, she learns that she can regain her balance. She can "stand on her own two feet," in an upright position, against the pull of gravity. She can differentiate her body movements so she can function with an economy of motion.

She can also discriminate among the sounds vibrating in her inner ear, and she learns to listen. She can coordinate her own body movements with visual sensations, and she learns to discriminate what she sees.

She learns to enjoy all kinds of movement. One kind is linear movement—back and forth, side to side, or up and down. Linear movement is usually soothing; parents have known since time immemorial that they can comfort a baby in a rocking chair, in a cradle, or with gentle bounces. In fact, many children (and adults) rock when they are upset, as a kind of tranquilizing self-therapy.

Another kind of movement is rotary—moving in circles, either on a tight axis (as an ice skater does when he spins) or in a wide arc (as a speed skater does when he sprints around the track). The child enjoys twirling on the tire swing—even to the point of getting dizzy. Rotary movement stimulates the vestibular system. Usually, it feels good, and that's why it is so much fun!

THE OUT-OF-SYNC VESTIBULAR SENSE

Vestibular dysfunction is the inefficient processing in the brain of sensations perceived through the inner ear.

The child with vestibular dysfunction is inefficient at integrating information about movement, gravity, balance, and space. She may be oversensitive to movement, or undersensitive, or both over- and undersensitive.

The child may not develop the postural responses necessary to keep upright. She may never have learned to crawl and creep. She may be late learning to walk. She may sprawl on the floor, slump when she sits, and lean her head on her hands when she is at the table.

As she grows, she may be awkward, uncoordinated, and clumsy at playground games. She may fall often and easily, tripping on air when she moves, bumping into furniture, and losing her balance when someone moves her slightly off the center of gravity.

As eye movements are influenced by the vestibular system, she may have visual problems. She may have inadequate gaze stability and be unable to focus on moving objects or on objects that stay still while she moves. At school, she may become confused when looking up at the chalkboard and back down to her desk. Reading problems may arise if she hasn't developed brain functions imperative for coordinating left-to-right eye movements.

Vestibular dysfunction may also contribute to difficulty processing language—a great disadvantage in everyday life. The child who misperceives language may have problems learning to communicate, read, and write.

Many types of movement provide a calming effect. The out-of-sync child, however, can't always calm herself because her brain can't modulate vestibular messages. Neural activity that organizes movement is either stuck "on," or turned off. Difficulty moving in an organized way interferes with her behavior, attention, and emotions.

The child with an inefficient vestibular system may have one or more problems with the integration of movement sensations. The child may:

1. Be hypersensitive to movement, like Kevin, and have:
    A) Intolerance to movement, and/or
    B) Gravitational insecurity, or

2. Be hyposensitive to movement, with increased tolerance and desire for movement, like Jason.

1. *Vestibular Hypersensitivity: "Oh, No!"*

Vigorous movement, or the possibility of being moved, causes the child with vestibular hypersensitivity to react negatively and emotionally, or to become overexcited.

Her brain can't regulate movement sensations. It processes too many, and her vestibular system is on overload. Particularly when her head or eyes move, her brain is bombarded with sensory stimuli that it can't organize.

A) INTOLERANCE TO MOVEMENT: "NO, DON'T!"

The child who is hypersensitive to vestibular sensations may be intolerant of movement. "Oh, no, don't make me move! Moving quickly is too much for me."

For her, linear movement is not comforting, especially when it is rapid. Riding in an automobile—particularly in the back seat—often causes car sickness. The child may avoid riding a bicycle, sliding and swinging at the playground, or just walking down the street.

Rotary movement can be even more distressing. She may become easily dizzy and nauseated on a tire swing. Even watching someone or something spinning can make her feel queasy. Moving in circles may make her head ache and stomach hurt.

If she avoids moving, she may lose the ability to keep up with others. She may become breathless and easily fatigued. Her motor coordination and motor planning skills may suffer, because she can't practice them with confidence.

HOW INTOLERANCE TO MOVEMENT
AFFECTS A CHILD'S BEHAVIOR

A Child with Normal SI	A Child with SI Dysfunction
Brian's favorite preschool activities are music and movement. Today, the class plays "Noncompetitive Musical Chairs." In this game, no chair is ever taken away. The object is to stand up, move around the chairs while the music plays, and sit down on any available seat when the music stops. Everyone gets to play the whole time; nobody is ever "out." When the music starts, Brian jumps up and circles the chairs with the other children. When the music stops, he slithers into a chair. Once, he lands on another child's lap, but he looks around quickly, sees an empty chair, and runs to it. Safe!	Sean, four, dislikes most music and movement activities. "Noncompetitive Musical Chairs" makes him especially uncomfortable. While the other children run freely around the circle, he inches along, clinging to the seats of the chairs. By the time he has circled the chairs twice, his forehead is sweaty, and his stomach is churning. The music finally stops, and Sean sits down with a sigh of relief. When the music resumes, he remains seated.

B) GRAVITATIONAL INSECURITY:
"I'M FALLING!"

Being connected to the earth is a primal need for survival. The vestibular system tells us where we are in relation to the ground. The trust that we are attached to the earth is called gravitational security.

Usually, a child has an inner drive to experiment with gravity. Jumping, swinging and somersaulting, she can relinquish her grip on earth for an instant, because she knows she will always return. With this basic sense of stability, she can develop emotional security.

The child with dysfunction may not enjoy this sense of stability. She feels vulnerable if her feet leave the ground. Lacking a basic sense of belonging to the earth, she has gravitational insecurity.

Gravitational insecurity is manifested by abnormal distress and anxiety in reaction to falling or the possibility of falling. *It is a primal fear.* It occurs when the child's brain overreacts to changes in gravity, even as subtle as standing up.

Movement for this child is not fun; it is scary. When her head moves, she responds, "I'm falling! I'm out of control!" She overreacts with a fight-or-flight response.

The "fight" response plays out as negative, defiant behavior, particularly when she is passively moved. She may resist being picked up, rocked, or pushed in the stroller. She may become angry and stubborn when someone suggests riding in the car or sledding down a hill.

The "flight" response plays out as extreme caution or avoidance of movement. She prefers keeping her head up and feet down, firmly planted. She may avoid playing "Ring Around the Rosy," riding a bicycle, sliding, and swinging. She may be fearful of unstable surfaces, such as a sandy beach or a climbing net at the playground. She may avoid novel experiences, such as visiting a friend's house, for any place other than home is unpredictable.

The child with this terror tends to be inflexible and controlling. She often has social and emotional problems, because she is so worried about falling that she always feels vulnerable when around other people. The result is that she can't get organized for other tasks, such as playing and socializing.

HOW GRAVITATIONAL INSECURITY
AFFECTS A CHILD'S BEHAVIOR

A Child with Normal SI	*A Child with SI Dysfunction*
With his class, Cal, nine, goes for a hike up a little mountain. At one point, a thick vine hangs down from a branch. Cal takes a turn swinging on the vine, screaming "Tarzan!" Cal's efficient vestibular system permits him to enjoy exploring gravity as he swings and soars through the air.	The day his class goes hiking, Brad, nine, watches each step. He is grouchy, silent, and slow. While his classmates swing on a vine, he stands aloof. When it's his turn, he takes the vine reluctantly. He can't move. The others cry, "Come on, Brad! It's fun! What's your problem?" Brad senses that if his feet leave the ground, he'll fall into the void. Saying, "I'm really not interested in this stupid game," he drops the vine and stalks away.

2) *Vestibular Hyposensitivity: "More!"*

At the other end of the spectrum, the child may be hyposensitive to movement experiences. This child's brain doesn't facilitate enough movement messages. She doesn't react negatively; she just doesn't get enough of movements that are sufficiently satisfying for others.

The child has an increased tolerance for movement and needs a lot of vigorous activity in order to "get into gear." To get vestibular sensations, the child may seek to resist gravity in unusual ways. For instance, she may assume upside-down positions, hang over the edge of her bed, or place her head down on the floor and pivot around it.

The child may be a "bumper and crasher," frequently seeking intense movement sensations, such as jumping from the top of the jungle gym or running fast when a sedate pace would do. Climbing may be her passion; for this child, everything is a ladder.

HOW HYPOSENSITIVITY AFFECTS A CHILD'S BEHAVIOR

A Child with Normal SI	A Child with SI Dysfunction
Justin, three, is at the swim center with his mother. He paddles in the kiddie pool, occasionally pausing to watch the big kids climb the ladder to the high diving board and jump into the water. When it is time to go home, he takes his mother's hand and says, "Let's go see that big ladder." He looks up, longingly. It's so high! So scary! Someday he'll be big and brave enough to climb it, but not yet.	Billy, three, is at the swim center with his mother. He starts to jump into the big pool, but she restrains him and guides him into the kiddie pool enclosure. While she and the lifeguard discuss scheduling Billy's first swimming lesson, he escapes. He clambers up to the high diving board. He teeters on the edge, ready to jump into the deep water. His mother notices his absence and springs up the ladder, just in time to catch him before he falls.

She may crave linear movement and enjoy rocking or swinging for exceptionally long times. She may especially seek rotary movement, such as twirling in circles, shaking her head vigorously from side to side, or spinning on the playground merry-go-round or tire swing.

She may flit and dart from one activity to another, always seeking a new thrill. Her attention span may be short, even for activities she enjoys. Although she may be constantly on the go, she may move without caution or good motor coordination.

HOW THE VESTIBULAR SENSE AFFECTS EVERYDAY SKILLS

The vestibular sense gives us information that is necessary for many kinds of everyday skills:

- Gravitational security (*see p. 104*)
- Auditory-language processing
- Movement and balance
- Visual-spatial processing
- Muscle tone
- Bilateral coordination
- Motor planning
- Emotional security

Movement and Balance

Automatic, coordinated movement is possible when the central nervous system connects vestibular sensations with other sensations. The vestibular system tells us which way is up, and that *up is where we want to be.* When we're upright, we're alert and in control.

To keep upright, we make unconscious, physical adaptations, called postural background adjustments. These subtle adjustments allow us to stabilize our bodies, to correct and maintain our balance, and to move easily.

The child with vestibular dysfunction has problems with movement and balance. She moves too little or too much, with too much or too little caution. Her movements may be uncoordinated and awkward.

HOW MOVEMENT AND BALANCE
AFFECT A CHILD'S BEHAVIOR

A Child with Normal SI	A Child with SI Dysfunction
When Jeremy, ten, first got his skateboard, he fell frequently, but he has gradually learned to adjust his weight to keep his balance. He sets up obstacle courses in the street, with ramps and traffic cones, and invites his pals to try new tricks. When Joe collides with him and throws him off balance, Jeremy can usually land on his feet.	Joe, ten, can't quite get the hang of riding his skateboard, although he practices every day. He keeps losing his balance. Frequently, he crashes into Jeremy's ramps and traffic cones, and even into Jeremy. Even when Joe feels himself falling, he can't stop himself, because his postural background adjustments are ineffective.

Muscle Tone

Muscle tone is the degree of tension normally present when our muscles are in a resting state. (Muscles never relax completely unless we are unconscious.) If you exercise regularly, you probably have firm tone when you are resting. If you are a "couch potato," you probably have low tone.

HOW MUSCLE TONE AFFECTS A CHILD'S BEHAVIOR

A Child with Normal SI	A Child with SI Dysfunction
Scotty, four, pulls on his socks and his high-top sneakers. He doesn't yet know how to tie his shoes. He grips with his toes to keep the loose sneakers on his feet and thumps to his father for help. His father says, "You're growing so fast, soon you'll be able to tie your shoes all by yourself." Scotty says, "But I can make them sparkle. Want to see, Daddy?" He jumps into the air, and when he lands, the heels of the sneakers light up.	Ted's father parks him on the bed and tries to push his limp feet into a pair of socks. "Can you help me, son?" he asks. "It seems as if I'm doing all the work here." Ted tries to cooperate, but his feet don't always do what he wants them to do. Finally, the socks are on. While his father wiggles Ted's feet into his sneakers, Ted sprawls backwards on the bed. "Can you help me, please?" asks his father. "Too tired," says Ted.

The vestibular system affects tone by regulating neurological information from the brain to the muscles, telling them exactly how much to contract, so that we can resist gravity to perform skilled tasks. Usually, our muscle tone is neither too tight nor too loose; it is just right, so we don't have to use much effort to move our bodies or keep ourselves upright.

The child with vestibular dysfunction may have a "loose and floppy" body, or low tone. Nothing is wrong structurally with her muscles, but her brain is not sending out sufficient messages to give them "oomph." Without that energizing oomph, the child's muscles lack the readiness or tension necessary to move with ease.

The child may often lay her head on the table, or sprawl on the floor, or slouch in her chair. She may have difficulty turning knobs and pressing levers. She may handle objects loosely or with a very tight grasp in order to compensate for the underlying low muscle tone. She may tire easily, because resisting the pull of gravity requires a great deal of energy.

Bilateral Coordination

Bilateral (from the Latin for "both sides") coordination means that we can use both sides of the body to cooperate as a team. A well-regulated vestibular system helps us to integrate both sides of our body.

By the age of three or four, a child should have mastered a bilateral skill called "crossing the midline." This is the ability to move one hand, foot, or eye into the space of the other hand, foot, or eye. We cross the midline when we scratch an elbow, cross our ankles, and read left to right.

For the child who avoids crossing the midline, coordinating both body sides may be difficult. When she paints at an easel she may switch the brush from one hand to the other at the midway point separating her right and left sides. She may appear not to have established a hand preference, sometimes using her left and sometimes her right to eat, draw, write, or throw. It may also be hard to survey a scene or to track a moving object visually without stopping at the midline to blink and refocus.

The child with poor bilateral coordination may have trouble using both feet together to jump from a ledge, or both hands together to catch a ball or play clapping games. She may have difficulty coordinating her hands to hold a paper while she cuts or to stabilize the paper with one hand while she writes with the other.

Poor bilateral coordination is often misinterpreted as a learning disability such as dyslexia. In fact, this subtle, but significant, difficulty can lead to learning or behavior problems, but it does not ordinarily mean that a child is lacking in intelligence or academic ability.

HOW BILATERAL COORDINATION
AFFECTS A CHILD'S BEHAVIOR

A Child with Normal SI	*A Child with SI Dysfunction*
Chelsea, eight, is making a Valentine. On a piece of red paper, she steadies a cardboard heart with her left hand and traces its outline with her right. She uses her right hand to cut out the heart and her left hand to hold and turn the paper. She makes four more Valentines during art period.	Celia, eight, wants to make a pink Valentine. She has trouble steadying the cardboard heart on the paper while she traces. Her outline is misshapen, but it will have to do. She picks up the paper in her right hand and the scissors in her left. No, that's not correct, so she switches hands. She cuts awkwardly. Instead of rotating the paper with her left hand, she moves her right hand, holding the scissors, around the paper. Her Valentine isn't very good, but she hopes her mother will like it.

Auditory-Language Processing

The vestibular and auditory systems work together as they process sensations of movement and sound. These sensations are closely intertwined, because they both begin to be processed in the receptors of the ear.

Audition, or hearing, is the ability to receive sounds. We are born with this basic skill. We can't learn how to do it; either we hear, or we don't.

The ability to hear does not guarantee, however, that we understand sounds. We are not born with the skill of comprehension; we acquire it, as we integrate vestibular sensations. Gradually, as we interact purposefully with our environment, we learn to interpret what we hear and to develop sophisticated auditory processing skills. Some auditory processing skills are:

- Auditory discrimination—differentiating among sounds,

- Auditory figure-ground—discriminating between sounds in the foreground and in the background, and, of utmost importance,

- Language!

Language is the meaningful use of words, which are symbols representing objects and ideas. Thus, language is a code for deciphering what words imply and how we use them to communicate. Language that we take in, by listening and reading, is called "receptive." Language that we put out, by speaking or writing, is "expressive."

(Language and speech are closely related, but they are not the same. Speech is the physical production of sound. Speech skills depend on smoothly functioning muscles in the throat, tongue, lips and jaw. The vestibular system influences motor control and motor planning that are necessary to use those fine muscles to produce intelligible speech.)

Because the vestibular system is crucial for effective auditory processing, the child with dysfunction frequently develops problems with language. How do these problems play out?

The child may have difficulty detecting likenesses and differences in words. She may find it hard to attend to the teacher's voice without being distracted by background noises. Her receptive language may suffer: she may be a poor listener, have trouble following directions, and struggle to read. Her expressive language may be inadequate: she may have trouble participating in conversations, answering questions, and putting her thoughts into writing.

She may not talk very much or very well . . . until she moves around. Indeed, when she begins to run or swing, she may suddenly talk, sing, or shout. As self-therapy, she may jump up to walk around the room when she begins to talk. The reason is that moving activates the ability to speak.

The child with vestibular and language problems benefits greatly from therapy that simultaneously addresses both types of dysfunction. Speech-and-language therapists report that just putting the child in a swing during treatment can have remarkable results. Occupational therapists have found that when they treat a child for vestibular dysfunction, speech-and-language skills can improve along with balance, movement, and motor planning skills. And even without the assistance of therapists, children who move spontaneously often show enhanced ability to verbalize their thoughts.

HOW AUDITORY PERCEPTION
AFFECTS A CHILD'S BEHAVIOR

A Child with Normal SI	A Child with SI Dysfunction
The fourth-graders can't go outside for recess because it's raining, so Hayley chatters with her friends as they work on a jigsaw puzzle. When math begins after recess, the kids can't settle down. The teacher begins class with the "Hokey-Pokey." Shaking her arms, legs, and head, and turning herself about, Hayley begins to feel alert again. When the teacher asks her for the answer to a math problem, Hayley responds correctly.	Caitlin looks forward to recess every day, but it's raining. Restless, she wanders around the room. The "Hokey-Pokey" doesn't help, because Caitlin can't understand the directions. When math begins, she feels sleepy. The teacher asks her an easy question. She jumps to her feet, but the teacher tells her to stay seated. She sits down again but can't give the answer. The next day, the weather is fine, and the kids play outside. Caitlin swings the whole time. During math class, the teacher asks her to answer another math problem. Caitlin gets it right. The teacher says, "Good!" and wonders why Caitlin is sometimes "on" and sometimes "off."

Visual-Spatial Processing

Vision is a complex process that enables us to identify sights, to anticipate what is "coming at us," and to prepare for a response. Vision should not be confused with eyesight. Eyesight, the basic ability to see the big "E" on the wall chart, is only one part of vision.

Healthy eyes and 20/20 eyesight are prerequisites for vision, just as hearing is a prerequisite for language skills. Eyesight contributes to our basic visual skills, called ocular-motor (eye movement, or eye motor) skills. The vestibular system has a profound effect on these motor skills, which include:

- Fixation—aiming our eyes or shifting our gaze from one object to another, such as reading from one word to another across a line of print,

- Tracking—following moving objects with ease and accuracy, such as when catching a ball or watching the quarterback run down the field,

- Focusing—switching our gaze quickly and smoothly between near and distant objects, such as looking back and forth from the desk to a tree outside the window, or when copying problems from the chalkboard, and

- Binocular vision, or eye-teaming—forming a single mental picture from the images that the two eyes separately record, such as looking into the sky with both eyes to see just one moon.

The vestibular system also has a huge influence on visual processing, including spatial awareness. Acquiring visual-spatial processing skills requires much practice in looking around, moving around, and actively participating in a variety of sensory experiences.

Some visual-spatial processing skills are:

• Visual discrimination—differentiating among symbols and forms, such as matching or separating colors, shapes, numbers, letters, and words,

• Visual figure-ground—differentiating objects in the foreground and background, to distinguish one word on a page, or a face in a crowd, and

• Visual-spatial functions—understanding that objects keep their basic shapes regardless of their position (form constancy); seeing the correct orientation of letters and objects (position in space); judging distances between objects, or between ourselves and objects (spatial awareness); and perceiving left and right, up and down, and front and back (directionality).

The child with vestibular dysfunction often has problems not only with basic eye motor skills but also with more refined visual-spatial processing. Because her brain does not efficiently integrate sensations from her eyes and body, the three "R's" may be enormously challenging. She may mix up words on the page, read and write letters backward, lose her place on work sheets, and confuse plus signs (+) with multiplication signs (x).

She may be overwhelmed by objects and people moving around her. She may overreach for objects. She may have difficulty climbing stairs. She may find it hard to fit pieces into a puzzle, paste stars on a paper, draw representational pictures, or do eye-hand activities. She may be unable to find her way to the cafeteria. When she plays soccer and basketball, she may run in the wrong direction. She is "lost in space."

HOW VISUAL-SPATIAL PROCESSING
AFFECTS A CHILD'S BEHAVIOR

A Child with Normal SI	*A Child with SI Dysfunction*
David, three, lines up with the other children to come inside for snack. As the line moves, David keeps his place, watching the girl in front of him so he won't step on her heels. At snack time, he pours juice into his cup, stopping just before the juice reaches the brim. After snack, he works on a jigsaw puzzle. One piece doesn't seem to fit. He studies it and realizes that it is upside down. He corrects his error and completes the puzzle. Then he does another, more complicated one.	Freddy lines up to come inside. He can't keep his place in line and several times bumps into the child in front of him. The other three-year-olds turn left toward the classroom, but Freddy turns right. After two months of school, he still doesn't know the way. He stands in the hall, bewildered, until the teacher finds him. At snack time, Freddy pours juice until the cup overflows. After cleaning him up, the teacher offers him a simple jigsaw puzzle. Freddy attempts to put the four pieces into the puzzle. It's too frustrating. He can't fit the four pieces. He asks if he may just sit in the cozy corner and hold the guinea pig.

Motor Planning

How do you learn to sit up? How do you figure out how to stand, walk, run, and skip? How do you get to Carnegie Hall?

Praxis, praxis, praxis!

HOW MOTOR PLANNING AFFECTS A CHILD'S BEHAVIOR

A Child with Normal SI	A Child with SI Dysfunction
Karen, seven, likes learning new dances. Today the Brownies are learning the Macarena. In this dance, the girls move their arms and hands in a complicated sequence, turning them in the air and moving them to touch one body part after another. After completing the sequence, they shimmy, jump a quarter turn, and repeat the motions. The Macarena is much more challenging than the Looby Loo. Karen loves it.	Libby, seven, likes being a Brownie, especially when the troop acts out stories and goes to museums, but she doesn't enjoy dancing. The Looby Loo was hard enough; now she must struggle with the Macarena. Moving her arms and hands is confusing and frustrating. Shimmying is difficult, so Libby just sways. Trying to jump a quarter turn, she goes in the wrong direction. Even when she stops to watch the other girls, it's hard to learn the sequence of movements. She wishes they could stick to familiar activities, instead of always tackling something new.

Motor planning is a generic term for praxis, which, as you have seen, is the ability to conceptualize, organize, and realize a complex sequence of unfamiliar movements. When our nervous system integrates vestibular sensations with tactile and proprioceptive sensations, we have a good body scheme. When we have a good body scheme, we can motor plan. Then, we can do what we set out to do.

Adapting her behavior to learn a new skill may be very hard for the child with vestibular dysfunction. For instance, she may be able to step into the bathtub but have trouble stepping into the car. She may have learned how to roller-skate but have difficulty ice-skating or roller-blading. If her central nervous system hasn't processed movement and balance sensations efficiently, then her brain can't remember how it feels to move in a certain way. Thus, she can't easily generalize a learned skill to plan and perform a new skill that is only slightly different.

Emotional Security

Emotional security is every child's birthright, but the child with vestibular dysfunction may not feel totally secure. Whether she is cautious due to hypersensitivity or gravitational insecurity, or is hyposensitive and daring, she will be disorganized in many aspects of her young life.

The child may have low self-esteem. Aware that ordinary tasks are beyond her ability, she may often say, "I can't do that." She may not even try. If she is uncertain about her abilities, even the best-loved child in the world may feel that she is unloved and unlovable.

HOW EMOTIONAL SECURITY
AFFECTS A CHILD'S BEHAVIOR

A Child with Normal SI	A Child with SI Dysfunction
Mark, four, gives Darius a plastic ball and bat for his birthday. After Darius opens the gift, Mark says, "Let's play!" A few kids manage to whack the ball. Mark hits it over the fence. He jumps up and down gleefully. "I knew I could do it! Now it's your turn, Darius." He offers the bat to his friend, but Darius frowns and turns away. When Mark's mother comes for him, he says, "Darius didn't like the bat, but I had a good time anyway."	Darius, four, opens Mark's present, but he doesn't want to play with the ball and bat. He knows he won't be any good. He watches the other children line up to swing the bat, but when Mark urges him to try, he turns away and says, "I can't." After the partygoers leave, he says to his mother, "Mark isn't my friend. He hates me." His eyes brim with tears, and he collapses in her arms. He whimpers, "Mommy, do you love me?"

CHARACTERISTICS OF VESTIBULAR
DYSFUNCTION

These checklists will help you gauge whether your child has vestibular dysfunction. As you check recognizable characteristics, you will begin to see emerging patterns that help to explain your child's out-of-sync behavior.

The hypersensitive child who shows **intolerance for movement** may:

☐ Dislike playground activities, such as swinging, spinning, and sliding.

☐ Be cautious, slow moving, and sedentary, hesitating to take risks.

☐ Appear to be a sissy.

☐ Seem willful and uncooperative.

☐ Be very uncomfortable in elevators and on escalators, perhaps experiencing car or motion sickness.

☐ Demand continual physical support from a trusted adult.

The child with **gravitational insecurity** may:

☐ Have a great fear of falling, even where no real danger exists. This fear is experienced as *primal terror*.

☐ Be fearful of heights, even slightly raised surfaces. The child may avoid walking on a curb or jumping down from the bottom step.

☐ Become anxious when her feet leave the ground, feeling that even the smallest movement will throw her into outer space.

☐ Be fearful of climbing or descending stairs and hold tightly to the banister.

☐ Feel threatened when her head is inverted, upside down or tilted, as when having her head shampooed over the sink.

☐ Be fearful when someone moves her, as when a teacher slides her chair closer to the table.

☐ For self-protection, try to manipulate her environment and other people.

The hyposensitive child with **increased tolerance for movement** may:

☐ Need to keep moving, as much as possible, in order to function. The child may have trouble sitting still or staying in a seat.

☐ Repeatedly and vigorously shake her head, rock back and forth, and jump up and down.

☐ Crave intense movement experiences, such as bouncing on furniture, using a rocking chair, turning in a swivel chair, assuming upside-down positions, or placing her head on the floor and pivoting around it.

☐ Be a "thrill seeker," enjoying fast-moving or spinning playground equipment, or seeking the fast and "scary" rides at an amusement park.

☐ Not get dizzy, even after twirling in circles or spinning rapidly for a lengthy amount of time.

☐ Enjoy swinging very high and/or for long periods of time.

☐ Like seesaws, teeter-totters, or trampolines more than other children.

The child who has difficulty with **movement, balance, and posture** may:

☐ Easily lose her balance when climbing stairs, riding a bicycle, stretching on tiptoes, jumping, hopping, standing on one foot, or standing on both feet when her eyes are closed.

☐ Move in an uncoordinated, awkward way.

☐ Be fidgety and clumsy.

The child with low **muscle tone** may:

☐ Have a loose and floppy body.

☐ Feel limp (like a wet noodle) when you lift her, move her limbs to help her get dressed, or try to help her balance on a teeter-totter or balance beam.

☐ Tend to slump or sprawl in a chair or over a table, prefer to lie down rather than sit upright, and constantly lean her head on a hand or arm.

☐ Find it hard to hold up her head, arms, and legs simultaneously when lying on her stomach.

☐ Sit on the floor with her legs in a "W," i.e., with her knees bent and her feet extended out to the sides, to stabilize her body.

☐ Have difficulty turning doorknobs or handles that require pressure, and have a loose grasp on "tools" such as pencils, scissors, or spoons.

☐ Have a tight, tense grasp on objects (to compensate for looseness).

☐ Have problems with digestion and elimination, such as frequent constipation or poor bladder control.

☐ Fatigue easily during physical activities or family outings.

☐ Be unable to catch herself from falling.

The child with poor **bilateral coordination** may:

☐ Not have crawled or crept as a baby.

☐ Have poor body awareness.

☐ Have poor gross motor skills and frequently stumble and trip, or be clumsy at sports and active games. She may seem to have "two left feet."

☐ Have poor fine motor skills and difficulty using "tools" such as eating utensils, crayons, pencils, and combs.

☐ Have difficulty making both feet or both hands work together, such as when jumping up and down or throwing and catching a ball.

☐ Have difficulty using one foot or hand to assist the other during tasks such as standing on one foot to kick a ball, or holding the paper steady when writing or cutting.

☐ Have trouble using both hands in a smooth, alternating manner, as when striking rhythm instruments together to keep a musical beat.

☐ Not have an established hand preference by the age of four or five. The child may use either hand for coloring, drawing, and writing, or may switch the crayon, pen, or pencil from one hand to the other.

☐ Avoid crossing the midline. The child may switch the brush from hand to hand while painting a horizontal line, or may have trouble tapping a hand on her opposite shoulder in games like "Simon Says."

☐ Have a hard time with organization and structured activities.

The child with **poor auditory-language processing** may:

☐ Seem unaware of the source of sounds and may look all around to locate where they come from.

☐ Have trouble identifying voices or discriminating between sounds, such as the difference between "bear" and "bore."

☐ Be unable to pay attention to one voice or sound without being distracted by other sounds.

☐ Be distressed by noises that are loud, sudden, metallic, or high-pitched, or by sounds that don't bother others.

☐ Have trouble attending to, understanding, or remembering what she reads or hears. She may misinterpret requests, frequently ask for repetition, and be able to follow only one or two instructions in sequence.

☐ Look to others before responding.

☐ Have trouble putting thoughts into spoken or written words.

☐ Talk "off topic," e.g., talk about her new shirt when others are discussing a soccer game.

☐ Have trouble "closing circles of communication," i.e., responding to others' questions and comments.

☐ Have trouble correcting or revising what she has said to be understood.

☐ Have a weak vocabulary and use immature sentence structure (poor grammar and syntax).

☐ Have difficulty with reading (dyslexia), especially out loud.

☐ Have trouble making up rhymes and singing in tune.

☐ Have difficulty speaking and articulating clearly.

☐ Improve her speaking ability after she experiences intense movement.

The child with poor **visual-spatial processing** may:

☐ Shield her eyes to screen out sights, close or cover one eye, or squint.

☐ Complain of seeing double.

☐ Have difficulty shifting her gaze from one object to another, such as when looking from the blackboard to her own paper.

☐ Turn or tilt her head as she reads across a page.

☐ Have difficulty tracking or following a moving object, such as a Ping-Pong ball, or following along a line of printed words.

☐ Fail to comprehend what she is reading or quickly lose interest.

☐ Confuse likenesses and differences in pictures, words, symbols, and objects.

☐ Omit words or numbers and lose her place while reading and writing.

☐ Have difficulty with schoolwork involving the size constancy of letters, the spacing of letters and words, and the lining up of numbers.

☐ Have difficulty with fine motor tasks involving spatial relationships, such as fitting pieces into jigsaw puzzles and cutting along lines.

☐ Orient drawings poorly on the page, or write uphill or downhill.

☐ Misjudge spatial relationships of objects in the environment, often bumping into furniture or misstepping on stairs and curbs.

☐ Confuse right and left, have a poor sense of direction, and frequently head the wrong way.

☐ Not understand concepts such as up/down, before/after, and first/second.

☐ Reverse letters ("b/d") or words ("saw/was") while reading and writing.

☐ Fail to visualize what she reads. It may be hard to call up mental images of objects and people, not relating pictures and words to "the real thing."

☐ Be uncomfortable or overwhelmed by moving objects or people.

☐ Fatigue easily during schoolwork.

☐ Withdraw from classroom participation and avoid group activities in which movement is required.

The child with poor **motor planning** may:

☐ Have difficulty conceptualizing, organizing, and carrying out a sequence of unfamiliar movements.

☐ Be unable to generalize what she has already learned in order to accomplish a new task.

The child who is **emotionally insecure** may:

☐ Get easily frustrated and give up quickly.

☐ Be reluctant to try new activities.

☐ Have a low tolerance for potentially stressful situations.

☐ Have low self-esteem.

☐ Be irritable in others' company, and avoid or withdraw from people.

☐ Have difficulty making friends and relating to peers.

Vestibular dysfunction may be your child's primary difficulty, but the tactile sense (chapter 3) and the proprioceptive sense may cause problems, too.

Chapter Five

How to Tell If Your Child Has a Problem with the Proprioceptive Sense

One Nine-Year-Old at the Swimming Pool

Jeff has tried to play team sports, but it's hard for him to get his body to work in a coordinated way. He hates it when other kids, including his siblings, say mean things like "You sure have a lousy sense of timing," or "Nobody picks you for a team because you don't help."

Knowing how Jeff longs to participate in a sport, his mother persuades him to join the beginners' swim team at the neighborhood pool. After shopping for goggles, a team suit, and a new athletic bag, Jeff begins to think that swimming might be okay. At least it doesn't involve hitting balls.

The first day of practice, Jeff inches into the locker room. The other boys dart in and out, joking and laughing, while Jeff struggles to change his clothes. He watches every move carefully, especially when he ties the waistband string of his swimsuit. He wants to be sure that his suit is on right, so nobody will laugh at him.

He goes out to the concrete pool deck and heads for the coach. He walks awkwardly, thudding his heels. He's watching his feet, not where he's going. He collides with a chair, which clatters across the concrete.

The coach glances up and beckons. He calls, "Come on! Get your goggles on! Dive in! Let's go!"

Getting the goggles on is tricky because Jeff can't see what he is doing. By the time he adjusts them, the other kids have dived in and begun swimming toward the far end of the pool.

Jeff doesn't know how to dive yet, so getting into the pool is another problem. He goes to the ladder and faces the water. With his arms awkwardly stretched behind him as he clings to the railings, he tries to descend. Then he remembers to face the ladder, not the water. He turns around, gropes for the rungs with his feet, and backs slowly into the pool.

Jeff begins to swim. He had swimming lessons, so he knows the basics. However, the pattern of his strokes is uneven. He stretches his right arm nicely but bends his left elbow too much, so he swims with a "limp." The result is that he keeps veering to the left and bumping into the rope.

Another problem is breathing. He concentrates hard: right arm, left arm, breathe, right, left, breathe—but he gets the sequence mixed up. When he breathes, his arms stop moving, and he feels as if he is about to sink.

When he gets to the end of the pool, Jeff is exhausted. The other kids are already swimming back to the other end. He's always the last one. He thinks maybe swimming isn't such a good idea after all.

Atypical Pattern of Behavior

Jeff is out of sync with his body and moves in an atypical pattern. He strikes his heels on the pool deck to get additional information to his muscles and joints. His awkward gait makes him look like a robot.

Jeff has poor body awareness and poor kinesthesia: he can't perceive how his individual body parts move, or where they are in space. He relies on vision to figure out how to make his body move. Changing into his swimsuit takes a long time because he must watch his hands. Positioning his goggles over his eyes is hard because he can't see what he's doing.

Another challenge is orienting his body to get into the pool. First, Jeff has trouble aligning his body properly on the ladder. Then, when he remembers to turn toward the ladder and to back into the water, he labors to find secure footing on the rungs.

In the pool, Jeff's swimming is irregular. His strokes are erratic because he has trouble matching the movements of his right and left arms.

Jeff works hard to swim; he likes the water and wants to be successful. He is easily frustrated, however, and decides that swimming isn't his thing. Uncoordinated and unaware of his body, Jeff has proprioceptive dysfunction, and, as is common, some vestibular dysfunction, as well.

Following are explanations of how the proprioceptive sense is supposed to function, and how proprioceptive dysfunction inundates Jeff.

THE SMOOTHLY FUNCTIONING PROPRIOCEPTIVE SENSE

Proprioception (from "proprio," Latin for "one's own") refers to sensory information telling us about our own movement or body position. It provides intake that helps integrate touch and movement sensations.

Receptors for the proprioceptive sense are in the muscles, joints, ligaments, tendons, and connective tissue. The stimuli for these receptors are movement and gravity.

Proprioception, the "position sense," sends messages about whether the muscles are stretching or contracting, and how the joints are bending and straightening. Even when we are motionless, gravity stimulates the receptors to create proprioceptive messages without our being consciously aware of them. For instance, if you're seated right now, you're relying on proprioception, not visual cues, to tell you that you're resting in a chair. Are your feet on a footstool? Do your hands hold this book? Proprioception gives you this information without the need to look at your feet and hands.

Joint and muscle sensations that come through this system are closely connected to both the tactile and the vestibular systems. Because they are so interrelated, professionals sometimes speak of "tactile-proprioceptive" or "vestibular-proprioceptive" processing.

Tactile-proprioceptive (or "somatosensory") perception refers to the simultaneous sensations of touch and of body position. This perception is necessary for such ordinary tasks as judging the weight of a glass of milk or holding a pencil efficiently in order to write.

Vestibular-proprioceptive perception refers to the simultaneous sensations of head and body position when the child actively moves. This perception is needed for throwing and catching a ball or climbing stairs.

The functions of proprioception are to increase body awareness and to contribute to motor control and motor planning. Proprioception helps us with body expression, the ability to move our body parts efficiently and economically. It allows us to walk smoothly, to run quickly, to climb stairs, to carry a suitcase, to sit, to stand, to stretch, and to lie down. It gives us emotional security, for when we can trust our bodies, we feel safe and secure.

Proprioception is the *unconscious* sense of body movement, such as when we automatically hold our bodies upright on a chair. Of course, we are often *conscious* of body position, such as when we uncross our legs before arising from the chair. Teachers and therapists use the term *kinesthesia* to describe the conscious awareness of joint position we use in learning.

THE OUT-OF-SYNC
PROPRIOCEPTIVE SENSE

Proprioceptive dysfunction is the inefficient processing of sensations perceived through the muscles, joints, ligaments, tendons, and connective tissue. Proprioceptive dysfunction is usually accompanied by problems with the tactile and/or vestibular systems. Whereas it is common for a child to have only tactile, or only vestibular, problems, it is less likely for a child to have only proprioceptive problems.

The child with poor proprioception has difficulty interpreting sensations about the position and movement of his head and limbs. The child lacks instinctive knowledge of these ordinarily subconscious sensations.

The child has a poor sense of body awareness and body position. Because he can't control or monitor his gross motor and fine motor muscles, motor planning is very challenging. He may be clumsy and easily frustrated. Other people perceive him to be a "klutz."

He may tackle everything and everybody. He may show confusion when walking down the street, getting in and out of the bathtub, or crossing the playground.

Manipulating objects may be difficult. He may exert too much or too little pressure on objects, struggling to turn doorknobs and regularly breaking toys and pencil points. He may spill the milk every time. The child may have a poor grip on heavy objects, such as buckets of water, or on light-weight objects, such as forks and combs. He may also have trouble lifting and holding on to objects of different weights.

Because of poor body awareness, the child needs to use his eyes to see what his body is doing. Ordinary tasks, like orienting his body to get dressed, zipping a jacket, buttoning a shirt, or getting out of bed in the dark, become very difficult without the aid of vision. Unless the child can watch every move, he may be unable to match a movement of one side of his body with a similar movement on the other side.

The child may be fearful when moving in space because he lacks postural stability. Because each new movement and each new position throw him off guard, he is emotionally insecure.

How the Proprioceptive Sense Affects Everyday Skills

Proprioception works closely with the tactile and vestibular systems, so some functions overlap. These functions include:

- Body awareness
- Motor control and motor planning
- Grading of movement
- Postural stability
- Emotional security

Body Awareness

Efficient proprioception provides information about body awareness. The child with poor proprioception may be unaware of his body position and body parts.

HOW BODY AWARENESS AFFECTS A CHILD'S BEHAVIOR

A Child with Normal SI	A Child with SI Dysfunction
To settle the children down before reading a story, the teacher of Jonathan's preschool class leads a stretching exercise. She says, "Close your eyes and stretch one arm way up toward the ceiling. Bring it down and now stretch the other arm, way up high." Jon, three, follows her directions without difficulty.	Kenny, three, keeps his eyes open during the stretching exercise. He looks at his right arm to make sure it is moving upward. When the teacher says to stretch the other arm, Kenny peeks at Jon to see what he is doing. Attempting to imitate Jon, he gets confused. He raises his right arm again, rather than his left.

Motor Control and Motor Planning

Proprioception provides information necessary to coordinate movements for efficient gross motor and fine motor activities.

For the child with poor proprioception, coordination of movements is a problem. Controlling large motor movements, such as getting from one position into another, is difficult. Fine motor movements, such as grasping objects or manipulating small toys, are also hard.

HOW MOTOR CONTROL AND MOTOR PLANNING
AFFECT A CHILD'S BEHAVIOR

A Child with Normal SI	A Child with SI Dysfunction
Todd, six, is practicing a marching routine in preparation for Field Day. "HUP, two, three, four, HUP, two, three, four," he chants as he smartly brings up his knees.	Collin lingers at the end of the line as his fellow first-graders practice marching. Even when he chants "HUP, two, three, four," he can't seem to coordinate his knees in a rhythmic pattern. This is so frustrating!

Grading of Movement

Proprioception helps us grade our movements. Grading of movement means that we sense how much pressure to exert as we flex and extend our muscles. We can judge what the quantity and quality of muscle movement should be, and how forcefully we should move. Thus, we can gauge the amount of effort necessary to pick up a fluffy dust ball, lift a heavy carton, or yank open a stubborn drawer.

Suppose you're at a picnic and you set down your lemonade on the table beside someone else's empty cup. Later, you return for another refreshing sip but pick up the other person's cup. You sense immediately that this cup is not yours, because it doesn't feel full. And how do you know? Proprioception tells you so!

Because the child with dysfunction doesn't receive efficient messages from his muscles and joints, he has difficulty grading his movements to adapt to changing demands.

HOW GRADING OF MOVEMENT
AFFECTS A CHILD'S BEHAVIOR

A Child with Normal SI	A Child with SI Dysfunction
Janie, seven, is going to help paint the bike shed at camp. She carries a brush in one hand and a paint bucket in the other. Walking to the shed, she adjusts her body to keep upright despite carrying different weights.	Ruth, seven, clenches a brush so she won't drop it. Her counselor hands her a bucket of paint. As Ruth can't perceive how heavy it is, she can't tighten her muscles to stand upright. She leans way over to one side as she lugs the bucket to the shed.

Postural Stability

Proprioception gives us the unconscious awareness of our body that helps stabilize us when we sit, stand, and move. The child with dysfunction lacks the stability to make fundamental postural adjustments for these everyday skills.

HOW POSTURAL STABILITY
AFFECTS A CHILD'S BEHAVIOR

A Child with Normal SI	A Child with SI Dysfunction
Larry, ten, pulls in his chair and surveys the dinner table. Yippee, corn on the cob! He eats, with his elbows on the table. His mother says, "Manners, please," and he straightens up.	Adam, ten, arranges himself on the chair: one foot tucked under his body and the other on the floor for stability. He knows his mother disapproves of elbows on the table, but he can't help it, especially when he eats corn.

Emotional Security

Proprioception contributes to our emotional security by orienting us to where our various body parts are and what we are doing with our bodies.

The child with poor proprioception isn't confident about his own body. Because he doesn't have the "feel" of it, he is emotionally insecure.

HOW EMOTIONAL SECURITY AFFECTS A CHILD'S BEHAVIOR

A Child with Normal SI	*A Child with SI Dysfunction*
Jenny, five, gets out of bed, dresses, walks to school, does her work sheets, plays outside, and goes on errands with her mother. She feels good about herself and the world she inhabits. Her sense of security results, in part, from dependable messages coming from her body. She can easily orient her body, and this ability gives her confidence as she moves through her day.	For Sara, five, almost everything she does requires effort—getting out of bed, dressing, walking to school, doing her work sheets, playing at the playground, and going on errands with her mother. She doesn't feel good about herself or the world she inhabits. Her sense of insecurity results from the undependable messages coming from her body, which doesn't move the way she wants it to. She has little self-confidence.

CHARACTERISTICS OF
PROPRIOCEPTIVE DYSFUNCTION

The following checklists will help you gauge whether your child has proprioceptive dysfunction. As you check recognizable characteristics, you'll begin to see emerging patterns that explain your child's out-of-sync behavior.

For **sensory feedback,** the child with dysfunction may:

☐ Deliberately "bump and crash" into objects in the environment, e.g., jump from high places, dive into a leaf pile, and "tackle" people.

☐ Stamp or slap his feet on the ground when walking.

☐ Kick his heels against the floor or chair.

☐ Bang a stick or other object on a wall or fence while walking.

☐ Rub his hands on tables, bite or suck on his fingers, or crack his knuckles.

☐ Like to be tightly swaddled in a blanket or tucked in tightly at bedtime.

☐ Prefer shoelaces, hoods, and belts to be tightly fastened.

☐ Chew constantly on objects like shirt collars and cuffs, hood strings, pencils, toys, and gum.

The child with inefficient **body awareness, motor planning,** and **motor control** may:

☐ Have difficulty planning and executing movement. Controlling and monitoring motor tasks such as adjusting a collar or putting on eyeglasses may be especially hard if the child can't see what he is doing.

☐ Have difficulty positioning his body, as when someone is helping him into a coat, or when he is trying to dress or undress himself.

☐ Have difficulty knowing where his body is in relation to objects and people, frequently falling, tripping, and bumping into obstacles.

☐ Have difficulty going up and down stairs.

☐ Show fear when moving in space.

The child with inefficient **grading of movement** may:

☐ Flex and extend his muscles more or less than necessary for tasks such as inserting his arms into sleeves, or climbing.

☐ Hold pencils and crayons too lightly to make a clear impression, or so tightly that the points break.

☐ Produce messy written work, often with large erasure holes.

☐ Frequently break delicate objects and seem like a "bull in a china shop."

☐ Break items that require simple manipulation, such as lamp switches, hair barrettes, and toys that require putting together and pulling apart.

☐ Pick up an object with more force than necessary, such as a glass of milk, causing the object to fly through the air.

☐ Pick up an object with less force than necessary— and thus be unable to lift it. He may complain that objects such as boots or toys are "too heavy."

☐ Have difficulty lifting or holding objects if they don't weigh the same. He may not understand concepts of "heavy" and "light."

The child with **postural instability** may:

☐ Have poor posture.

☐ Lean his head on his hands when he works at a desk.

☐ Slump in a chair, over a table, or while seated on the floor.

☐ Sit on the edge of the chair and keep one foot on the floor for extra stability.

☐ Be unable to keep his balance while standing on one foot.

The child with **emotional insecurity** may:

☐ Avoid participation in ordinary movement experiences, because they make him feel uncomfortable or inadequate.

☐ Become rigid, sticking to the activities that he has mastered and resisting new physical challenges.

☐ Lack self-confidence, saying "I can't do that," even before trying.

☐ Become timid in unfamiliar situations.

Part II of this book will give you specific, practical advice as you begin the process of evaluation, diagnosis, and treatment. You will also find many suggestions and activities to help your child at home and at school.

COPING WITH

SENSORY

INTEGRATION

DYSFUNCTION

Chapter Six

Diagnosis and

Treatment

This chapter will help you learn to recognize and document your child's out-of-sync behavior. It suggests when and how to seek a professional evaluation and diagnosis, and it includes descriptions of various kinds of intervention, with emphasis on occupational therapy.

A Parent's Search for Answers

A mother wrote me this letter:

"By the time Rob was two, I felt he had a special need, but I couldn't figure out what it was. He required constant attention. Time-outs didn't work because I couldn't contain him. He was defiant, disobedient, disrespectful, and demanding. He was always busy, always talking (great verbal skills!), strong willed, contrary, and easily frustrated. I felt blessed to have Rob, and wouldn't trade him for the world, of course, but he constantly tested and rejected me.

"What was the reason for his behavior? How could I regain control? What method of discipline would get through to him? If his behavior was an attempt to get my attention, how could I supply it in a way that would satisfy him? How could I help a high energy child channel his energy in a positive direction? I was desperate for answers.

"I started seeking information from my pediatrician. He recommended a neurologist who tested Rob for seizures (he tested normal) and who didn't think he had ADD. Next we saw a psychologist who said Rob was a normal, active little boy. Then we tried an allergist because he craves milk, and then an ENT because he seems tired a lot and snores. I thought he might have infected adenoids, but he doesn't.

"Then we saw a child development specialist who knew something about sensory problems. He didn't do a formal evaluation but could tell that Rob has an immature, under-reactive vestibular system with delays in auditory and visual processing. He gave us specific suggestions for activities to do at home, but they didn't work well because Rob didn't cooperate. Since home therapy wasn't working, we then tested Rob for ADD (negative).

"Finally, a neighbor gave me the name of an O.T. (occupational therapist) who did a formal evaluation. At three and a half, he was diagnosed with Sensory Integration Dysfunction. It was a double relief to have Rob's problem identified and to learn that therapy really helps! After four sessions with her, she feels that with a few months of therapy, Rob has good potential to benefit from O.T. and that his 'nerve problem' will be repaired, and then managing his behavior will be easier.

"The pediatrician feels the therapy won't change anything and suggests using more discipline and seeing a child psychologist. But we have already begun to see results and want to continue the occupational therapy for as long as the O.T. feels it is necessary. I am hoping we are on the right track.

"This is so unlike anything I have ever been through. This is so hard for me. I am a very 'up' person with lots of friends who call me for advice, and for the first time in my adult life I need advice, *big* time! I've always worked hard to make our lives 'perfect,' but just getting through the day with Rob has been an accomplishment.

"We're not done yet, but we're making progress. Instead of feeling all alone and desperate, now I'm excited and hopeful. When I see Rob's sweet, loving nature emerging, I feel certain we'll restore harmony in our home."

RECOGNIZING WHEN YOUR CHILD NEEDS PROFESSIONAL HELP

Ordinarily, growing older means that a child builds upon skills already acquired. A typical child develops the capacity to run after learning to walk, after learning to stand, after learning to creep.

For the out-of-sync child, however, growing older does not always mean getting better at many physical and intellectual tasks, because the basic foundation for efficiently organizing sensory information isn't solid enough.

If growing older doesn't help, what does? Early intervention! The most appropriate intervention for SI Dysfunction is occupational therapy, which helps the child develop his nervous system.

Before receiving occupational therapy or any other form of intervention, the child will need a professional evaluation and a diagnosis. How do you know if an evaluation is necessary?

Seven Rationalizations That Prevent Recognizing Dysfunction

At least seven rationalizations prevent some people from recognizing SI Dysfunction and thus seeking a diagnosis. Educators and therapists hear these comments all the time.

1. *"Looks like ADD, sounds like ADD, must be ADD."* Symptoms of SI Dysfunction may tend to look like symptoms of several other problems.

2. *"Never heard of it, so it can't be important."* SI Dysfunction is not well understood. Pediatricians don't study it in medical school, teachers don't learn about it in schools of education, and the mass media rarely cover it. Parents are hard-pressed to learn about SI Dysfunction when many early childhood experts are, themselves, unfamiliar with it.

3. *"Not MY kid!"* Even when parents do learn something about SI Dysfunction, they may be reluctant to believe that it affects their child. People don't go looking for answers if they are in denial that a problem exists.

4. *"So what if he's not a rocket scientist? We love him just the way he is."* Accepting a child "where he's at" is great, but sometimes parents are too accepting. They may be satisfied with their child's irregular development, even if their child is not.

5. *"So what if she doesn't do what other kids do? She's advanced for her age."* Parents may think their child's

unchildlike behavior signifies that she's "too smart" for playdough and playgrounds. However, every child needs to be able to play before she is able to succeed at school. The ability to read at the age of five doesn't guarantee that she has the physical, social, and emotional readiness for kindergarten.

What looks like precocious behavior may, in fact, indicate neurological dysfunction. A little boy I know pulled himself to a stand in his crib at five months. At nine months, he walked—on tiptoes! His parents thought he was way ahead of other babies until they learned that his tactile defensiveness made him seek to avoid touching the crib sheet and the ground.

The child may skip typical childhood experiences because she can't do them. It's illuminating to ask oneself what she avoids. The question may be hard to answer, for parents may not realize that moving, touching, and playing matter so much. This is a common scenario among families in which the child is the oldest or only one. Without another, more organized child to compare with the disorganized one, parents may be unfamiliar with age-appropriate skills.

6. *"He's so smart, so what if he can't tie his shoes?"* Despite having SI Dysfunction, the child may have many strengths. He may be a math whiz, a dinosaur expert, or a great storyteller. By contrast, the same child may be weak in self-help skills, sports, or handwriting.

Often, the out-of-sync child develops one or two "splinter skills." These are skills that the child works exceedingly hard to master, but they don't help him generalize his learning to accomplish more complex skills.

For example, one of my preschool students learned to play "Frère Jacques" on the xylophone. He was pleased as punch. (Me, too!) Unfortunately, that was his only tune. He played it repeatedly and could not be persuaded to try "Old MacDonald," another simple tune. Another child learned to ride a small bicycle at school—a great accomplishment. However, she had no concept of how to apply her skills to a slightly larger bike at home.

When the child is adept in several areas, or achieves a splinter skill, parents, teachers, and pediatricians frequently believe that she has no definable problems. They think she's "just lazy" about learning new skills.

7. *"He can do everything well, if he wants to."* The child may have good days, when he's cooperative, calm, and competent, and bad days, when he's furious, fidgety, and frustrated. Because SI Dysfunction can manifest itself in different ways, at different times, it is easy to be lulled into false confidence that dysfunction is not the problem.

Parents may believe that the child's erratic behavior is a matter of choice. It isn't. No child chooses to be disorganized, but the out-of-sync child is typically inconsistent in behavior.

Three Valid Reasons to Seek Help

Still uncertain whether to travel the rocky road to a diagnosis? If so, consider the following criteria.

1. *Does the problem get in the child's way?* The answer is yes if he struggles with "doing what comes naturally": creeping, running, jumping, climbing, talking, listening, hugging, and playing. The answer is also yes if he has low self-esteem. Indeed, low self-esteem is one of the red flags of SI Dysfunction. Sometimes the child will be referred to a mental health professional who can offer counseling and therapy. But, if the underlying neurological problems are not addressed, the child develops only compensatory techniques, at most.

2. *Does the child's problem get in other people's way?* Yes, if the problem causes behavior that may not bother the child but bothers everyone else. The child may annoy other children when he pushes, may vex his teacher when he fidgets, and may scare the bejeepers out of his parents when he's reckless— without comprehending why they are always upset with him.

Yes, if the child is an "angel at home," where it's safe, but a "devil on the street," where it's unpredictable and scary. Yes, if he's an angel at school, where he manages to pull himself together, but a demon at home, where he falls apart at the end of the day. When his behavior differs dramatically in different situations, he is sending out signals of distress.

3. *Should you listen when a teacher, pediatrician, or friend suggests you seek help?* Yes, if they have dealt with many children and can recognize disorganized behavior. While their advice may hurt, it may also confirm what you sense but have been unable to address. Think of it this way: If the gas station

attendant says your car needs a tune-up because it isn't functioning well, you would listen. How about a tune-up for your out-of-sync child?

DOCUMENTING YOUR CHILD'S BEHAVIOR

Parents know their child best but often can't make sense of what they know. Perhaps you're concerned about your child's difficulties, which don't fit into traditional medical categories of children's illnesses or disabilities. Perhaps the pediatrician can't identify the problem, either, and says, "Nothing is wrong. Everything will eventually turn out all right."

What should you do?

First, *trust your instincts*, and then document your observations.

Documentation is a critical part of the process of identifying and addressing your child's needs. Anecdotal evidence is just as important as professional diagnosis. Jot down observations you have made at home and incidents teachers have noted at school. Then, armed with specific data, you will be better equipped to notice patterns and to describe your child's difficulties to a doctor or therapist who is familiar with Sensory Integration Dysfunction.

Remember Tommy, Vicki, and Peter? (*See pp. 4–7.*) Tommy's problems are tactile; Vicki's are vestibular; Peter's are proprioceptive. (These imaginary children have obvious problems. In real life, dysfunction is not always so clear-cut.)

Below are examples of charts prepared by their parents. The first chart for each child documents the "bad times": situations that cause out-of-sync behavior. The second chart documents the "good times": situations in which Tommy, Vicki, and Peter function well.

The last charts are blank. Make several copies and fill them with clues to help you solve the mystery of your beautiful, but bewildering, child.

Tommy's Troubling Times
(Tactile Dysfunction)

Because no one seems able to help, Tommy's parents decide to do some detective work. They begin to chart his most difficult moments, hoping to discover patterns that will offer clues about his behavior. Here is their chart:

Behavior	Date, Time	Circumstances
Tantrum! Refused to get dressed.	Oct. 10, 8:30 A.M.	Says his socks are too tight and he hates his new turtleneck sweater.
Inconsolable at school.	Oct. 14, 10:00 A.M.	Teacher said he was fine until it was time for art project (finger painting).
Threw plate on kitchen floor.	Oct. 22, 12 noon	I thought he'd like cottage cheese (instead of yogurt) for a change. Wrong!
Screamed in grocery store and threw orange at friendly old woman.	Nov. 23, 4:30 P.M.	Day before Thanksgiving. Crowded store. Lots of noise and cart bumping. Old woman (stranger) tousled his hair.
Single-handedly destroyed toys at "Santa's Workshop."	Dec. 18, 2:00 p.m.	Excited by all the toys in the department store and couldn't seem to keep his hands off them. Completely out of control, like a bull in a china shop.

INTERPRETATION OF TOMMY'S
TROUBLING TIMES

Unrelated as the charted notations seem, they indicate a pattern of tactile dysfunction. Let's look at the incidents, one by one.

First incident: Tommy fusses over his clothes because he is uncomfortable in high collars and bumpy socks. He is not purposely ornery. He simply cannot explain why certain textures are irritating. His poorly regulated tactile system is the culprit, telling him on a subconscious level that his clothes are threatening his sense of well-being. His mother remarks, "The person who invents the truly seamless sock will make a fortune!"

Second incident: Tommy is inconsolable at school, because of fingerpainting. The teacher, believing that she offers pleasurable activities to her students, is mystified and urges Tommy to participate. He hates the thought of wet, messy hands, feels like a failure, and wishes the teacher would leave him alone. The scene escalates into a very unhappy situation.

Third incident: Tommy makes a scene at lunch. He has eating problems, for his mouth is overly sensitive to the food textures. If you remember the first time you put a raw oyster in your mouth, you can sympathize! Tommy will eat yogurt because it is familiar and safe. Lumpy cottage cheese, however, is not safe. Tommy can't explain that his defensive tactile system is sending up alert signals so he hurls down his plate.

Fourth incident: In the supermarket, Tommy bops a friendly woman on the head with an orange. Why does he lash out, making his mother wish she could just abandon him and the Thanksgiving turkey and go home to weep? The answer is simple: to Tommy, the woman is a threat.

She is unfamiliar, and she makes the "mistake" of patting him on the head.

For all of us, our heads are extra-sensitive to unexpected, light touch. Most of us react instantly to light touch in order to protect the body parts we need for survival. Because Tommy is more sensitive than most, he reacts with what we might consider an excessive response.

Fifth incident: Tommy tears into the toys at Santa's Workshop. Whereas others his age may be satisfied to look at and maybe caress the toys, with a discriminative touch, Tommy "attacks" them. An aspect of his out-of-sync touch system requires him to manhandle objects in order to learn about them. Poor Tommy! He wreaks havoc in Santa's Workshop because he wants to know (and, of course, own) all the toys.

In summary, Tommy has tactile dysfunction, involving oversensitivity to touch as well as difficulty getting the touch information he needs.

Tommy's Terrific Times

Noting Tommy's out-of-sync behavior gives only half the picture. Tommy's parents also chart his terrific times (*see next page*), when he is more positively in sync.

INTERPRETATION OF TOMMY'S TERRIFIC TIMES
First incident: Firm, predictable touch has always comforted Tommy. He asks for a back rub with downward strokes—the way hair grows. (Upward strokes "ruffle his feathers" and "rub him the wrong way.") He prefers his father's deep pressure to his mother's gentler caresses. Firm, soothing pressure suppresses his hypersensitivity and prepares him for sleep.

Behavior	Date, Time	Circumstances
Fell asleep easily.	Oct. 11, 7:30 P.M.	Asked for a back rub: "Daddy do it, not Mommy." (Art was pleased; usually Tommy prefers me to his Dad.) "Down, not up!" Art rubbed his back really hard with firm, downward strokes. Then Art gave him ten tight bear hugs. Tommy asked Art to put him to bed—a first!
Enjoyed bath and again fell asleep easily.	Oct. 12, 7:30 P.M.	Two good ideas: having Tommy help get the water temperature "just right" (lukewarm) and using Art's rubbing technique, first with a washcloth, then with a sponge. "More, Mommy, more!" The rubbing relaxed him.
Had a great day at school.	Oct. 15, 9 A.M.–12	After I told his teacher that he likes rubdowns, she tried the "People Sandwich" game. He was the "baloney," lying facedown at one end of a gym mat (the "bread"). With her hands, she patted pretend mustard and mayonnaise all over his body. Then she covered him with the other end of the mat, and a few kids crawled over the mat to squish out the excess mustard. Tommy loved it. Rest of the day went well.

Ate lunch without complaint.	Oct. 15, 12:30 P.M.	Gave him pureed soup—no lumps. He chowed it down and had a second bowl. Why did it take me so long to realize he'll eat only smooth food?
Actually enjoyed trip to grocery store.	Nov. 30, 3:00 P.M.	Went to supermarket that has miniature carts for kids. He liked pushing one, loaded with potatoes and apples, and was a great helper. Good idea to take him when store isn't crowded.
Sat on kitchen floor and kept me company for an hour while I baked.	Jan. 5, 2:00 P.M.	His teacher said he enjoyed handling dried beans in the big bin. (He avoids the bin when it has water or sand in it.) I filled a dishpan with peas, pinto beans, and lentils and gave him some measuring cups and a scoop. He busily measured and poured beans, chatting away. He said, "This is fun work."

Second incident: Tommy's mother invites him to help adjust the water temperature before he gets in the bath. He likes having some control, rather than being plunged into water that is "too hot!" or "too cold!" Tonight, he climbs in willingly. Also, she takes a cue from her husband and rubs Tommy's back and limbs firmly with a washcloth and sponge, instead of sprinkling him clean. He relaxes, and the result is another pleasant bedtime.

Third incident: The teacher tries a deep pressure activity at school, with much success. Tommy enjoys being pounded with "mustard" and crawled over by his classmates. Therapeutic and fun, the "People Sandwich" activity also helps him interact with his peers.

Fourth incident: Tommy cannot tolerate lumps in his food. When his mother prepares soup with a smooth texture, he likes it.

Fifth incident: Tommy likes pushing the little grocery cart. He can get a good grip on the smooth handlebar, which doesn't irritate his hands. The deep muscle work of pushing something with resistance feels good. Also, Tommy's mother is paying more attention to his fear of crowds. She notes that going to the store when it is quiet makes the outing enjoyable.

Sixth incident: Tommy likes handling the dried beans because they aren't sticky, and he becomes engrossed in his play. Comparing notes about his behavior, his mother and teacher can strategize ways to provide him with successful tactile experiences at home and school.

Vicki's Vicissitudes
(Vestibular Dysfunction)

Vicki's parents take notes about their child's inconsistent behavior:

Behavior	Date, Time	Circumstances
Strolling to corner mailbox, stumbled and fell. Cried, "So tired. Carry me!"	June 4, 9:30 A.M.	After a long night's sleep and good breakfast, why should she be so limp? By the end of the day, she's always raring to go!

Refused to let me leave her at Ellen's birthday party. Once the games began, she became wound up and uncontrollable.	June 9, 2:30 P.M.	So excited about the party, until we arrived. The whole class was invited to play tag and relay races. I was the only mom who had to stay, and Vicki was the only child who didn't play. When she finally left my side, the games really wound her up. She was in everybody's face, shouting, pushing, and running wildly. Everyone was in tears. We left early.
Fell apart at the playground. Tantrum lasted twenty minutes.	July 3, 2:30 P.M.	Yesterday she loved the playground; today she hated it. Same place, same time, same weather, but different child! All I did was spin her a few times on the tire swing. Usually, she loves the tire swing.
When we pointed to the moon, she kept looking at our fingers rather than the sky.	Sept. 4, 9:30 P.M.	Up later than usual. Other kids at neighborhood picnic excited about the bright moon and stars. Vicki didn't understand what she was supposed to be looking at.

INTERPRETATION OF VICKI'S VICISSITUDES

First incident: Vicki's early-morning fatigue is a symptom of low muscle tone; she has a loose and limp body. A short excursion to the corner mailbox requires more energy than she can muster at the moment. Also, her trunk is unstable, and she has poor postural responses, poor balance, and poor motor coordination. Her mother notes, however, that in the evening, Vicki is energetic. The reason is that her constant movement throughout the day revs her up.

Second incident: New situations distress Vicki. Difficulty controlling her movements causes her to be emotionally insecure, so she clings to her mother. Poor coordination and poor motor planning hinder her ability to socialize effectively with her classmates. Her need for vigorous movement is keen, but when she eventually joins in the games, she goes overboard, crashing and bumping into the other children.

Third incident: Knowing that Vicki often enjoys the tire swing, her mother thinks she'll enjoy it even more with a little help to make it spin faster. Vicki cannot tolerate the unexpected, passive movement, however. Vicki hates being on the tire swing when someone else moves it; she likes it only when she is in control.

Fourth incident: Looking at the moon poses another problem. Vicki's eye movements are not well coordinated. Because her eyes don't work well together, she has poor eye-teaming and poor depth perception. She looks at her parents' wagging fingers, within her visual range, and seems unable to gaze beyond her immediate space.

In summary, Vicki is hyposensitive to vestibular sensations. Associated problems are her loose, floppy muscle tone, poor postural responses, and poor ocular control.

Vicki's Victories

Vicki's parents also take notes about successful situations.

INTERPRETATION OF VICKI'S VICTORIES

First incident: Positioning herself upside down, feet in the air, is a form of self-therapy. Although this position seems odd, it helps regulate Vicki's inefficient processing. Through her inner ear she is receiving useful information about the pull of gravity.

Behavior	Date, Time	Circumstances
Spent 5 minutes standing on her head. Afterwards, was calm and attentive.	June 6, 8:00 A.M.	Tried to get Vicki into bed to listen to a story, but she was revved up, walking in circles. Finally, she went to the corner and got into an upside-down position. I read the story and she listened quietly. Then she came back to earth, climbed into bed, and fell instantly asleep.
At park, swung for forty-five minutes! Bubbly, bright, and talkative all afternoon.	July 2, 2:30 P.M.	First, she lay across the swing, tummy down, and pushed with her toes. Second, she sat on the swing and asked me to push her for a very long time. Third, she spun herself around on the tire swing. She wasn't dizzy, but I was, just watching!
Tipped to and fro on a makeshift teeter-totter. Later, seemed more in sync than usual.	July 12, 2:30 P.M.	Vicki joined her big brother and pals as they played on the teeter-totter they made by placing a big square plywood board over a railroad timber. She rocked from side to side and seemed to enjoy the jolt whenever the edge of the board hit the ground. She had a lot of fun coming up with different ways to balance.
Played happily (for a change!) with other kids at the lake.	August 1, 4 P.M.	Instead of throwing and catching the ball, she had fun sitting and lying on it. When she fell off onto the grass, she laughed. The other kids were interested in her ideas, and they all took turns. It's great to see her playing with others!

Second incident: Vicki enjoys swinging in different ways for an unusually long time. When she decides how to move and for how long, she is actively engaging in self-therapy. Hanging upside down provides one kind of intense vestibular intake that her brain craves. Swaying gently back and forth, a form of linear movement through space, is soothing. Spinning on the tire swing, a form of rotary movement, also helps regulate her vestibular system.

The fact that she does *not* get dizzy when she spins indicates that her vestibular system is out of sync. Normally, prolonged spinning would make a person feel woozy, but it makes Vicki feel wonderful.

After swinging, she is chatty and vivacious. The activities have aroused the language centers of her brain. Like all children, she has a lot to say; unlike most children, she often has trouble getting the words out. When she "primes the pump," the words begin to flow.

Third incident: Rocking from side to side is a form of linear motion called oscillation. Like swinging, it organizes Vicki's vestibular system. She likes the jolting sensation when the board strikes the ground. The jolts arouse her in a positive way by sending extra messages to her joints and muscles. When she directs her own play, she plays with purpose and with good attention.

Fourth incident: Tossing a beach ball is too great a challenge, due to Vicki's poor motor skills. However, she enjoys a different challenge: maintaining her balance while sitting on the ball. Every child has an inner drive to resist gravity. Sometimes all the child needs is the right equipment in the right place at the right time! When the other children join her game, Vicki's self-confidence soars, and she is able to play with them happily.

Peter's Problems
(Proprioceptive Dysfunction)

Peter's parents prepare this chart as they look for patterns:

Behavior	Date, Time	Circumstances
Walked into a telephone pole and required three stitches.	July 9, 3:30 P.M.	Leaving ice cream parlor, he was paying attention to his cone, not to where he was going. So exasperating and frustrating!
Picked up Granny's best china figurine; then smashed it to smithereens when he set it down.	Aug. 2, 8:00 P.M.	Maybe he was tired after long trip getting to Granny's, but even when he's rested he's clumsy. Granny's unhappiness worsened the situation. She wasn't angry at him, just sad, but he was inconsolable.
Trying to play catch with a beach ball, he missed the ball every time.	Aug. 4, noon	Peter either lunges at the ball at the wrong time or swats it away. His younger cousins are so mean and say, "Baby! Baby! Don't you even know how to catch a ball?"
At the restaurant, spilled his milk on the table and his clothes.	Labor Day, 6:30 P.M.	Sometimes Peter can't manage getting milk into his mouth. Even though the waitress was a sweetheart, Peter was distraught.
Late for first day of fourth grade because he had a fit buttoning his new shirt.	Sept. 6, 8:30 to 9:30 A.M.	First he resisted wearing the shirt, and then buttoned it incorrectly, crying, "They made it wrong. I never do things right." He works so hard to do the simplest things.

INTERPRETATION OF PETER'S PROBLEMS

First incident: Peter bumps into a pole because eating the cone requires his full attention. He really can't chew and walk at the same time. His mother's frustration is nothing compared to Peter's!

Second incident: Peter misjudges the weight of Granny's figurine. Of course, Granny is upset. It's hard to understand that poor control over the force he puts into every movement causes his carelessness.

Third incident: It's about as easy for Peter to catch a beach ball as it is for most of us to capture a butterfly. He has poor kinesthesia, the conscious awareness of his own movements. He has trouble moving through space, coordinating his arms and legs, and anticipating the impact of the ball. No wonder his cousins are "so mean!" They don't like to play with him because they can't predict what he will do and how he will do it. They notice his jerky movements and consider him a "jerk."

Fourth incident: The outing to a restaurant is a disaster. When Peter picks up a glass that feels unfamiliar, the sensations from his muscles and joints can't tell him how much effort to exert. The glass of milk flies through the air, and Peter, once again, makes a mess.

Fifth incident: Buttoning a stiff shirt is hard for Peter. Normal first-day-of-school anxiety, plus Mother's urgings to move faster, plus his clumsiness add up to Peter's deep despair. Because he moves inefficiently, he has low self-esteem. When he cries, "I never do anything right," he really believes what he says.

In summary, Peter's main problem is proprioceptive dysfunction.

Peter's Positives

Peter's parents also record his positive experiences:

Behavior	Date, Time	Circumstances
Pleased with himself after writing a brief note to Granny before our trip.	July 28, 3:30 P.M.	Before writing, Peter cracked his knuckles, pressed his hands together and squeezed his fingers. Said, "My hands will work better now." Wrote the note without breaking the pencil point!
Loved playing Granny's "Posture Game."	Aug. 4, 10 A.M.	His posture worries Granny, so, placing a cookbook on her head, she challenged him to walk with a book on his head longer than she can. Peter won (or she let him) and earned a trip to the baseball card shop with her. She makes him "shape up." He adores her.
Enjoyed a tug-of-war game on the beach.	Aug. 7, noon	We had to play a silly game of tug-of-war with the Smiths to prove that our branch of the family is just as strong as theirs. Surprise— Peter loved it! Said, "It's awesome to be on a team." Seems as if he's developing a competitive streak this summer. Astonishing.

Helped wash Ron's car; then volunteered to wash mine, too.	Dec. 28, 2 P.M.	The cars were encrusted with salt after the last snowstorm. As Ron had already turned off the outside hose faucets to prevent the pipes from freezing, they had to lug buckets of water from the house. We didn't realize Peter could lift such a heavy weight! He enjoyed helping his dad sponge and dry the car. He said, "I bet you're glad to have a son like me." It's a joy to hear him say that. Maybe we need to assign him more chores.

INTERPRETATION OF PETER'S POSITIVES

First incident: Peter is "waking up" his writing muscles when he cracks his knuckles and squeezes his fingers. He needs extra stimulation in his joints and ligaments in order to manipulate a pencil. His mother remarks that after this exercise he doesn't break the pencil point, as usual.

Second incident: Granny's technique to improve Peter's posture is therapeutically sound. The weight of the book compresses the muscles in his neck and shoulders and gives him extra sensory information. He stands up straighter, in an adaptive behavior to resist gravity. Granny's technique is also psychologically sound. She guesses correctly that he will accept her challenge because it is fun and not too demanding. Succeeding boosts his self-esteem, and tomorrow he may try a bigger challenge—like a dictionary!

Third incident: Pulling the rope organizes Peter's proprioceptive system. He enjoys the tug-of-war because tensing his muscles feels good. He also likes being on a team where everyone is working together and no one can be singled out as the "loser." Like all children, Peter has the inner drive to use his muscles effectively, but he is not a "self-starter." He doesn't know how to engage in activities that benefit his proprioceptive system unless the opportunity is literally put into his hands.

Fourth incident: Peter uses his muscles vigorously when he hoists the heavy buckets of water, squeezes the sponge, and wipes the car with towels. This activity energizes him, and he likes it so much that he's ready to wash another car. His mother's plan to give him more chores will help Peter, for every child needs to feel useful and competent.

Make several copies of the charts on the next pages, pick up your pencil, and fill in the blanks to document your child's behavior.

_____'S OUT-OF-SYNC BEHAVIOR

Behavior	Date, Time	Circumstances

_____'S IN-SYNC BEHAVIOR

Behavior	Date, Time	Circumstances

DIAGNOSING THE PROBLEM

Consider the adage "When you hear hoofbeats, look for horses, not zebras." Documenting your child's responses will help you locate those "horses," the specific situations causing out-of-sync behavior.

Maybe you can spot the problem clearly. Maybe you can't. What should you do? Where do you start? You have three choices.

Three Choices

1. You could take the "wait-and-see" approach—but please don't! It is not advisable to sit back and wait for your out-of-sync child to catch up, if his dysfunction gets in his way every day. Possibly, with time, he will function better—but probably his life will just get harder. Why take a chance, when getting help now may make a tremendous difference in his coping skills?

2. You could improve your child's "sensory diet." Joining forces with the teacher, you could develop a home-and-school program that will help your child strengthen his skills. (*See chapter 7.*)

3. You could seek a specialist or team of specialists who will either screen your child for possible risk factors or do a full evaluation. (Screenings and evaluations are described below.) Ask the pediatrician first for a referral to a specialist. If the doctor resists this idea for some reason, try one of the support systems listed below. (*Also see Resources.*)

Where to Turn for Support

If you aren't certain what your child's needs are and you want a global picture of his problems, start with one of these resources:

- Your child's preschool, early childhood center, or elementary school. Some schools maintain a list of local occupational therapists who are familiar with sensory integration dysfunction and who have worked successfully with other students. The school may suggest one or two for you to call.

- Your local public school, even if your child is too young to attend or is not enrolled there. Your child has the legal right to obtain free services in the school system of the jurisdiction in which you pay taxes. IDEA and subsequent legislation require states to provide early identification of, and treatment for, developmental delays. The public early intervention/childhood program, often called Child Find, provides evaluations and connects parents with appropriate educational services.

- Private, nonprofit mental health and social service organizations (listed in the telephone directory), which also provide services, often on a sliding scale.

- A multidisciplinary teaching hospital, where a team of specialists can make a complete evaluation ("total workup").

If you are fairly certain that your child has Sensory Integration Dysfunction and you want to locate an occupational therapist to screen or evaluate the child, start here:

• The Occupational Therapy Department of your local children's hospital.

• Private practitioners listed in the telephone directory.

• The American Occupational Therapy Association, Inc. (AOTA).

• Sensory Integration International (SII). The mission of SII is to develop awareness, knowledge, skills, and services in sensory integration. SII can provide you with a list of occupational therapists in your community who are experienced in sensory integration therapy.

What if no O.T.s in your area practice sensory integration therapy? One option is to contact SII for the name of the nearest professional who can help you. Another option is to arrange for your child's initial consultation with an O.T. who is familiar with SI, although that O.T. may be some distance away. The therapist whom your child sees for a screening or evaluation can at least provide you with ideas for a home or school program.

WHAT IS A SCREENING?

A screening is a quick and simple procedure that checks whether children have acquired specific skills. Often, groups of children are screened at the same time at schools or early childhood centers.

The purpose of a screening is the early identification of children who may have one or more developmental deficiencies: cognitive, physical, speech and language, psychosocial, self-help, or adaptive.

A screening is a short, informal "look-see." It is neither a test nor an in-depth examination. When it suggests that a child may have a problem, parents are notified and encouraged to have the child fully evaluated.

WHAT IS AN EVALUATION?

A formal evaluation is a thorough, individualized examination to measure a person's skills. Depending on the child's problem, the professional would be a pediatrician, a pediatric eye doctor, an audiologist, a speech/language clinician or pathologist, or an occupational therapist.

One part of the evaluation is a questionnaire that parents complete, such as a medical, sensorimotor, developmental, or family history. Sometimes teachers are asked to fill out questionnaires, too (*see examples, pp. 28–33*). Your answers will help the professional assess your child, since patterns of behavior since birth may confirm clinical observations.

Providing information about your child will help you, too. Indeed, after completing a sensorimotor questionnaire, one mother noted, "We've been puzzled by our four-year-old's cautiousness, language delay, and sensitivity to touch, but we never understood the connection. Now the pieces are beginning to fit!"

Another part of the evaluation is the child's visit with the professional in a hospital, clinic, office, school, or your home. The evaluation is based on standardized tests and structured observations of your child. Depending on how much testing is required, the evaluation will take from one hour to several hours, spread over several days.

Before making a diagnosis, the professional considers the "W" questions: What are the child's strengths and weaknesses? Where, when, how often, and with what intensity do problems occur? What length of time has the child exhibited the problem behavior? What is the age level at which the child performs? What is happening at home or school that may be affecting his ability to function? Who brings out the worst and the best in him? Why, in the professional's opinion, is the child out of sync?

After careful consideration of these factors, the professional makes a diagnosis, writes a detailed report, and confers with the parents to help them interpret the results. Often, the report is informative and understandable. If you receive one that is full of bewildering terms, call the professional back for a better explanation. He or she wants to help you, not confuse you.

Sometimes the professional will say that therapy is not indicated. It happens occasionally that a child is simply immature. If so, then time, rather than extensive therapy, will be his best teacher. The professional may suggest games and activities that you can do as a family at home to help your child develop lagging skills.

If, however, a definitive problem is diagnosed, the professional will recommend direct, individual therapy sessions. If you decide to enroll your child, you will not be obligated to stick with the professional who conducted the evaluation. Finding the right therapist is important, because a good fit between therapist and child will affect your child's progress.

You will also need to consider the cost. Although therapy may be clearly indicated for your child, most health insurance policies do not cover the expense. You have a slight chance of getting coverage if your pediatrician puts into writing that therapy is a medical necessity. However, SI Dysfunction is not a health problem.

Financial assistance from the government is also difficult to procure. Money is scarce, and many children with multiple special needs require assistance. Public funds are not usually available for the child who has only SI Dysfunction.

However, you may receive assistance if you can prove that SI Dysfunction is so severe that it interferes with the child's ability to benefit from education. Whether or not your child has been identified as being learning disabled, a pronounced problem with educational functioning is sometimes considered to be a sufficient criterion for funding.

If, in addition to SI Dysfunction, your child has significant medical, physical, and developmental problems, such as mental retardation, then you are eligible to receive funds under IDEA. If your child is enrolled in a special-education class in a public school, then related services such as occupational therapy, physical therapy, and speech/language therapy are part of the free educational package, if your child qualifies for them.

Otherwise, paying for therapy is up to you.

So—you will need to weigh the expense versus the benefits.

One benefit is what a therapist offers: her training and expertise, her therapeutic equipment, and her ability to provide experiences that your child can't get elsewhere. Another, most important, benefit is knowing that you are acting in your child's best interest. By investing in treatment now, you forestall problems that may later cause greater pain and more expensive therapy.

You will have many decisions to make, but should you get early intervention for your child, you will probably see an enormous change in his behavior, his feelings, his skills, and your family life.

THE OCCUPATIONAL
THERAPIST'S EVALUATION

An occupational therapist will usually evaluate the child in her office. The evaluation is ordinarily a pleasant experience. While costs vary, expect to spend several hundred dollars. This will be money well spent, and it may be covered by health insurance.

Here are some of the areas an O.T. investigates:

• Fine and gross motor developmental levels
• Visual-motor integration (doing puzzles or copying shapes)
• Visual perception
• Neuromuscular control (balance and posture)
• Responses to sensory stimulation (tactile, vestibular, and proprioceptive)
• Bilateral coordination
• Motor planning

Sensory integration is just one of several issues the O.T. is qualified to address. She may identify needs in other areas as well, such as attention deficit, language delay, or a visual or emotional problem. If she finds that your child has a difficulty different from SI Dysfunction, or that his needs are greater than her skills can serve, she may refer you to another professional.

DIFFERENT THERAPIES,
DIFFERENT APPROACHES

After an evaluation, the next step is to arrange for treatment. The most beneficial treatment for SI Dysfunction is occupational therapy.

Occupational Therapy

Utilizing both science and art, occupational therapy (O.T.) is a health profession devoted to helping people with motor and behavior problems learn how to perform purposeful activities. For a child, purposeful activities include making mud pies, climbing, jumping, buttoning, drawing, and writing. Such activities are the child's "occupation."

In general, O.T. improves the functioning of a person's nervous system, which may be damaged, as in an accident victim, or may be inefficient, as in a child whose behavior is ineffective and inappropriate.

THE OCCUPATIONAL THERAPIST

An occupational therapist (also abbreviated as O.T.) is an allied health professional. He or she has received a baccalaureate or master's degree after completing a course of study, plus internship experience, in the biological, physical, medical, and behavioral sciences. Course work includes neurology, anatomy, orthopedics, psychology, and psychiatry.

The O.T. may work with your child at school, in his or her office or clinic, in a hospital, in a community mental health center, or sometimes in your home. The ideal O.T. is one who specializes in pediatrics and who has received additional, postgraduate training in sensory integration theory and treatment.

Under the guidance of a therapist, the child actively takes in movement and touch information in playful, meaningful, and natural ways that help his brain modulate these fundamental neural messages. The child responds favorably to SI treatment, because his nervous system is pliable and changeable. Therapy teaches the child to succeed—and he *loves* it!

ACTIVITIES THE O.T. MAY PROVIDE

Every child is different, so the sequence and kinds of activity that an occupational therapist provides for your child will be individualized. She will design a program based on his particular needs, and, following his lead, she will guide him through activities that challenge his ability to respond successfully to sensory stimuli in an organized way.

For instance, your child may have difficulty jumping, climbing, pedaling tricycles, and getting dressed. These problems can't be "fixed" by teaching him specifically how to jump, climb, pedal, and put on a jacket, when the underlying problem is SI Dysfunction. He doesn't need jumping lessons but opportunities to integrate all sensations. With her appealing equipment and professional knowledge, a qualified therapist can weave art and science together to offer these opportunities.

Here is a small sampling of activities that an O.T. may provide:

• To develop better body awareness and improve postural security—swinging prone in a special swing suspended from the ceiling, in order to experience specific movement sensations

• To improve tactile discrimination—finding hidden toys by manipulating a ball of therapeutic putty

- To reduce tactile defensiveness—having arms and legs rubbed with differently textured sponges and cloths

- To improve balance—lying or sitting on large, inflated therapy balls

- To improve bilateral coordination—using a rolling pin with both hands to bat at a ball hanging from the ceiling, while lying prone

- To improve motor planning—moving through obstacle courses

- To improve fine motor skills—playing with magnets to build up the muscles of the hand to stabilize loose joints

- To improve extension against the pull of gravity—riding across the floor, or riding headfirst down a ramp, while lying prone on a scooter

- To improve flexion—clinging to a cylindrical swing that is suspended from the ceiling

- To reduce gravitational insecurity—swinging gently on a flat glider swing; jumping on a bounce pad

- To improve ocular control and visual-spatial perception—playing games with beanbags, balloons, and suspended balls

The most important factor that will determine the success of therapy is the child's own inner drive to explore and learn from the environment. The child's motivation to spin on a swing, to touch certain textures, or to be gently pressed between two gym mats tells the therapist what the child's nervous system seeks.

According to Dr. Ayres, "Sensations that make a child happy tend to be integrating." When the child is actively involved in his own therapy, he becomes more organized, he has fun, and he feels in sync.

Other Types of Therapy

While the out-of-sync child will benefit most from occupational therapy, sometimes another highly specific type of therapy will also help.*

SPEECH-AND-LANGUAGE THERAPY

Speech-language therapy includes activities designed to meet specific goals for the child. The child may need help with speech skills, such as pronouncing "L," "K," or "Sh" sounds; monitoring the pitch of his voice; and strengthening oral-motor control in the muscles of his mouth. He may also benefit from activities designed to expand his language skills, such as retelling stories, conversing, and playing games to develop memory and vocabulary.

AUDITORY INTEGRATION TRAINING

Auditory integration training is a method of sound stimulation designed to improve a person's listening and communicative skills, learning capabilities, motor coordination, body awareness, and self-esteem. The methods developed by Dr. Alfred Tomatis and Dr. Guy Berard both employ the use of special headphones. During a course of several days, the child listens passively to music and voices filtered through the headphones. Then he participates in active voice work, such as repeating sounds, reading

---

*Neurologists are physicians who diagnose and treat seizures and other diseases of the brain and central nervous system. While SI Dysfunction is a neurological problem, it is not a medical condition. Neurologists are not trained to evaluate SI Dysfunction in children, and they do not provide SI therapy.

aloud, and conversing. Therapy helps the ear to attend to and discriminate among sounds, the vestibular system to integrate sensory messages of balance and posture, and the person to become more focused, centered, and organized.

VISION THERAPY

Vision therapy, or optometric visual training, helps the person improve visual skills. It can also prevent learning-related visual problems. In conjunction with lenses or prisms, therapy helps the child integrate visual information with intake from the other senses, such as hearing, touching, and moving. A developmental (or behavioral) optometrist provides sensorimotor and educational activities for the child to do in the specialist's office and at home. These activities strengthen eye-motor control, eye-hand coordination and depth perception, and they help develop visual perception.

PSYCHOTHERAPY

Psychotherapy is sometimes appropriate, particularly if the child is depressed or has a poor self-image or behavior problems. (Psychotherapy deals with the effects of SI Dysfunction but not the underlying causes.) Types of psychotherapy include behavioral therapy, to help the child deal with problematical symptoms and behaviors; family therapy, to help the child, parents, and siblings become a healthier unit; and play therapy, to promote the child's social-emotional development. Therapists include clinical psychologists, licensed clinical social workers, and child psychiatrists.

PHYSICAL THERAPY

Physical therapy is a health profession devoted to improving an individual's physical abilities. It involves activities that strengthen the child's muscular control and motor coordination, especially of his large muscles. Sometimes using physical agents such as massage, whirlpool baths, or ultrasound, physical therapists help the child get his muscles ready for voluntary movement. Some physical therapists receive additional training in sensory integration theory and treatment.

BRINGING THERAPIST AND CHILD TOGETHER

Before the first session with the O.T. (or other therapist), you will want to prepare your child. You can say, "Today you'll meet someone who will help you get stronger. She has great toys and games to play. Her place is like a gym where you will do things that feel good. I think you'll have lots of fun."

Emphasizing that therapy will be fun is important. Many children with Sensory Integration Dysfunction don't have much fun. They wish they could but simply don't know how.

When you think and speak positively about therapy, you help make it work for your child. You reassure your child that this is not punishment or something to feel defensive about. The child may blame himself for being frequently clumsy or tired, saying, "I'm no good." He needs frequent confirmation that he *is* good, and that therapy will make him even better.

Whether treatment takes place in a busy clinic, at school, or in your very own basement, you will be involved, too. Part of the therapist's job is to collaborate with parents to design activities that help the child function better at home. The therapist may also give suggestions to the teacher, if the teacher agrees to modify the classroom environment.

Because treatment will become a part of your child's life, you and your child should get along well with the therapist. Goodness-of-fit is essential! If your child resists going for treatment, or if you lack confidence in the therapist, then something is amiss, and you should switch to another one, if possible. Treatment will be most successful when all the parties have a respectful and pleasant working relationship.

Working with the therapist will take some time and effort, but your involvement is definitely worthwhile. The therapy itself may not last forever, but the results will last a lifetime.

KEEPING A RECORD

If you aren't already keeping a running record of your child's behavior and development, please begin one now! Your record should include:

• Your own documented observations,

• Teachers' comments and reports,

• Names, addresses, and telephone numbers of professionals you have consulted or intend to consult,

• Detailed, dated notes of consultations and telephone conversations with professionals,

• Written confirmation of information you have received orally, and

• Specialists' evaluations, diagnoses, and recommendations.

An orderly, chronological notebook is a valuable tool. It will help you see patterns that you may have missed. It will provide evidence of your child's uneven development, should you need to prove at some point that your child requires special services. It will also help you feel more organized and in control.

A professional diagnosis, along with therapy, should bring some relief. Meanwhile, life at home may improve when you follow some of the suggestions offered in the next chapter.

Chapter Seven

YOUR CHILD AT HOME

Parents can make home life easier both for themselves and their child by introducing a balanced "sensory diet," including activities that strengthen neurological development and improve self-help skills.

A PARENT'S REVELATION

When Tonya was three, she entered St. Columba's. Reluctantly. She was fearful and limp. She spoke in a breathy voice, shrank from physical contact, and cried when it was time to go outdoors. However, she was very bright and loved stories, music, and dressing up.

During the fall, we screened the three-year-olds for sensory integration dysfunction. Tonya's results suggested a possibility of some dysfunction, but we weren't sure. She might have been simply immature.

While we usually observe late bloomers carefully before recommending occupational therapy, we decided to have a conference with Tonya's parents. We felt we could promote Tonya's social and physical development if we could persuade them to improve her sensory diet.

During the conference they listened politely to our suggestions to get Tonya outside every day, to give her more hands-on experiences, and to invite children over to play.

"Well, those ideas won't work," her mother said. "Tonya hates being cold and messy. She dislikes going outside and playing with other kids. She just wants to be with the baby and me and listen to stories." Rising to her feet, she added, "And that's fine with us." Unsatisfactorily for all of us, the conference ended.

And so it went. Since the parents repeatedly resisted our suggestions, we decided to back off.

Then, just as we stepped back, Tonya's little sister took charge at home. This two-year-old began to clamor for changes in the family's lifestyle. Sociable and energetic, she loved playing outside with the neighborhood children. Her mother found that the best way to gratify her was to take her daily to the playground. Of course, Tonya had to go, too.

After Christmas vacation, we noticed a "new" Tonya. She was participating more and playing happily with other children. She laughed, spoke up, and even shouted. Her development amazed and delighted us.

One day, her mother said, "I must tell you, I've had a revelation. We've been going to the park every day, even when it's freezing. Tonya resisted at first, but now she asks to go. You had to tell me over and over again about a sensory diet, until I finally listened. Now I realize that for both girls, a sensory diet makes good sense and a huge difference!"

A BALANCED SENSORY DIET

A balanced sensory diet is defined as a planned and scheduled activity program that an occupational therapist develops specifically to meet the needs of the child's own nervous system. Its purpose is to help the child become more focused, adaptable, and skillful.

Just as the five main food groups provide daily nutritional requirements, a daily sensory diet fulfills physical and emotional needs. The out-of-sync child needs an individualized diet of tactile, vestibular, and proprioceptive nourishment more than most but doesn't know how to get it. So, we must and can help.

A sensory diet includes a combination of alerting, organizing, and calming activities. An alerting or calming activity may come first, depending on your child's needs.

Alerting activities benefit the undersensitive child, who needs a boost to become effectively aroused. These include:

- Crunching dry cereal, popcorn, chips, crackers, nuts, pretzels, carrots, celery, apples, or ice cubes,

- Taking a shower,

- Bouncing on a therapy ball or beach ball, or

- Jumping up and down on a mattress or trampoline.

Organizing activities help regulate the child's responses. They include:

- Chewing granola bars, fruit bars, licorice, dried apricots, cheese, gum, bagels, or bread crusts,

- Hanging by the hands from a chinning bar,

- Pushing or pulling heavy loads, or

- Getting into an upside-down position.

Calming activities help the oversensitive child decrease hyper-responsiveness to sensory stimulation. They include:

• Sucking a pacifier, hard candy, frozen fruit bar, or spoonful of peanut butter,

• Pushing against walls with the hands, shoulders, back, buttocks, and head,

• Rocking, swaying, or swinging slowly back and forth,

• Cuddling or back rubbing, or

• Taking a bath.

When you initiate your own home program for a sensory diet, it is always best to consult a therapist about your child's requirements. What are appropriate activities? Where should your child do them? When? How often? For how long?

Here are some guidelines:

• Set up specific times during the day for a structured sequence, such as after breakfast, after school, and before bedtime.

• If possible, supply the activity that your child wants. Often, the child will tell you. Even if he can't say, "My nervous system desperately requires an intense movement experience," you may be able to read his mind as he prepares to leap from the playhouse roof. Find another way to let him jump!

• Let the child direct the play. While "more!" may mean more, do supervise carefully so the child doesn't become overaroused. "Stop!" means stop, immediately.

During the activity, watch and listen for nonverbal signals: relaxation and pleased facial expressions suggest that the activity feels good; whimpers or raucous laughter suggest that it is time to cool down.

• For variety, occasionally change the routine and environment.

• Check periodically with the therapist to ensure your home diet is "nutritious" and is meeting your child's varying needs.

A balanced sensory diet is like a fitness plan. It will enhance every child's ability to function smoothly, whether the child is in or out of sync.

PROMOTING HEALTHY
SENSORY INTEGRATION AT HOME

Many children seek more touch and movement than others. They are Touchers-and-Feelers, Bumpers-and-Crashers. Their high activity level tells us that if they can play "bumpety-bump" on the tire swing, or soar into a leaf pile, or wallow in mud puddles, they will "get it all together." They are right.

Other children avoid touch and movement experiences, which make them uncomfortable. These children need guidance to explore their environment and to feel safe. Once they learn how to play actively, they, too, begin to get it all together.

Following are some ideas for multisensory activities that parents and caregivers can provide for children at home. Every little body can benefit from these suggestions—not only the children who seek such activities, but also the children who are more tentative about exploring their environment.

Activities to Develop Tactile Integration

• Rub-a-Dub-Dub—Encourage the child to rub a variety of textures against her skin. Offer different kinds of soap (oatmeal soap, shaving cream, lotion soap) and differently textured scrubbers (loofa sponges, thick washcloths, foam pot-scrubbers, plastic brushes).

• Water Play—Fill the kitchen sink with sudsy water and a variety of unbreakable pitchers and bottles, turkey basters, sponges, eggbeaters, and toy water pumps. Alternatively, fill a large washtub with water and toys and set it outside on the grass. Pouring and measuring are excellent for developing the tactile system as well as high forms of entertainment.

• Water Painting—Outdoors, give the child a bucket of water and a paintbrush to paint the porch steps, the sidewalk, the fence, or her own body. Another good water toy is a squirt bottle filled with clean water (because the squirts often go in the child's mouth).

• Finger Painting—If your child craves it, let him wallow in this literally "sensational" activity. If he shuns it, encourage him to stick a finger or two into the goop, but don't force him if he's uncomfortable. For a different tactile experience, mix sand into the paint. Or, instead of commercial paint and paper, place a blob of shaving cream, peanut butter, or pudding on a plastic tray. If the child is old enough, encourage him to draw shapes, letters and numbers. If he "messes up," he can erase the error with his hand and begin again.

• Finger Drawing—With your finger, "draw" a shape, letter, number, or design on the child's back or hand. Ask the child to guess what it is and then to pass the design on to another person.

• Sand Play—In a sandbox or on a sand table, add small toys (cars, trucks, people, and dinosaurs), which the child can arrange and rearrange, bury, and rediscover. Alternatives to sand are dried beans, rice, pasta, cornmeal, popcorn, and mud. Making mud pies and getting messy are therapeutic, too.

• Feelie Box—Cut a hole in the top of a shoe box. Place different objects in the box, such as spools, marbles, plastic animals, and little airplanes. The game is for the child to insert a hand through the hole and guess what toy she is touching—without looking. This activity improves the child's ability to discriminate the form of an object without the use of vision.

• "Can You Find It?" Game—Hide small objects in the sandbox or feelie box. Ask your child to find a button or car without looking. Or, show him a toy, coin, or block and ask him to find one that matches.

• "Can You Describe It?" Game—Provide play objects with different textures, temperatures, and weights. Ask her to tell you about an object she is touching. (If you can persuade her not to look at it, the game is more challenging.) Is the object round? Cool? Smooth? Soft? Heavy?

• Oral Activities—Licking stickers and putting them in books, blowing whistles and kazoos, blowing bubbles through wands or straws, drinking through straws or sports bottles, tasting new foods, and chewing on gum or rubber tubing may satisfy the child's need to use his mouth.

• Hands-on Cooking—Put cookie dough, bread dough, or meat loaf in a shallow roasting pan (not a high-sided bowl) for the child to mix.

• Science Activities—Touching worms and egg yolks, catching fireflies, collecting acorns and chestnuts, planting seeds, and digging in the garden provide interesting tactile experiences.

• Handling Pets—What could be more satisfying than stroking a kitten, brushing a dog, or cradling a rabbit?

• Box Play—Collect boxes of different sizes. The child can stack them like skyscrapers and line them up like houses to make a Box City. He can nest them, load them with treasures, and rearrange them. He can decorate them with stickers, paint them, and punch them. He can design his own obstacle course and move on, in, and around them.

• Swaddling—Roll the child up tightly in a blanket or carpet. Being wrapped up provides deep pressure and is usually pleasurable. The child with tactile dysfunction will often roll himself up in a blanket as a form of self-therapy, but it is a special treat to have a trusted grown-up do the rolling.

• People Sandwich—Have the "salami" or "cheese" (your child) lie facedown on the "bread" (a gym mat or large couch pillow) with her head extended beyond the edge. With a "spreader" (a sponge, pot scrubber, basting or vegetable brush, paintbrush, or washcloth) smear her arms, legs, and torso with pretend mustard, mayonnaise, relish, ketchup, etc. Use firm, downward strokes. Cover the child, from neck to toe, with another piece of "bread" (the folded mat or a second pillow). Now press firmly up and down the mat to squish out the excess mustard, so the child feels the deep, soothing pressure. You can even roll or crawl across your child; the mat will distribute your weight. Your child will be in heaven.

• Back Rubs—Apply deep, firm pressure to your child's back and limbs. Rub downward, the way hair grows.

• Dress Up—Prepare a special carton just for dress up. Include hats, shoes, gloves, furry or feathery boas, and silk scarves.

• Secret Hideaway—Supply towels, blankets, sheets, sleeping bags, down comforters, pillows, etc., for a fort or hideaway under a table.

Activities to Develop Vestibular Integration

• Hoppity Hopping—Like a big balloon with handles, a Hoppity Hop is great for bouncing up and down. Let the child try it first on the grass or rug, before trying it on the sidewalk or floor.

• Rolling—Cut out the bottom of a cardboard box, so the child's head and arms are free at one end and feet are free at the other. Let her roll down a grassy hill. Wrap her up in a beach towel for a different rolling experience.

• Swinging in a Blanket—Two adults hold opposite corners of a blanket and the child gets an exciting ride. A hammock works, too.

• Swinging—Encourage (but never force) the child to swing. Gentle, linear movement is therapeutic. If he has gravitational insecurity, start him on a low swing so his feet can touch the ground, or hold him on your lap.

• Spinning—At the playground, let the child spin on the tire swing or merry-go-round. Indoors, offer a swivel chair or Sit 'n Spin. It is very important to monitor the spinning activity, as the child may become easily overstimulated. Don't spin her without her permission!

• Sliding—How many ways can a child swoosh down a slide? Sitting up, lying down, frontwards, backwards, holding on to the sides, not holding on, with legs straddling the sides, etc.

• Riding Vehicles—Trikes, bikes, and scooters help children improve their sense of balance as well as motor planning and motor coordination.

• Jumping on a Trampoline—A kid-sized trampoline with a handle is a good investment. Jumping is hard work—and so much fun!

• Walking on Unstable Surfaces—A sandy beach, a playground "clatter bridge," a grassy meadow, and a water bed are examples of shaky ground that require children to adjust their bodies as they move.

• Rhythmic Rocking—Provide a rocking chair for your child to get energized, organized, or tranquilized.

• Riding, balancing, and walking on a seesaw.

• Balancing on a Teeter-Totter—Center a one-by-three-foot board or a three-foot-square sheet of plywood over a four-by-four or railroad timber. (Don't use a cylindrical piece of wood underneath; the board will slip off.) Let the child walk back and forth, jump up and down, and balance in the center at the fulcrum.

Teeter-Totter:

• Sitting on a T-Stool—A T-stool helps a child improve his sense of balance, his posture, and his ability to pay attention. Sitting on a T-stool is challenging at first, but the more practice a child has balancing, the easier balancing becomes. To make a one-legged T-stool, get a two-by-four and cut two twelve-inch lengths of wood. Screw the pieces together to form a "T" shape.

T-Stool:

• Perching on a "Sitting Ball"—Get a playground ball for your child to sit on while watching television or listening to a story. A twelve-inch ball is the appropriate size for most preschoolers. The ball's diameter should equal the distance between the child's buttocks and the floor when his knees are bent at a right angle and his feet are flat on the floor.

• Balancing on a Large Therapy Ball—Your child can lie on her stomach, on her back, or sit and bounce.

• Tummy Down, Head Up Activities—Have the child lie on her stomach. On the floor, she can rock forward and back to "Row, Row, Row Your Boat"; draw on newspaper while listening to music, using crayons, which require her to bear down to make a mark; and play with Legos and small toys. On a swing or therapy ball, she can "draw" on the ground or carpet with a stick; throw sponges into a laundry basket; and bat a suspended ball with a cardboard tube.

• Ascending and descending stairs.

• Somersaulting.

• "Tightrope" walking on low walls.

• Jogging—Run around the block together!

Activities to Develop Proprioceptive Integration

• Carrying Heavy Loads—Have the child carry large soft-drink bottles to the picnic site, or filled laundry baskets from room to room, or grocery bags, filled with nonbreakables, into the house. The child can also carry a load of books, a bucket of blocks, or a pail of water from one spot to another.

• Pushing and Pulling—Set grocery bags down inside the front door and have the child drag them to the kitchen. Let him push the wheelbarrow or stroller, vacuum, rake, shove heavy boxes, tow a friend on a sled, or pull a loaded wagon. Hard muscular work jazzes up the muscles and joints.

• Hanging by the Arms—Mount a chinning bar in the child's bedroom doorway, or take her to the park to hang from the monkey bars. When she suspends her weight from her hands, her muscles and joints send sensory messages to her brain. When she shifts from hand to hand as she travels underneath the monkey bars, she is developing upper-body strength.

• Pillow Crashing—Pile several large cushions, beanbag chairs, or downy comforters in a corner. Invite the child to dive, jump, roll, stretch, and burrow in the cushions. You could also make a "crash cushion": stuff large foam scraps into a comforter cover or into a huge bag made by sewing two sheets together.

• Hermit Crab—Place a large bag of rice or beans on the child's back and let her move around with a heavy "shell" on her back.

• Joint Squeeze—Put one hand on the child's forearm and the other hand on his upper arm. With slow, firm pressure, push his forearm and upper arm toward the elbow; then, pull them away. Push and pull the muscles near his knees and shoulders. To activate his proprioceptors in other ways, press both hands down on his head; slowly straighten and bend his fingers, wrists, elbows, knees, ankles and toes. These extension and flexion techniques provide traction and compression to his joints and are effec tive when he's stuck in tight spaces, such as church pews, movie theaters, cars, trains, and especially airplanes where the gravity changes.

• Body Squeeze—Sit on the floor behind your child, straddling him with your legs. Put your arms around his knees, draw them toward his chest, and squeeze hard. Holding tight, rock him forward and back.

• Bear Hugs—It is said that everyone needs twelve hugs a day.

• Pouring—Put different amounts of sand, beans, or water into a cup or pitcher. Let the child pour from one container to another.

• Opening Doors—Is this hard for your child? Then she needs practice! Take the time to let her do it alone, without help.

• Ripping Paper—Give your child yesterday's newspaper and let him tear strips to make a big heap of confetti.

• Playing "Bumpety-Bump" on the Tire Swing.

• Back-to-Back Standing Up—Position two children on the floor, back to back. Ask them to "dig their feet into the floor" and to stand up together by pressing against each other's back.

• Tug-of-War—Get a long, thick rope and tie knots or loops into it to make it easier to grip. Divide up equal teams. (It's okay to cheat a little, so your child can "win.") Try this game as you sit, stand, or kneel.

• "Bulldozer"—One child sits in a large cardboard box or on a folded gym mat, and another child pushes the load across the floor, using his head, shoulders, back, or feet to make it move.

• Playing Catch—Toss a big ball or pillow back and forth.

• Roughhousing—Pushing, pulling, rolling, and tumbling with an adult or friend can feel good all over, but this activity must be carefully supervised so no one gets hurt or overloaded with sensory stimulation. Two important reminders: Never pull on each other's clothes, and never tickle.

• Arm wrestling—If you are stronger than your child, please let him win once in a while.

• Leapfrog—or horsie, or any playful "contact sport."

More Activities to Develop Sensorimotor Skills

Sensory integration is the foundation for fine motor skills, motor planning, bilateral coordination, auditory skills, and visual skills. All these sensorimotor skills will improve as the child tries the following activities, which integrate many tactile, vestibular, and proprioceptive sensations.

FINE MOTOR SKILLS

• Flour Sifting—Spread newspaper on the kitchen floor and provide a bag of flour, scoop, and flour sifter. (A turn handle is easier to manipulate than a squeeze handle, but both develop fine motor muscles in the hand and fingers.) Let the child scoop and sift.

• Manipulating Small Toys and Objects—Working with Legos, building with blocks, playing with magnets, and doing jigsaw puzzles develop a child's tactile and proprioceptive systems.

• Stringing and Lacing—Provide shoelaces, lengths of yarn on plastic needles, or pipe cleaners and a variety of buttons, macaroni, cereal "Os," beads, thread spools, paper clips, and jingle bells. Making bracelets and necklaces develops eye-hand coordination, tactile discrimination, and bilateral coordination.

• Egg Carton Collections—The child may enjoy sorting shells, pinecones, pebbles, nuts, beans, beads, buttons, bottle caps, and other found objects and storing them in the individual egg compartments.

• Household Tools—Picking up cereal pieces with tweezers; stretching rubber bands over a box to make a "guitar"; hanging napkins, doll clothes, and paper towels on a rope with clothespins; smashing egg cartons with a hammer or crab mallet; and pounding nails or golf tees into foam blocks are activities that strengthen sensory integration in many ways.

• Office and Classroom Tools—Have the child cut with scissors; draw with markers, crayons and pencils; paint with brushes (feathers, sticks, and eyedroppers are fun to paint with, too); squeeze a hole puncher and press a stapler through paper and cardboard; squeeze glue onto paper in letters or designs, sprinkle sparkles on the glue, and shake off the excess; press office stamps in ink pads and make designs on paper; lick decorative stamps and make designs on paper; and wrap boxes with brown paper, tape, and string.

• Playdough—Your child can knead, shape, pinch, squeeze, and pound it; roll snakes, form balls, and flatten pancakes. Offer coins, keys, paper clips, and hair curlers to press imprints into the dough. For more fun, provide cookie cutters, blunt scissors, a rolling pin, a garlic press, and an egg slicer. These activities strengthen hand muscles, improve finger dexterity, and give the child a multisensory workout.

Note: To make homemade playdough, mix two cups flour, one cup salt, four teaspoons cream of tartar, two cups water, and four tablespoons vegetable oil in a cooking pot. Stir over low heat until the dough comes away from the sides and makes a soft ball. Blend in a few drops of food coloring and peppermint extract, if you wish. Let it cool.

MOTOR PLANNING

• Moving through Obstacle Courses—Build an obstacle course that requires a child to change her body positions and forms of locomotion. Include tunnels, rising and descending ramps, balance beams, boards, stepping stones, stairs, ladders, and monkey bars, placed in a wide circle, indoors or out. For different sensory challenges, have the child try the course barefoot, in stocking feet, or walking in shoe boxes.

• Jumping from a Table—Place a gym mat beside a low table and encourage the child to jump. After each landing, stick a piece of masking tape on the mat to mark the spot. Encourage the child to jump farther each time.

• The Feet-Beat Game—Recite a nursery rhyme, clap, or beat a drum in a steady rhythmic pattern. Ask the child to jump or hop to the rhythm. For a greater motor planning challenge, alternate your tempo between slow and fast and encourage him to keep the beat.

• Walking like Animals—Encourage the child to walk like a bear, on all fours; a crab, from side to side on all fours; a turtle, creeping; a snake, crawling; an inchworm, by stretching flat and pulling her knees toward her chest; an ostrich, while grasping her ankles; a duck, squatting; a frog, squatting and jumping; a kangaroo or bunny, jumping; a lame dog, with an "injured" leg; a gorilla, bending her knees; a horse, galloping.

• Rolling and Curling—Spread a blanket on the floor and have your child roll up and unroll himself. Have him move from one position to another: first curl up, then stretch out; first curl, then roll; first kneel, then roll; first squat, then roll; first roll, then stand. Ask him to stand with his back to a wall and roll against it.

• Wheelbarrow Walking—Lay a string on the floor in a serpentine path. Hold the child's knees or ankles. How far can he walk on his hands?

• Playground Games—Remember Simon Says, Ring-Around-the-Rosy, The Hokey-Pokey, London Bridge, Shoo Fly, and Mother, May I?

• Insy-Outsy—Teach the child to get in and out of clothes, the front door, and the car. With a little help, the child may become able to perform these tasks independently, even if it takes a l-o-o-n-n-g time!

BILATERAL COORDINATION

• Ball Roll—Face your child, sitting or lying on the floor. Roll a ball or orange back and forth, using both hands. For variety, hold a paper towel tube in both hands and push the ball back and forth.

• Ball Catch—Toss a large or medium-sized beach ball gently to the child from a short distance. As the child becomes more competent at catching, use a smaller ball and step farther away.

• Ball Whack—Have the child hold a baseball bat, rolling pin, broomstick, book, cardboard tube, or ruler in both hands. Remind her to keep her feet still. Toss her a big ball. As she swings, her arms will cross the midline.

• Two-Handed Tetherball—Suspend a plastic or sponge ball, at the child's eye level, from a string attached to a wide door frame. Let your child choose different "bats." Have her count how many hits she makes without missing. Try four-handed tetherball, in which you play, too.

• Balloon Fun—Always using both hands together, the child throws a balloon into the air and 1) catches it, 2) keeps it afloat by repeatedly whacking it with open hands, or 3) bats it repeatedly with both hands clasped together in one large "fist." Another activity is bouncing and catching a balloon.

• Rolling Pin Fun—Provide the child with a cylindrical block or a rolling pin without handles, so he presses down with his opened hands. Have him roll real dough, playdough, crackers, clay—or mud!

• Clapping and Tapping—Have your child imitate your rhythmic hand motions as you clap your hands and tap different body parts. (Counting to eight gives your child a chance to catch on and join in.) Add alternating hand motions. Then, cross the midline.

• Clapping to Rhymes—Sit facing each other. You each tap your own knees, clap your own hands, and clap each other's hands. Recite rhymes and jump-rope chants. For variety, use rhythm sticks, which you can buy or make.

• Body Rhythms—Clapping and tapping are good; getting the whole body into the act is better! While you chant or sing, have your child imitate your motions. Tip your head from side to side, wave your arms overhead, shake icky sticky glue off your hands, pound your fists and chest, slap your hips, bend from side to side, hunch and relax your shoulders, stamp your feet, and hop from one foot to the other. Use both hands together or alternately.

• Drumbeats—Give your child a drum to beat while you chant rhymes or play music. She can use mallets or spoons, or beat the drum with her hands. No drums? Use cooking pots, tin cans, and oatmeal boxes.

• Homemade "Jai Alai"—Cut out the bottom of a milk carton or a laundry detergent bottle. Have the child toss a bean bag or light-weight ball into the air and catch it with the milk carton "basket."

• Eggbeater Fun—Give your child an eggbeater to whip up soapsuds or mix up a bowl of birdseed, or of uncooked beans and rice.

• Marble Painting—Line a tray or cookie sheet with paper. Put a few dabs of finger paint in the center of the paper. Provide a marble or small ball to roll through the paint to make a design. Great wrapping paper!

• Screwing and Unscrewing—Let your child open and close the lids of a variety of jars, or screw and unscrew a variety of nuts and bolts.

• Ribbon Dancing—Attach ribbons, streamers, or scarves to the ends of a dowel. Holding the dowel with both hands, the child swirls the ribbons overhead, from side to side, and up and down. (No dowel? Give him a ribbon for each hand.) This activity also improves eye-hand coordination.

• Two-Sided Activities—Encourage the child to jump rope, swim, bike, hike, row, paddle, and do morning calisthenics.

AUDITORY SKILLS

• Become an active listener. Pay attention. Look your child in the eye when she speaks. Show her that her thoughts interest you.

• Simplify your language. Speak slowly, shorten your comments, abbreviate instructions, and repeat what you have said. Reinforce verbal messages with gestural communication: facial expressions, hand movements, and body language.

• Take the time to let your child respond to your words and express his thoughts. Don't rush him, interrupt him, or pressure him to talk.

• Reward her comments with nonverbal gestures, such as smiles and hugs, and with verbal praise, such as, "That's a great idea!" Your positive feedback will encourage her.

• Help the child communicate more clearly. If you catch one word, say, "Tell me more about the truck." If you can't catch his meaning, have him show you by gesturing.

• Talk to your child while she dresses, eats, or bathes, to teach her words and concepts, such as nouns (sunglasses, casserole), body parts (thumb, buttocks), prepositions (around, through), adjectives (juicy, soapy), time (yesterday, later), categories (vegetables/fruits, play clothes/dressy clothes), actions (zip, scrub), and emotions (pleased, sorry).

• Share your own thoughts. Model good speech and communication skills. Even if the child has trouble responding verbally, she may understand what you say.

• Use rhythm and beat to improve the child's memory. Give directions or teach facts with a "piggyback song," in which you substitute your own words to a familiar tune. Example: To the tune of "Mary Had a Little Lamb," sing, "Now it's time to wash your face, Brush your teeth, comb your hair, Now it's time to put on clothes, So start with underwear!"

• Tell "add-a-line-stories" in which you take turns saying one line at a time to create an open-ended story.

• Play "Fill-in-the-Rhyme," in which you make up a ditty and leave the last rhyming word out for your child to say. Example: "A little bird lives in the tree, A little fish lives in the——."

• Encourage your child to pantomime while listening to stories and poems, or to music without words.

• Read to your child every day!

VISUAL SKILLS

• Flashlight Fun—With two flashlights, try these activities with your child in a darkened room. Focus your light on the wall or ceiling and ask the child to meet your spot. Flash your light briefly on the wall and ask her to beam onto the same spot. Slowly trace a path on the wall and ask her to follow it with her beam. Trace shapes and ask her to name them. Have her trace shapes for you to guess.

• Making Shapes—Let your child draw or form shapes, letters, and numbers in different materials, such as playdough, finger paint, shaving cream, soap foam, sand, clay, string, pudding, or pizza dough.

• Mazes and Dot-to-Dot Activities—Buy a maze book, or make your own mazes on paper, the sidewalk, or the beach. Have the child follow the mazes with his finger, a toy car, a crayon, a marker, or chalk. Buy a dot-to-dot book or, on graph paper, make your own patterns for the child to follow.

• Geoboard—Buy a geoboard or make one by hammering rows of nails into a block of wood. Stretch rubber bands across the nails to make a design or shape and have your child reproduce the design.

• Peg Board—Have the child reproduce your design or make his own.

• Cutting Activities—Provide paper and scissors and have your child cut fringe and strips. Draw curved lines on the paper for her to cut. Cutting playdough is fun, too.

• Jigsaw Puzzles!

• Block Building!!

Suggestions to Develop Self-Help Skills

Self-help skills improve along with sensory integration. The following suggestions may make your child's life easier—and yours, too!

DRESSING

• Buy or make a "dressing board" with a variety of snaps, zippers, buttons and buttonholes, hooks and eyes, buckles and shoelaces.

• Provide things that are not her own clothes for the child to zip, button, and fasten, such as sleeping bags, backpacks, handbags, coin purses, lunch boxes, doll clothes, suitcases, and cosmetic cases.

• Provide alluring dress-up clothes with zippers, buttons, buckles, and snaps. Oversized clothes are easiest to put on and take off.

• Play make-believe "Shoe Store." Gather a few pairs of shoes and boots, a shoehorn, and new shoelaces. Take turns pretending to be the customer and the salesperson. Practice lacing or tying shoelaces.

• Eliminate unnecessary choices in your child's bureau and closet. Clothes that are inappropriate for the season and that jam the drawers are sources of frustration.

• Put large hooks inside closet doors at the child's eye level so he can hang up his own coat and pajamas.

• Attach loops to coats and pajamas on the outside (so they won't irritate the child's skin).

• Supply cellophane bags for the child to slip her feet into before pulling on boots. The cellophane prevents shoes from getting stuck and makes the job much easier.

• Let your child choose what to wear. If she gets overheated easily, let her go outdoors wearing several loose layers rather than a coat. If he complains that new clothes are stiff or scratchy, let him wear soft, worn clothes, even if they're not very fashionable. Comfort is most important.

• Set out tomorrow's clothes the night before.

• Encourage the child to dress himself. Allow for extra time, and be available to help. If learning a dressing skill is difficult, help him into the clothes but let him do the finishing touch: start the coat zipper but let him zip it up, button all but one of his buttons, buckle his belt but let him secure the end through a loop.

• Motivate the child to dress himself with clothes he likes. For example, when my son was four, he wanted sneakers with four blue stripes. We went to four shoe stores before finding them, but the search was worthwhile because he was motivated to learn to tie shoelaces. When he was five, he wanted a cowboy belt with colorful studs and then learned to buckle it. Little things can make a big difference.

GROOMING

• Play make-believe "Barber Shop." Gather combs and brushes, barrettes and bobby pins, ribbons and elastic bands, a mirror and chair, a smock or towel, and a bowl of warm water. Take turns pretending to be the customer and the barber or beauty salon operator.

• Keep a stool handy so the child can see herself in the bathroom mirror. On the sink, keep a kid-sized, broad-handled toothbrush in a plastic cup, within arm's reach. Even if the child resists brushing teeth and hair, be firm, if possible. Some things in life are nonnegotiable.

SNACK TIME AND MEALTIME

• Provide a chair that allows the child's elbows to be at table height and feet to be flat on the floor. A stool or pillow may help. (Kids fidget less when they feel grounded.)

• Offer a variety of ways to eat food. For instance, she can eat pudding with a spoon or scoop it up with her fingers and lick them. She can use a spoon or a fork to eat corn kernels, or use both hands to munch corn on the cob. She can spoon chicken broth or lift the bowl to her mouth to drink.

• Offer a variety of foods with different textures: lumpy, smooth, crunchy, chewy. Keep portions small, especially when introducing new foods.

• Let the child pour juice or milk into a cup. A tip-less cup will help prevent accidents. The child who frequently spills juice needs much practice.

• Give the child straws to sip drinks through.

• Encourage the child to handle snack-time or meal-time objects. Opening cracker packages, spreading peanut butter, and eating with utensils are good for proprioception, bilateral coordination, and fine motor skills.

CHORES

• Together, make a list of chores he can do to help around the house: make his bed, walk the dog, empty wastebaskets, take out trash, pull weeds, rake, shovel, sweep, vacuum, fold laundry, empty the dishwasher, set and clear the table. Let him know you need and appreciate him.

• Make a routine, and stick to it.

• If the child is forgetful, make a chart and post it on the refrigerator. When he finishes a chore, let him stick a star on the chart. Reward him with a special privilege or outing when he accumulates several stars.

• Break chores down into small steps. Let her clear the table one plate at a time. (She doesn't have to clear all the dishes.)

BATHING

• Let the child help regulate the water temperature.

• Provide an assortment of bath toys, soaps, and scrubbers.

• Scrub the child with firm, downward strokes.

• Provide a large bath sheet for a tight wrap-up.

SLEEPING

• Give your child notice: "Half an hour until bed-time!" or "You can draw for five more minutes."

• Stick to a bedtime routine. It may include stories and songs, a look at a sticker collection, a chat about today's events or tomorrow's plans, a back rub and snug tuck-in.

• Children with tactile defensiveness are very partic-ular about clothing, so provide comfortable pajamas. Some like them loose, some like them tight; some like them silky, some don't like them at all. Nobody likes them bumpy, scratchy, lacy, or with elasticized cuffs.

• Use percale or silk sheets for a smooth and bump-less bed.

• Let your child sleep with extra pillows and blankets, in a sleeping bag or bed tent, or on a water bed.

Life at home can improve with a sensory diet and attention to your child's special needs, and life at school can improve as well.

Chapter Eight

Your Child at School

Becoming an advocate for your child, communicating with school personnel, finding a good school-and-child match, and sharing ideas with teachers can all promote your child's success at school.

What a Difference Communication Makes!

Last year, Nicky hated fourth grade. Mrs. Colladay, his teacher, was mean. She always scolded him when he was slow, disorganized, or fidgety. She would say, "I wish you'd just try harder." He *was* trying.

This year, Nicky loves fifth grade. Ms. Berry is nice. She makes sure he understands the assignments and shows him how to break them down into manageable parts. She got him a chair that doesn't wiggle and thick pencils that don't break. She made him captain of the Flying Aces Math Team. She never makes him miss recess. She likes him.

What a difference a teacher makes! And what a difference a parent makes when she becomes her child's advocate!

Nicky is in a classroom that meets his needs because his mother took action. After years of seeking to avoid stigma and labels, she decided to inform the school about his sensory processing problems and about the benefits of therapy and a sensory diet. If Nicky could function more smoothly at home, surely he could gain confidence and competence at school.

During the summer, Nicky's mother met with the principal and Ms. Berry and was relieved to find them eager for information. They wanted to understand Nicky's strengths and weaknesses, so they could promote his success. They told her they would explain his needs to the art, science, and physical education teachers. They would arrange for special services at school. They would call her with questions and would welcome her calls.

What a difference communication makes!

IF ONLY SCHOOL WERE MORE LIKE HOME

The child with SI Dysfunction often has enormous difficulty in the classroom. His problem is not a lack of intelligence or willingness to learn. His problem may be dyspraxia, which is difficulty in knowing what to do and how to go about doing it.

The preschooler who has difficulty stringing beads often becomes the school-age child who can't organize the parts of a research project. He wants to interact successfully with the world around him, but he can't easily adapt his behavior to meet increasingly complex demands.

The out-of-sync child may be unable to settle down to work. Everything may be distracting—the proximity of a classmate, the sound of rustling paper, the movement of children playing outside the window, the itchy label inside his shirt collar, and even the classroom furniture. She may be disorganized in her movements, verbal responses, and interactions with teachers and classmates.

For many reasons, school may be grueling:

1. School puts pressure on children to perform and conform. While the average child buckles down to meet expectations, the out-of-sync child buckles under pressure.

2. The school milieu is ever-changing. Abrupt transitions from circle time to art projects, from math to reading, or from cafeteria to gymnasium may overwhelm the child who switches gears slowly.

3. Sensory stimuli may be excessive. People mill around. Lights, sounds, and odors abound. The child may become overloaded easily.

4. Sensory stimuli may be insufficient. A long stretch of sitting may pose problems for the child who regularly needs short stretch breaks to organize his body. A spoken or written lesson, directed toward aural and visual learners, may not reach the kinesthetic and tactile learner.

5. School administrators and teachers often misunderstand SI Dysfunction. They may be truly interested in helping the child, but they can't accommodate his unique learning style if they don't know where to begin.

6. School is not like home. For many children, school is unpredictable and risky, while home is familiar and safe.* The behavior of the child will differ because the environments differ. School can become more like home, however, when parents share information about their child with the adults who can make a difference in the child's success.

Years ago, before we became savvy about sensory integration, the St. Columba's director and I met with Allen's mother to learn how we could help her boy. At preschool, he hardly spoke, hardly moved. He would park himself in the sandbox corner, behind a barricade of trucks. He had no self-help skills, no playmates, no affect. We described a sad, scared, helpless loner.

His mother was astonished. "But he isn't that way at all!" she said. Her description was 180 degrees different from ours. At home, he was a chatterbox. He was lively and cheerful. He jumped on the furniture, dug in the garden, and played with neighborhood kids. True, the kids he played with were all younger. True, he had trouble getting dressed. True, he had definite likes and dislikes in foods and activities. But he wasn't a problem at home. "If only school were more like home," she said with a sigh.

The conference was an eye-opener for everyone. As we talked, his mother realized that Allen functioned well at home because she fulfilled his need for consistent routines, just-right stimulation, physical security, and constant reminders of love. We, the teachers, realized that we

---

*On the other hand, sometimes school is orderly and predictable, while home is stressful and chaotic.

could fulfill some of those needs at school, now that we understood what they were.

We entered a home-and-school partnership to help Allen succeed. The teachers became more sensitive to his cautious behavior and learned to guide him gently into preschool activities. They gave him more structure and protected him from overstimulation. Many small changes had a big, positive effect on his behavior.

Meanwhile, his mother adapted Allen's home environment to meet his special needs. She purchased some special equipment, like a trampoline and a crawling tunnel, and turned the basement into a mini-gym. She also became aware of her obligation to share her observations, selectively, with his school and teachers.

DECIDING WHOM TO TELL

The out-of-sync child needs an articulate advocate. Usually, it is up to a parent to make teachers and other caregivers aware of his special needs.

The thought of revealing their child's difficulties makes many parents anxious. They worry that the child may be stigmatized and labeled, that they may be blamed for the child's behavior, or that insensitive school personnel may be indiscreet or may use the information in the wrong way. Besides, talking about the child's inadequacies is painful. Nonetheless, for the child's sake, communication is essential.

Why is it necessary to provide information? Adults who work with children, like sculptors who work with clay, must have a feel for the material they shape. With some understanding of Sensory Integration Dysfunction, they can become more attuned to the child's differing abilities. Without information, however, they can't be expected to change their classroom environment, alter their teaching style, or redirect their thinking.

Who needs to know? Classroom teachers should be informed. The principal, the art, science, music and physical education teachers, and the computer and media specialists may need to know. School bus and carpool drivers, religious school teachers, scout leaders, coaches, and baby-sitters may also be more considerate when told.

What information should be shared? Briefly, tell the teacher what the child's problem is. (Avoid terms such as "hyporesponsiveness to vestibular sensations," unless pressed for details.) Then, give specific suggestions about what works at home, so the teacher can consider doing the same at school.

Examples: "My daughter is very sensitive to being touched or jostled. At home, we've noticed she does best when she doesn't feel crowded. Would you remember her need for space when you plan the seating arrangement?" Or, "My son has difficulty with motor coordination. He is receiving therapy to help him move more smoothly. At home, we find that frequent breaks to move and stretch help him get organized."

When you find that the teacher is receptive, you may also choose to share your own documented observations, therapists' evaluations, sensory diet suggestions, and tips for teachers, included at the end of this chapter.

How should information be shared? Frame the information positively: "She concentrates beautifully if . . . ," or "His motor coordination improves when . . ." Stress the child's abilities: "She adores art projects," or "He has a great sense of humor." Enlist the teacher's goodwill: "We hope we can work together. Please keep me posted!"

Where should information be shared? Arrange meetings in advance, so you and the teacher can talk uninterrupted. Confer in the classroom before or after school, in the teachers' lounge at lunchtime, or by telephone at night.

When should information be shared? Before the school year starts, anticipate your child's difficulties and communicate with those who need to know. Help them be proactive, rather than reactive, when problems arise.

A Good School-and-Child Match

Communicating regularly with school personnel should make a positive difference for your child. Sometimes, however, the teacher will resist taking suggestions and making modifications in the classroom. You will then have to decide whether to step in or step back.

For instance, one mother knew that chewing gum helped her son get organized while reading and writing. She asked the teacher if gum would be permissible. The teacher refused: "He can't have special privileges, just because he has special needs." Although the mother was reluctant to go over the teacher's head and make a fuss, she decided to complain to the principal. The principal intervened, the teacher relented, and the child was allowed to chew (but not crack) gum. His performance improved, and, several months later, the teacher apologized.

Sometimes the teacher is willing to make adjustments, but the school puts up obstacles. The child may require a chair that lets him keep his feet flat on the floor, or a desk of his own rather than a shared table, or a locker he can open easily, while the school insists on regulation furnishings. In such cases, hard as it may be, try to pick the most important battles—and keep fighting.

If goodness-of-fit at school is lacking, you have several options:

- Ask to move the child to another teacher's classroom.

- Investigate special-education programs. Special-education classes are usually smaller and less distracting than regular classrooms. Special educators are trained to address children's differing abilities. With an IEP (Individualized Education Program), the out-of-sync child may flourish.

- Enroll the child in another school. Transferring from one public school to another is a possibility. An advantage of public education is the availability of facilities, including O.T.s, speech therapists, and remedial reading specialists. If the child is eligible for special-education services under the IDEA, then these services are provided during the school day, at no charge.

- Another possibility is enrolling the child in a private school, with smaller class size and more individualized attention. In a private school the immature child can repeat a grade, if necessary, whereas in a public school the child may not get this chance to "pause" before promotion to a more challenging grade.

Each school year, reopen the channels of communication. Teachers will come and go, some sensitive, some not so sensitive, and your steady support and voice will help your child succeed.

Below you will find some classroom strategies to share with your child's teacher. He or she may learn from these guidelines how to be supportive, how to gauge when to encourage and when to step back; how to refrain from overloading the child with excessive stimulation and unmanageable work; and how to control his or her own frustrations when dealing with an out-of-sync child.

PROMOTING YOUR CHILD'S
SUCCESS AT SCHOOL

The child with Sensory Integration Dysfunction needs understanding and support if he is going to succeed at school, whether that school is public or private. A teacher may want to help an out-of-sync student but may lack training in the appropriate techniques. If so, it may work to try some of the following classroom strategies, proposed by experienced educators and experts in Sensory Integration Dysfunction.

These commonsense strategies help the out-of-sync child. They also help every other child.

Yes, every child!

Every child benefits from a safe, calm, and distraction-free environment. Every child requires occasional breaks from work to move and stretch. Every child needs to know that someone is paying attention to his strengths and weaknesses, likes and dislikes, ups and downs. Every child needs to be shown how to find solutions to problems. Every child needs assurance that it's okay to have differing abilities, that he can be successful, that his ideas have merit, that his personhood is valued.

When the out-of-sync child begins to feel more in control, his schoolwork and social skills will improve. When he is less distracted, he distracts the other children less. Then, when all the students are working to their best ability, the teacher can teach!

Classroom Strategies

1. CONTROLLING THE ENVIRONMENT
• *Reduce sensory overload.*

You may have to intuit what kind of sensory stimulation is getting in the child's way, because he may be unable to tell you. Remember that stimuli that bother him today may not bother him tomorrow, and vice versa. If you can remove or diminish most distractions, you will increase the child's ability to attend to the important job of learning. Help the child focus on one idea at a time by minimizing unrelated sensory stimuli. Simplify, simplify, simplify.

Tactile distractions may divert the child's attention. If the proximity of classmates irritates the child, help him find a spot where he will feel safe. Steer the younger child to a seat at the head of the table, or at the edge of the rug, to lessen the possibility of contact with other children. Station the older child's desk in a classroom corner, or up front near you.

Let her bring up the rear when the class tiptoes single file down the corridor so that no one can bump her from behind. Provide her with the space she needs.

Visual distractions may interfere with the child's concentration. Eliminate clutter on bulletin boards. Secure artwork, maps, and graphics on the walls so they don't flutter. Tack a sheet over open shelves to cover art materials, games, and toys that may attract the child's attention. Remove mobiles swaying from light fixtures. Adjust venetian blinds to prevent sunshine from flickering through.

The movements of other children may also be visually distracting. Have the child sit near you at the front of the room, with his back to his classmates. Surround him with children who sit quietly, pay attention, and serve as good role models.

When preparing work sheets for the school-age child, keep to a minimum instructions to read and math problems to solve. White space around each written problem helps the child focus on one at a time. He may do best when he can frame each problem with a cardboard template.

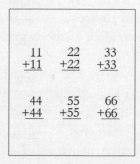
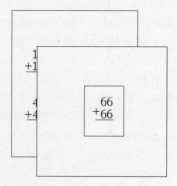

Auditory distractions may make the room seem like an echo chamber for the child with auditory processing problems. A classroom's hard surfaces, such as desktops, linoleum tiles, and painted walls, reflect sound. Wherever possible, cover hard surfaces with carpet, cloth, or corkboard. Be sure the child isn't seated near the humming fish tank, under the buzzing fluorescent bulb, or beside the window where he may be distracted by children's voices outside.

When the children are working at their desks, you may find that playing classical music, such as Bach and

Mozart, softens the auditory environment and helps organize everybody.

Olfactory distractions may include the smells coming from the lunchroom or from the gerbil cage. If it is possible to adjust the schedule, time your lessons so that the child's most difficult subject is not being taught as the fragrance of grilled cheese wafts through the door. Keep animals, paint supplies, and other aromatic materials away from the child's desk.

• *Provide comfortable furniture.*

This prescription may be hard to fill for a teacher who must make do with regulation chairs and desks. However, the child who frequently falls off his chair because of inefficient body awareness may be able to align his body and maintain stable posture if the furniture fits.

Find the child a chair that does not tip. The height of the chair should allow him to place his feet flat on the floor. The height of the desk should be at his waist level.

Sometimes a special type of chair helps. If the preschooler is fidgety at circle time, for instance, a ball to sit on will help focus his attention. The ball's diameter should equal the distance between his buttocks and the floor when his knees are bent at a right angle and his feet are flat on the floor.

An older child who is expected to sit at a desk for long periods might benefit from a corduroy cushion that will help him stick to the seat.* If the other students want to try the cushion, let them. Soon they'll forget about it, and you can get on with your job while the child who needs it stays put.

• *Keep chalkboards and work sheets clean.*

Fuzzy lines present problems for the child with visual processing difficulties. Most helpful are crisp white lines on a dark chalkboard and clear dark lines on white paper so that the child can discriminate between the background and the letters or numbers you want her to understand.

2. MANAGING THE CLASSROOM
• *Develop a consistent routine.*

The out-of-sync child may have trouble getting organized to do what is necessary. He may struggle to overcome a feeling of chaos, internally and externally. Thus, he is most comfortable when things are "just so," exactly as they were yesterday and will be tomorrow. His rigidity is a manifestation of his need to organize his world.

For this child, a classroom that is clearly structured is preferable to one that runs on spontaneity. Help him by writing classroom routines on the board, sticking to the schedule, keeping the room arranged in a predictable way, and remembering whose turn it is to be line leader or to play with the new set of magnets.

---

*A teenage boy, whose dysfunction had been overlooked for years, glued thumbtacks—points UP—to the seat of his desk chair at home. The tacks, he explained, reminded him when he was about to slide off the chair! A cushion would seem to be a preferable alternative.

• *Plan transitions as carefully as lessons.*

If focusing on a task is difficult, changing focus is even harder for the out-of-sync child.

Notify students about impending transitions: "In ten minutes, we'll go to the all-purpose room," or "After recess, you'll get the new reading books." Give plenty of notice when something out-of-the-ordinary will occur, such as a field trip, a visit from a reptile trainer, or a change in seating arrangements.

To facilitate transitions, signify what will happen next by clapping or beating drum rhythms. For instance, two long claps followed by three short claps may say that it is time to put away math books and stand up to stretch.

—   —   –   –   –
long,   long,   short,   short,   short

A sequence of one long clap followed by four short claps and a final long clap may mean that it is time to come in off the playground.

—   –   –   –   –   —
long,   short,   short,   short,   short,   long

Prepare transition fillers to turn empty time into teachable moments. Recite poems and sing activity songs with motions. Offer activities to strengthen language and critical thinking skills, such as passing around laminated "What's Missing?" pages from children's magazines, or playing "What If?" games (What if we had wings? What if we had no electricity?).

Brainstorm together. Write down everyone's suggestions for class plays or for science projects. Assure each child that his idea is valid.

Take a vote. Who wants a happy face on the jack o' lantern, and who wants a scary face? Who hopes the

Democrat will win, and who chooses the Republican? Who wants to study rain forests, and who prefers deserts?

• *Plan movement breaks between and during activities.*

Provide acceptable ways for the fidgety child to move. Incorporate movement into the routine, so children can stand and stretch, or move across the room from math to science center, or march to a drumbeat. Try activities such as Simon Says (where nobody loses), Follow the Leader, Jumping Jacks, or relay races. Play "Silent Speed Ball," in which the children pass a ball quickly around a circle, without making a peep. Movement "primes the pump" and helps every child pay attention, think, speak, and write.

• *Devise team or club efforts.*

Teams that read the most books, solve the most math problems, or produce cooperative projects earn a reward that you can decide on together. Earning team points can be a strong incentive for out-of-sync students, as well as for better-organized classmates who may not choose to work with them.

3. HELPING CHILDREN BECOME BETTER ORGANIZED

• *Encourage students to be active rather than passive learners.*

All children have an inner drive to learn, and they learn best when they can move and touch. Remember that *reading and listening are not every child's main avenue of learning*. Therefore, provide multisensory lessons so that the learning arrives through every possible route.

For example, the preschooler with inefficient auditory processing may learn best through tactile and visual experiences. Thus, he may learn more about rhythm and pitch by playing "Jingle Bells" on the xylophone than by hearing a recording. The older child, whose visual processing problem makes work sheets a chore, may learn well in hands-on, "real-life" situations. Thus, he can absorb math concepts while making change in a school store.

Dr. Mel Levine, a specialist in children's learning disorders, says that the best way to learn to read is to read widely in the area in which one has expertise. Even prereaders learn best when they can investigate subjects that are interesting and relevant.

Find out what the child has an affinity for, and lead her to explore the subject she is passionate about, through her preferred sensory path. Is she interested in spiders? Aerospace? Native Americans? If she is a tactile learner, let her draw a picture or build a model. If she likes to talk, let her give a short oral presentation. If she loves to move, let her demonstrate ritual dances. Build on the child's sensory strengths.

Post this Chinese proverb in your classroom as a constant reminder:

> *I hear, and I forget.*
> *I see, and I remember.*
> *I do, and I understand.*

• *Give children time.*

Nobody likes to feel rushed, especially the child with SI Dysfunction who may take longer than others to process new information. This child needs warm-up time, just as much as cool-down time.

Give this child the luxury of time to learn new material:

A) Before presenting a lesson, tell the class what you will teach them,

B) Teach them,

C) Tell them what you have taught them, and then

D) Allow them time to absorb the lesson or to practice it. Drill is particularly valuable for the child who, lacking an internal sense of order, requires repetition of academic tasks before catching on.

Give the child time to process a question and answer. The special child often has the knowledge but just takes longer to prove it. Ten seconds is not too long to wait for an answer that someone else may produce in three.

• *Simplify instructions.*

When you give instructions, make eye contact with the child. Give one or two directions at a time. Be concise and specific. Repeat the instructions if necessary. When assigning daily homework, say it in words and put it in writing. Have the child repeat it and write it down herself.

Short assignments will match the child's short attention span, will help him see an end to the task, and will give him a series of little successes.

Break down big assignments into small chunks. He may be a great reader but have difficulty planning long-term research projects. Provide a schedule and your clear expectations. For example, Week 1: each child will tell you his chosen topic. Week 2: he will submit a tentative reading list. Week 3: an outline. Week 4: a rough draft. Week 5: a finished report.

• *Provide a choice of writing implements.*

Some children do better with standard pencils, others with fat primary pencils; some with standard crayons, others with chubby crayons. While fine motor skills generally develop later in boys than in girls, these skills are especially late-blooming in the boy or girl with SI Dysfunction. Help the child choose the writing tool that fits him or her best.

• *Respect the child's needs.*

The child's primary need is to feel safe. When he feels safe, his brain is available for learning.

Many fine teachers, with the best intentions, commonly err with out-of-sync children by trying to "jolly them out" of their difficulties. For instance, a teacher may tell the preschooler with tactile defensiveness that "everyone likes finger paint, so take your turn," hoping to change his tendency to withdraw from touch. A physical education teacher of the older child with vestibular hypersensitivity may try to position him to do a somersault on the tumbling mat. These encouragements won't "fix" the child's dysfunction but, instead, may cause an aversive response, because he feels threatened.

Unless you know exactly what you're doing, it is probably better to respect the child's sensory defensiveness. Remember that the child's behavior is out of line not because he won't do things right but because he can't. It is unfair to force the child to do things he is unready to do.

• *Give the child alternatives.*

Anticipate problems, and help the child find suitable alternatives to situations that cause problems. For example, the child who is uncoordinated may avoid boisterous recess games. Guide him to other activities he can excel in that will strengthen his motor skills and that won't make him feel like a bystander or a sissy.

For the preschooler, going through an obstacle course at his own pace, after everyone else has completed it, is one possibility. If he resists a particular obstacle, such as the balance beam or tunnel, let him be! Praise him for conquering the obstacles he can manage.

For the older child, ball skills may improve after playing tetherball, one-on-one catching and throwing games, or dribbling activities with a teacher or a buddy.

In the classroom, the child who is easily distracted by too many choices may seem unable to choose any. He may say he's bored, when he is really confused. Help him find an activity or project that he can do while socializing with just one or two other children.

If possible, consult with an occupational therapist about activities and techniques you can use to address the child's needs.

4. ADAPTING YOUR OWN BEHAVIOR

• *Emphasize the positive.*

Give each child what psychotherapist Carl R. Rogers calls "unconditional, positive regard." The out-of-sync child needs constant assurance that her efforts are appreciated and worthwhile. She may not feel competent, even when she is! Reward the child for what she did accomplish, rather than remarking about what she left undone. Success breeds success.

• *Keep your voice low.*

The child with a supersensitive auditory system can become very uncomfortable when he hears a high-pitched or loud voice. He may even misinterpret your tone of voice and become distraught.

One day I had to use a more forceful voice than usual to move a group of preschoolers through a Halloween song in which different rhythm instruments represent witches, skeletons, and pumpkins. Midway through the song, I raised my voice to be heard: "Now, please put down your tambourines and pick up your wood blocks."

I didn't understand then, although I do now, why a particularly anxious boy cried, "Don't talk to me that way! Don't you know I can't do anything right when you talk to me that way?" My words hadn't been threatening; my directions hadn't been complicated. It was my louder, higher voice that made him fall apart. More effective would have been whispering, the technique I use now, especially in a noisy room.

• *Provide physical feedback.*

When you want to be certain that the child is paying attention, get up close. Look the child in the eye. While speaking, put your hands on the child's shoulders and press down firmly. These techniques may help the child focus better on what you are saying.

• *Keep your expectations realistic.*

So what if the child doesn't complete a task or doesn't do it the way other children do? Remember what is most important in learning: process rather than product, and participation rather than perfection.

Chapter Nine

COPING WITH YOUR
CHILD'S EMOTIONS

For the child to become more self-regulated and for families to deal with the emotional fallout of sensory integration dysfunction, there are positive words and actions that may improve the child's skills and self-esteem, as well as pitfalls to avoid.

A TYPICALLY DREADFUL MORNING

Marge, the mother of two, tells this story:

"This morning was typically dreadful. Chip, my eight-year-old, got out of bed on the wrong side. Actually, he fell out of bed. Then, on his way to the bathroom, he crashed into Melissa and knocked her down. He yelled at her, 'You're always in my way, dumb head!' She ran downstairs, bawling. He's always so mean to her, and she's only three.

"While I comforted her, I heard Chip slamming his bureau drawers and shouting. He finally came downstairs wearing his T-shirt inside out. He said this way the tags

wouldn't hurt him. I thought that was pretty good problem-solving, but my husband disagreed. Before I could
say anything, he ordered Chip to change. Chip refused.
My husband was furious. He pulled off Chip's shirt,
turned it right side out and stuffed Chip into it. Chip was
really upset and fighting back tears.

"Finally, he sat down and poured orange juice over his
cereal. When I said that wasn't a good idea, he began to
cry. He said, 'It was an accident! I didn't do it on purpose!'
Then he poured the rest of the juice on Melissa's head.
On purpose.

"Okay. I kept my temper, because it was time to meet
the school bus. But Chip couldn't find his reading book. It
took ten minutes to find it behind the couch. He missed the
bus, so I drove him to school. When we got there, we saw a
classmate getting out of her car. She had a model of an igloo
made of sugar cubes. Then Chip really lost control. He had
forgotten about the 'Homes around the World' assignment.
I felt just awful because I had forgotten, too. Chip hunkered
down and refused to get out of the car.

"The girl's mother waved to me and said, 'These special
projects take a lot out of me! What a dreadful morning!'

"If she only knew!"

What do we see here? Poor motor coordination. Tactile
defensiveness. Sibling rivalry. Conflict between parents.
Anger. Rage. Frustration. Loss of autonomy. Poor self-
help skills. Passive aggression. Disorganization. Loss of
self-control. Defiance. Helplessness. Despair. Guilt. Inad-
equacy. Isolation.

If you have an out-of-sync child, these problems may
be all too familiar. The effects of SI Dysfunction can per-
meate your lives.

Is it possible to learn to cope with the emotional fallout? Yes, if you understand your child, if you have support and understanding, and if you educate yourself.

EXPERTS' ADVICE

Many books are available that offer coping techniques for parents of challenging children. A. Jean Ayres, Ph.D., O.T.R., and Maryann Colby Trott, M.A., have written specifically about sensory integration. Other experts who refer to sensory processing problems include Stanley I. Greenspan, M.D.; Mary Sheedy Kurcinka, M.A.; Larry B. Silver, M.D.; and Stanley Turecki, M.D. Their methods may help you develop consistent, positive, and workable coping skills. (*See Recommended Reading.*) Here are some of their ideas.

Pay Attention to Your Child

• Remember that the child's problem is a physical one. "Indigestion of the brain" causes his unusual behavior. Just as another child with measles can't help itching, the out-of-sync child can't help being clumsy or afraid.

• Tune in to the kinds of stimulation that the hypersensitive child avoids, or that the hyposensitive child craves.

• Find the best way to reach your child, through his preferred sensory channel. Use a variety of ways to communicate (talking, writing, drawing, gesturing, and demonstrating). Keep your messages simple.

• Identify your child's temperament, by analyzing traits such as activity level, distractibility, intensity, regularity, persistence, sensory threshold, flexibility, and mood. Evaluating his temperament will help you define his problems.

• Know your child's strengths and weaknesses. If your child has been evaluated and diagnosed, study the reports carefully. Read everything you can. Get information from teachers, special educators, and other experts who are familiar with differing abilities and learning styles.

• Set up "floor time," Stanley Greenspan's term for an unstructured, special play time, at least thirty minutes daily. Sit on the floor with your child. Let him choose and lead the activity. Follow along in the play, paying attention to whatever interests him. Engaging with your child on his terms establishes a warm, trusting attachment, the basis of all future relationships.

Anticipate Responses

• Anticipate emotional crises. Too much stimulation at a birthday party or a crowded mall may trigger a negative response. Be ready to remove the child from sensations that will overwhelm her, before she loses control.

• Help the child learn to notice her increasing intensity. Give her opportunities to remove herself from the action and to recharge by being alone. Help her understand her need for space.

• Develop strategies with your child to cope with negative emotions before they occur. "Let's lay out your clothes tonight, so in the morning you won't feel rushed."

• To diffuse her strong reactions, be prepared to provide soothing activities, such as warm baths, stories, or quiet imaginative play. A rocking chair, a back rub, or a trip to the playground may also be calming.

• If she is slow to react to sensory stimuli, allow her extra time before responding.

Empathize

• Identify and empathize with the child's point of view. Empathizing with his motives and goals helps you understand why he behaves as he does, so you will have an easier time changing his behavior.

• Give him the words to describe the emotions and sensations he experiences.

• Understand the child's feelings and reflect them back: "It's hard to fall asleep when you're worried about the monster in the closet." Reflective listening helps him identify and master his emotions.

• Tell him repeatedly that you understand his difficulties. The child needs your reassurance.

• Share your own similar emotions, to show that we all have fears. "I think roller coasters are scary, too," or "We both get nervous in crowds."

• Take the time to reevaluate your child's emotions. He may behave aggressively because he is afraid, not because he is angry. Respond to the primary emotion, rather than to the defensive behavior.

• Give your child coping skills for regaining self-control. After an emotional storm, provide a quiet space, a firm hug, a walk, or appropriate words or actions to use to restore harmony. "Do you need to do something to feel better about what happened?"

• Accentuate the positive. Notice and comment upon your child's abilities, interests, and good behavior. Build his self-concept by reinforcing his growing self-awareness and accomplishments.

• Build on his strengths and help him compensate for his weaknesses. Welcome him to the world; do not excuse him from life.

Provide Structure

• Establish routines and schedules, and keep to them consistently. Explain the daily plans. Give notice of upcoming activities.

• Make transitions as smooth as possible. Allow time for ending one activity and making the transition to another.

• Limit transitions as much as possible. Avoid surprises.

• Expect the child to take longer than others to adapt to routines.

• Help your child become organized in his own work. Together, set up schedules and job charts. Eliminate distractions. Give him an uncluttered space and sufficient time to complete projects and homework. Provide guidance so he has the satisfaction of doing his work independently.

Have Realistic Expectations

• While your child may function very well some-times, at other times, she will resist going to school, spill her milk, and fall. Expect inconsistency, and when she stumbles, try to be understanding.

• Break challenges into small pieces. Encourage the child to achieve one goal at a time to help her feel the satisfaction of a series of little successes.

• Remember that you have had years of experience in learning to deal with the world, and that the child who is out of control has not.

Discipline

• When the child loses control, avoid punishment. Loss of self-control is scary enough; punishment adds guilt and shame.

• Comment on the child's negative behavior, not on the child: "Your yelling makes me angry," rather than "You infuriate me!"

• Help the out-of-control child find a quiet space, away from sensory overload. Teach him that time-out is not punishment but a technique to regain self-control. Let him decide the length of the time-out, if possible.

• Set limits. Limits make a child feel secure. Pick one battle at a time to help him develop self-control and appropriate behavior.

• Be firm about the limits you set. Show him that his feelings won't change the outcome; a rule is a rule. "I know you're frustrated because you want to play with the puppy, but we're all sitting down for supper now."

• Explain why you are disciplining the child. Accompany the explanations with gestures and empathy.

• Discipline consistently. (Discipline means to teach or instruct, not punish.) After you tell the child what you are going to do, then do it.

• Develop management techniques based on understanding the child's difficulty. Decide whether to deal with the problem now or to disengage yourself for a moment. Evaluate the situation before taking action.

• Determine appropriate consequences for misbehavior. A natural consequence is best, because it is reasonable, factual, and you don't impose it: "If you skip breakfast, you will be hungry." A logical consequence, in which the child is responsible for the outcome of his behavior, is second best: "If you throw food, you must mop it up." An applied consequence, in which the punishment doesn't exactly fit the crime, is useful when nothing else works: "If you spit on the baby, you won't be allowed to play with your friends," or "If you hit me, you may not watch TV."

• Reward appropriate behavior with approval.

Problem-Solve

• Set up problem-solving time, in which you become an equal partner with your child to discuss problems, negotiate differences, and arrive at solutions.

Elevating his problem-solving ability helps him anticipate challenges, take responsibility, cope with his feelings independently, become a logical and flexible thinker, and learn to compromise. "What else can you do when you're angry besides throwing toys? Can you say, 'I don't like that!' and jump up and down?"

• Help your child learn to find appropriate outlets for emotions. Let her know when she can scream, where she can let loose, and what she can punch. Teach her that some expressions of anger or frustration are acceptable and safe, while others are inappropriate.

• When the child's intense emotions overwhelm you, first get control of your own feelings. You will show your child that strong emotions are a fact of life; everyone must learn to cope with them. You will also show him that he, too, can learn to calm himself.

• Ask him for advice on how you can help him.

• Think up ways you can have fun together. Life does not need to be serious all the time.

• If necessary, seek extra support to help with the "ripple effect" of your hard-to-raise child. Professionals can help you improve family life and relations with relatives, peers, and other people outside your nuclear family.

• Join a support group to share child-rearing concerns with others.

Become Your Child's Advocate

• Educate adults who need to know about your child's abilities. Not only classroom teachers, but also art, gym, music, and Sunday school teachers, soccer and Little League coaches, camp counselors, and Scout leaders probably need to know. Because SI Dysfunction is invisible, people tend to forget or disbelieve that a significant problem affects your child. Your job is to inform them, so they can help your child learn.

• Monitor your child's classroom and group activities. If you see that a teacher or coach is insensitive, uncooperative, or too demanding, take action.

• Offer your protection or intervention when the child can't handle a stressful situation alone. Reinforce the message that asking for help is a positive coping strategy, not an admission of failure.

DOS AND DON'TS FOR COPING

Now here are my suggestions for dealing with the out-of-sync child on a daily basis.

Please Do . . .

Do build on the child's strengths: "You are such a good cook! Help me remember what we need for our meat loaf recipe. Then you can mix it." Or, "You have energy to spare. Could you run over to Mrs. Johnson's house and get a magazine she has for me?" Think "ability," not "disability."

Do build on the child's interests: "Your collection of rocks is growing fast. Let's read some books about rocks. We can make a list of the different kinds you have found." Your interest and support will encourage the child to learn more and do more.

Do suggest small, manageable goals to strengthen your child's abilities: "How about if you walk with me just as far as the mailbox? You can drop the letter in. Then I'll carry you piggy-back, all the way home." Or, "It's fine if you take just one dish at a time to clear the table. We aren't in a hurry."

Do encourage your child to develop self-help skills: To avoid "learned helplessness," sponsor your child's independence. "I know it's hard to tie your shoes, but each time you do it, it will get easier." Stress how capable she is, and how much faith you have in her, to build her self-esteem and autonomy. Show her you have expectations that she can help herself, and remember to keep those expectations realistic.

Do let your child engage in appropriate self-therapy: If your child craves spinning, let him spin on the tire swing as long as he wants. If he likes to jump on the bed, get him a trampoline, or put a mattress on the floor. If he likes to hang upside down, install a chinning bar in his bedroom doorway. If he insists on wearing boots every day, let him wear boots. If he frequently puts inedible objects into his mouth, give him chewing gum. If he can't sit still, give him opportunities to move and balance, such as sitting on a beach ball while he listens to music or a story. Your child will seek sensations that will nourish his hungry brain, so help him find safe ways to do so.

Do offer new sensory experiences: "This lavender soap smells wonderful. Want to sniff it?" Or, "Turnips have the same texture as apples but taste different. Would you like a bite?"

Do touch your child, in ways that the child can tolerate and enjoy: "I'll rub your back with this sponge. Do you like me to rub hard or gently?" (Stop if it doesn't feel good.) Or, "Do you know what it means when I squeeze your hand three times, like this? It means I-LOVE-YOU!"

Do encourage movement: "Let's swing our arms to the beat of this music. I always feel better when I move and stretch a little, don't you?" Movement—especially rhythmic movement—improves sensory processing.

Do encourage the child to try a new movement experience: "If you're interested in trying that swing, I'll help you get on." Some children are not adept at motor planning. They may enjoy new movement experiences but need help figuring out how to initiate them.

Do offer your physical and emotional support: "I'm interested in trying that swing. Want to try it with me? You can sit on my lap, and we'll swing together." The child who is fearful of movement may agree to swing at the playground if he has the security of a loving lap. (Stop if he resists.)

Do allow your child to experience unhappiness, frustration, or anger: "Wow, it really hurts when the other kids don't pick you for the team." Acknowledging your child's feelings allows him to deal with them, whereas rushing in to make it better every time he's hurt prevents the child from developing the ability to cope with negative emotions.

Do provide appropriate outlets for negative emotions: Make it possible and acceptable for the child to vent pent-up feelings. Give her a ball or a bucketful of wet sponges to hurl against the fence. Designate a "screaming space" (her room, the basement, or garage) where she can go to pound her chest and shout.

Do reinforce what is good about your child's feelings and actions, even when something goes wrong: "You didn't mean for the egg to miss the bowl. Cracking eggs takes practice. I'm glad you want to learn. Try again." Help her assess her experience in a positive way by talking over what she did right and what she may do better the next time.

Do praise: "I noticed that you fed and walked the dog. Thank you for being so responsible." Reward the child for goodness, empathy, and being mindful of the needs of others. "You are a wonderful friend," or "You really know how to make animals feel safe."

Do give the child a sense of control: "If you go to bed now, we'll have time for a long story. If you choose to play a little longer, that's fine, but then there won't be time for a story. You decide." Or, "I'm ready to go to the shoe store whenever you are. Tell me when you're ready to leave." Impress on the child that others don't have to make every decision that affects him.

Do set reasonable limits: To become civilized, every child needs limits. "It's okay to be angry but not okay to hurt someone. We do not pinch," or "I can see you're angry with the way the game is going, but you may not be destructive."

Do understand: "I know writing spelling words makes you tired." How wonderful to hear that an adult is sympathetic, rather than judgmental!

Do put yourself in your child's shoes: "I know how frustrating it is when you spill your soda. I get upset, too, when I spill my coffee. Nobody makes mistakes on purpose. It's okay."

Do recall how you behaved as a child: Maybe your child is just like you once were. (The apple doesn't fall far from the tree!) Ask yourself what you would have liked to make your childhood easier and more pleasurable. More trips to the playground? More free time to mess around? More cuddling? Fewer demands? Lower expectations? Try saying, "When I was a kid and life got rough, I liked to climb trees. How about you?"

Do respect your child's needs, even if they seem unusual: "You sure do like a tight tuck-in! There, now you're as snug as a bug in a rug." Or, "I'll stand in front of you while we're on the escalator. I won't let you fall."

Do respect your child's fears, even if they seem senseless: "I see that your ball bounced into the sandbox where the big kids are digging. I'll go with you to get it. Let's hold hands." Your frequent reassurances will help her build her trust in others.

Do say "I love you": Assure your child that you accept who she is. Frequent reminders that you love and value her will strengthen her emotional foundation. You cannot say "I love you" too often!

Do follow your instincts: Your instincts will tell you that everyone needs to touch and be touchable, to move and be movable. If your child's responses to ordinary touch and movement sensations "just don't seem right," keep pressing to identify the problem. Ask questions; get information; follow up with appropriate action.

Do listen when others express concerns: When teachers or caregivers suggest that your child's behavior is unusual, you may react with denial or anger. But remember that they see your child away from home, among many other children. Their perspective is worth considering.

Do educate yourself about normal child development: Read. Take parent education classes. Learn about invariable stages of human development, as well as variable temperaments and learning styles. It's comforting to know that a wide variety of behaviors falls within the normal range. Then, you'll find it easier to differentiate between typical and atypical behavior. Sometimes a cigar is just a cigar, and a six-year-old is just a six-year-old!

Do seek professional help: SI Dysfunction is a problem that a child can't overcome alone. Parents and teachers can't "cure" a child, just as a child can't cure himself. Early intervention is crucial in dealing with a difficulty that lies below the child's conscious level.

Do keep your cool: When your child drives you crazy, collect your thoughts before responding, especially if you are angry, upset, or unpleasantly surprised. A child who is out of control needs the calm reassurance of someone who is in control. She needs a grown-up.

Do take care of yourself: When you're having a hard day, take a break! Hire a baby-sitter, if necessary, and remove yourself from your child. Go for a walk, read a book, take a bath, dine out, make love. Nobody can be expected to give another person twenty-four hours of undivided attention, and still cope.

Please Don't . . .

Don't try to persuade your child that he will outgrow his difficulties: "You'll be able to climb Mt. Everest when you're older!" Growing older does not always mean growing stronger, or more agile, or more sociable. For children with Sensory Integration Dysfunction, growing older often means inventing new ways to avoid everyday experiences.

Don't tell your child she is bound to get stronger, better organized, or more in control, if she applies herself: "You can do better if you'll just try!" The child *is* trying.

Don't joke: "Why are you so tired? Did you just run a four-minute mile, ha ha?" Being tired is not a laughing matter to the child. Jokes make him feel laughed at, and they produce self-defeating anger and humiliation.

Don't plead: "Do it for Mommy. If you loved me, you'd sit up like a nice young lady." Your child does love you, and she yearns to please you, but she can't. Besides, she would sit up straight if she could, for her own sake, even if she didn't love you!

Don't shame: "A big boy like you can open the door all by himself." He may be big yet have little strength.

Don't threaten: "If you don't pick your feet up when you walk, then you'll ruin your shoes and you won't get any new ones." Threats backfire.

Don't talk about your child in demeaning ways in front of him: "This dopey-looking kid is my son. Wake up, Lazybones, and give our new neighbor a high-five!" Such comments aren't funny to the listener.

Don't talk about your child in demeaning ways behind his back: "My kid is such a lazy good-for-nothing. I just can't get him to understand the importance of hard work." What do you want your boss, relatives, and friends to remember about your child?

Don't compare, aloud, one child with another: "Your brother rode a two-wheeler when he was six. What's wrong with you?" (But do note to yourself the abilities your child seems to lack, compared with others of the same age.)

Don't do for your child what your child can do for himself: "I'll sharpen your pencils, while you get out your homework." Pampering a child gets you both nowhere fast.

Don't expect consistency: "You could hang your coat up yesterday. Why can't you do it today?" Inconsistency is common in out-of-sync children. What worked yesterday may not work today, and vice versa!

Don't make your child do things that distress him: "You must put your hand into this paint to make a handprint for Grandpa," or "You'll love riding the elevator up the Empire State Building." You can't make him enjoy touch or movement experiences until his neurological system is ready.

Don't overload your child with multisensory experiences: "Let's eat some chili, put on some steel-band music, and dance the rumba. We're going to have a terrific South-of-the-Border night." Slow down! Offering your child a variety of sensations, one at a time, is fine; offering her a variety of sensations, all at the same time, will overload her system.

Don't be afraid of "labeling" your child: Many parents fear the stigma attached to SI Dysfunction. They don't want their son or daughter to be labeled as a child with special needs. That fear is normal, but it doesn't help your child. Consider the identification of SI Dysfunction as a benefit, for now you know that your child can get help before the problem turns into a serious learning disability.

Don't feel helpless: The world is full of children with sensory integration dysfunction, and people who love them. You and your child are not alone. Support is out there; it awaits you, and you can find it.

Chapter Ten

LOOKING AT YOUR CHILD IN A NEW LIGHT

A PARENT'S EPIPHANY

A father writes, "When I first heard the words 'sensory integration' and 'low muscle tone' used in connection with my daughter Julie, I both didn't know what they meant and also dismissed them as yet another example of my wife's overprotectiveness. These terms were used by Stanley Greenspan, M.D.—one of the city's (and country's) top child psychiatrists—whom we had consulted on Julie's sleep problems. Such technical jargon was testimony, in my mind, to the unspoken alliance that surely persisted between high-paid child experts and jittery mothers.

"True, at twelve months, Julie did flop around a little more than I would have expected (she did not yet crawl or stand), and true, she didn't snuggle as I had hoped. But I chalked it up to her being a little prickly and thought she was fine just as she was. The fact is, I hadn't seen enough other kids (as my wife and the doctor had) to know that her behavior was out of the ordinary.

"While I was either objecting or standing aside, my wife persisted. She took Julie to an occupational therapist—also well paid and ready to agree with the diagnosis—and put Julie into a twice-a-week course of therapy. I remained skeptical.

"The turning point came when I attended a workshop called 'Understanding Sensory Integration.' While the presentation initially had limited impact on me, I was impressed with the number of parents there. 'So maybe this sensory stuff is for real,' I thought, 'and we're not the only ones who are concerned.'

"More important than the large turnout were the 'experience' stations in the back of the room. When I tried to accomplish simple tasks with some of my senses impaired—walking a straight line while looking through the wrong end of a pair of binoculars, for example—it started to penetrate my thick skull that Julie may in fact have entered the world with some special needs, and would have to compete with her peers at an unfair disadvantage as long as she had them.

"Suddenly, the significance of all this dawned on me—and I began to look at my daughter in a new light.

"From that point on I became increasingly supportive of whatever would expand Julie's sensory and gross motor horizons. I remember our glee when Julie started mashing food with her hands. I am now aghast that, out of ignorance and bravado, I would probably have denied Julie help at a critical time in her life, when she had her best chance to keep sensory deficiencies from becoming deep and lasting scars. And I applaud my wife who was forced to do battle on two fronts—Julie's deficiencies and my resistance—to allow Julie to overcome her deficiencies before she ever knew she had them."

BECOMING ENLIGHTENED

When you begin to understand sensory integration dysfunction, you, too, will begin to look at your child in a new
light. Recognizing that he is struggling to master the simplest tasks of everyday life is the first step toward helping
him while he is still young.

Accepting your child's limitations isn't easy. It's natural to want to deny that your child's difficulties are out of
the ordinary. It's natural to feel sad when you understand
how hard he must work. It's natural to feel guilty for the
times you scolded him or got impatient because of his
behavior.

It takes time to become enlightened. It will take psy-
chic and physical energy to begin the journey toward
making him feel better about himself and about what he
can achieve. If you're reading this, you are already on the
road, so take heart. It's going to get better.

• *Your child is unable, not unwilling, to perform routine tasks.*
Maybe she often says that she is "just too tired."
Maybe she slumps over the dining room table instead of
sitting upright, or hasn't the energy to turn a doorknob,
although she seems to be eating and sleeping enough.

Redirect your thinking: When she says she's tired, she
means it. She really is unable—not unwilling—to perform
routine tasks. No matter how much she wants to be independent and peppy, her sensory processing problem hin-
ders her motoric ability. She knows, subconsciously, that
her strength is limited. She has deduced how to reserve it
for the jobs she knows she must do, which may be chewing, getting in and out of the car, or bending down to
retrieve a dropped mitten.

Your child isn't lazy; in fact, she is using enormous energy just to get through the day.

• *Your child has developed some clever compensatory skills.*

Away from home, it could be that your child doesn't appear to be as smart as you know he is. He may not talk much, giving the impression that he has little to discuss. Conversely, he may talk nonstop, yet be a poor conversationalist.

He may seem uncommonly shy with unfamiliar adults and other children. He may choose the same old games and toys, as if he lacks curiosity and a sense of intellectual adventure.

Redirect your thinking: Sensory Integration Dysfunction affects all kinds of children, including those who are extremely intelligent. Give your child credit for being so bright that he has figured out how to avoid making a fool of himself when he knows he can't meet others' expectations.

Perhaps your child has lofty thoughts but can't express them well because of a language disability that is sometimes associated with vestibular dysfunction. Or, he may be verbally adept with a repertoire of excuses for evading intolerable movement or tactile experiences: "I can't paint today, because I'm wearing my new shirt and I shouldn't get it dirty."

Perhaps he has learned that if you see him digging in the sandbox, you will leave him alone. If he's busy, maybe you won't urge him to get on the swing, an activity that makes him feel that he is falling off the earth. You may notice that he looks up at you frequently, checking in for your approval, rather than concentrating on digging all the way to China.

Perhaps, if he can't climb stairs easily, he has figured out a way to get you to carry him. When a child reaches up two small arms for an embrace and says, "Hug me up the stairs," what parent would believe that neurological dysfunction is a problem?

Your child has developed compensatory skills that allow him to devise acceptable methods of avoiding the areas he knows will give him trouble.

• *Your child has courage.*

Perhaps your child resists descending the playground slide, doesn't like to play at other children's houses, shuns new foods, or becomes very anxious before visiting the doctor for an annual checkup. You may be exasperated by what you see as her excessive and inappropriate fearfulness.

Redirect your thinking: People need fear; fear alerts us to danger. Your child's apprehensions may seem excessive, but they are appropriate for her, because her world seems dangerous. Each day she must face the same scary situations, such as a fear of losing her balance or of being touched. No wonder she is cautious about new situations, which are even scarier because they are unpredictable.

Furthermore, it takes courage to resist enjoyable experiences, resist change, or resist a parent. The penalty for disappointing an important grown-up is disapproval. No one seeks disapproval. But disapproval is preferable to proceeding with an activity that the child perceives as life threatening.

Your child is brave, not a coward.

• *Your child has a tender heart.*

Perhaps your child has a "bad boy" reputation. He behaves aggressively, confronting the world with a stick in his hand, slugging the playmate who brushes against him, and shouting "I hate that!" "This is boring!" "You're stupid!" "Get away or I'll kill you!" These antagonistic responses may make your child appear to be a truly unpleasant person, even if you know that within the bully beats a tender heart.

Redirect your thinking: Perhaps your child can't differentiate between benign and hostile tactile experiences. Because he must protect himself from situations that he senses are dangerous, he instinctively chooses "fight" over "flight." He puts up a "don't mess with me" façade, not because he is misanthropic, but because he is scared.

The child who is inwardly on the defensive will often be outwardly offensive. An air of arrogance or a tough-guy image is common among people (adults, too) who feel uncertain about their abilities and self-worth.

You know how loving your child can be at home, in his familiar surroundings. He would be gentle outside the family circle, too, if he felt more comfortable in the world.

• *Your child has many abilities.*

Your child may not be skillful at reading, running, or paying attention. Her shortcomings may disappoint you.

Redirect your thinking: She may show extraordinary empathy and compassion for other living things. She may have a rare talent for creative thinking and be artistic, musical, or poetic. She may be observant where others are oblivious. She may have a wonderful sense of humor. Her special sensitivities may be a tremendous asset. Think abilities, not disabilities.

• *Your child has a special need for love and approval.*

Maybe she strikes you as being too possessive. She grabs all the toys but may not play with them; she just wants to have them. She demands all your time, but when you give it to her, she is unsatisfied. If she loses a round of Candyland, she cries and mopes. She wants it all.

Redirect your thinking: She requires things and attention to bolster her own small store of self-esteem. She has to be the winner because she usually feels like a loser. She seems greedy because she is needy.

More than anything, your child has a special need to be loved and appreciated.

• *Your child's "hardheadedness" is a survival skill.*

Perhaps he says things like "I'm the boss of my own body. You can't tell me what to do." Perhaps he is rigid, always wanting to wear the same clothes and eat the same cereal in the same bowl. Perhaps he insists on elaborate rituals for bath or bedtime.

Redirect your thinking: Nobody awakens in the morning thinking, "Today I'm going to resist everything." Human beings learn to cope with a changing environment by being flexible. Your little fellow appears stubborn, however, because he is not the boss of his own body, and he is not in control. His life is full of uncertainties and obstacles.

An inefficient tactile system, with an attendant fussiness about clothing, may be the reason that he wants to wear shorts when it snows. Because the inside of his mouth may be overly sensitive to food textures, he may insist on the same kind of cereal, day after day.

Sameness and rituals are tools that help him accomplish basic jobs, like getting dressed or preparing for bed. His apparent stubbornness is rooted in his need to survive.

He isn't willfully stubborn; he is stubborn because he has trouble adapting his behavior to meet changing demands, so he sticks to what he knows will work.

• *Your child truly requires your attention, tailored to his needs.*

Let's suppose you dress your little boy in the morning, because he takes so long and becomes tearfully frustrated when you leave the job up to him. Then let's suppose that his preschool teacher mentions how much extra time is required for her to attend to his needs. She suggests that you urge him to become independent in the getting-dressed department. Even if you know more than she does about problems caused by Sensory Integration Dysfunction, you may still believe that your parenting skills are inadequate.

Redirect your thinking: Giving your child attention when he needs it and when a job must get done quickly is perfectly okay. Particularly when your family runs on a tight schedule, you will do whatever works to move everybody from Point A to Point B.

Unenlightened parents ignore their children. Enlightened parents do what they can to make their children's lives pleasant and safe.

• *Your child can function better—with help.*

If your child has sensory difficulties now, her problems will grow with her. Certainly, she may develop strategies to avoid or compensate for stressful sensory experiences. Certainly, she may develop talents that are not dependent upon her shaky sense of balance, or hypersensitivity to touch. But she will always have to work very, very hard to function smoothly.

Redirect your thinking: Sensory Integration Dysfunction is like indigestion of the brain. Just as antacid can soothe upset stomachs, so can occupational therapy and a sensory diet smooth neural pathways.

Most of all, your everyday love and empathy will boost your child's emotional security. We all need to know that someone is there for us, especially when times are rough. We all need to know that someone applauds our strengths, understands our weaknesses, and honors our individuality. With your help, your son or daughter can become in sync with the world.

A PARENT'S ENCOURAGING WORDS

A mother writes: "If we had only known. If only there had been a book like this to read. If only our long- and eagerly-awaited child had been 'normal.'

"Initially, we thought he was. He had great APGAR scores and was on schedule with all developmental checklists. Certainly, he had no obvious physical abnormalities; he was beautiful. Moreover, he was alert, learning to talk at six months! When he was two years old, all the pediatricians at the clinic dropped what they were doing to observe his phenomenal verbal skills. We were so proud.

"But at the same time, we knew that something was not right. Something had not been right all along. In the newborn nursery, he cried so loudly that he kept all the other babies awake. Then there was the traumatic transition from breast to bottle feeding. In fact, any kind of transition from one experience to another was horrendous.

"He was also extremely sensitive to light touch and new textures. It was difficult to dress him. Then came Gymboree, with terror and screaming at physical activities the other children loved. I had to face the stares from critical instructors and parents of more 'cooperative' children. With time, his behavior became more and more troublesome.

"What was wrong with my child? My beautiful and funny child.

"Finally, I contacted the Public School's Early Childhood Screening program, and we were scheduled for a group screening.

"When we arrived at the appointed time and place, we found many children with obvious handicaps and a play table to occupy them until their turn to go through the stations. Those with mental retardation, braces, and missing limbs went ahead smoothly.

"At our turn, the transition from play to screening activity resulted in a screaming, limp child who could not be handled by all the experts assembled. We left in tears. Our son, the only child with no discernible problem, couldn't even be tested.

"Upon subsequent individual evaluation by a team including an educational specialist, occupational therapist, speech pathologist, and psychologist, we were finally introduced to the 'something wrong.' Its name was Sensory Integration Dysfunction. It required 'occupational therapy' and 'a good nursery school.'

"Why had it taken so long? Why hadn't *anyone* known? Why had my family suffered so much?

"It didn't matter now. The good nursery school was at hand.

"Upon the recommendation of the evaluation team, I contacted St. Columba's. I will never forget my first conversation with Carol Kranowitz. It was the first day my fear began to abate. She was the Music and Movement teacher, but she was so much more. She was the first person to whom I had ever spoken who knew my child without ever having met him. That is because she knew about SI Dysfunction and had undertaken to inform and train other staff in its idiosyncrasies and, even more important, its management.

"These people at St. Columba's were not afraid of my child. They didn't see him as 'bad' or 'uncontrolled.' They saw him struggling with Sensory Integration Dysfunction, and though he challenged them mightily, they never gave up.

"With occupational therapy, we began to overcome such hurdles as fear of movement and revulsion caused by unfamiliar textures. As his fear of new things diminished, as the world became a less scary place, transitions also improved. With a psychologist's help, we structured the environment and managed behavioral responses (i.e., tantrums) consistently.

"Gradually, our child has blossomed and we have learned to do something with him which I never thought would be possible. We learned to enjoy him. He is our favorite companion.

"As I look back upon two years of O.T. and a nurturing nursery school, I shudder to think what a mess we would all have been without them. They were our lifeline, our hold on hope.

"Here is my charge to you: If you have concerns about your own or another child, no matter how vague they seem or how inarticulate you feel verbalizing them, pursue them. A child can have less pronounced problems than mine and still need help. And in your pursuit, continue until you find hope. In doing so, you may free other wonderful, enjoyable little people held hostage by SI Dysfunction. They are too small and frightened to free themselves."

APPENDIX: THE SENSORY PROCESSING MACHINE

Here is a brief anatomy lesson of the central nervous system, and an explanation of how sensory integration occurs therein. This overview may help you appreciate the marvel of sensory integration.

THE SYNCHRONIZED NERVOUS SYSTEM

All animals respond to sensations of touch, movement and gravity, and body position. Thus, human animals share the hidden senses with goldfish and goats, falcons and frogs, caterpillars and clams. Through eons of evolution, humankind refined these senses in order to survive in a hazardous world.

As life forms gradually arose from sea to land to treetops, they had to adapt to differing environments. Hands to pluck berries, limbs to climb trees, eyes to see moving as well as stationary objects, and ears to detect prey and predators developed over time.

Along with these skills came increasingly complex sensations. The human brain evolved to integrate these sensations, so that the hand would pick a berry rather than a thorn, the limb would cling to a branch, the eye would discern a motionless tiger poised to pounce, and the ear would hear faraway hoofbeats.

With the most complex brain in the animal kingdom, humans have the most complex nervous system. Its main task is to integrate the senses.

The nervous system has three main parts, working in harmony. One is the peripheral nervous system, running through organs and muscles, such as the eyes, ears, and limbs. The second part is the autonomic nervous system, controlling involuntary functions of heart rate, breathing, digestion, and reproduction. The third part is the central nervous system (CNS), consisting of countless neurons, a spinal cord, and a brain.

THREE COMPONENTS OF THE CENTRAL NERVOUS SYSTEM

A) The Neurons

Neurons, or nerve cells, are the structural and functional units of the nervous system. Neurons tell us what is happening inside and outside our bodies. The brain has approximately one hundred billion neurons. Each neuron has:

- A cell body, with its nucleus inside.
- Many short dendrites (Greek for "little branches"), reaching out to other neurons to receive messages, or impulses, and carrying them into the cell body.

• A long axon, like a stem with roots, which sends impulses from the cell body to the dendrites of other neurons.

A Neuron

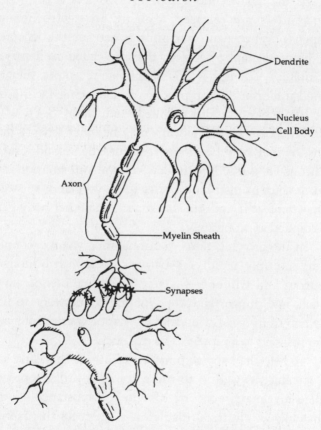

Two kinds of neurons connect the brain and spinal cord to the rest of the body: sensory and motor. Sensory neurons receive impulses from sensory receptors in our eyes, ears, skin, muscles, joints, and organs.

Impulses travel along the sensory neuron's axon and communicate messages to other neurons at contact points called synapses (Greek for "point of juncture"). Each neuron makes thousands of synaptic connections every time it fires. The neuron firing off the message is called presynaptic; the neuron receiving the message is called postsynaptic.

At the nanosecond that the message is fired, neurotransmitters are released, causing an electrochemical response. When neurotransmitters activate the receptors of the postsynaptic neurons, they are called excitatory or facilitatory. When they do not activate receptors, they are called inhibitory. (The process of balancing facilitatory and inhibitory messages is called modulation. *See p. 42.*)

The postsynaptic neurons may be other sensory neurons, or they may be motor neurons, the second kind of neurons in our CNS. Receiving the information, the motor neurons instruct muscles to move, glands to sweat, lungs to breathe, intestines to digest, and other body parts to respond appropriately.

In the growing fetus, neurons and synaptic connections multiply rapidly. A baby is born with billions of neurons and trillions of synapses. Sensations of smell, touch, and hunger activate synaptic connections to help the baby survive. For instance, synaptic connections help him respond to a nipple so he can suck.

To help the baby respond efficiently to this early skill of sucking, as well as to more complex skills, a process called myelination occurs. Myelin is a substance—somewhat like an electrical insulator—that coats the axon of the neuron to protect it, to smooth the path, and to speed up the connections.

At about eighteen months, the child stops developing new neurons, because his brain already has all that it needs—and his skull has all that will fit! New synapses, however, keep multiplying as the child integrates new sensations. That is, synapses multiply if synaptic connections are useful for everyday functioning and if they are repeatedly used. Otherwise, they vanish.*

By about twelve years, the child will lose many synapses he was born with, through a normal and necessary process called pruning. Pruning eliminates synapses the child does not need and stabilizes those he does. If he is Japanese, his brain will prune synapses necessary to pronounce the sound of "r," because "r" isn't used in his language. If he is French, his brain will strengthen these synapses, so he can roll his "r's" with fluency.

Normally, as the child actively responds to sensations, useful synaptic connections increase. The more connections, the more myelination; the more myelination, the stronger the neurological structure; and the stronger the neurological structure, the better equipped the child is to learn new skills.

Two Examples of the Function of Neurotransmitters

City Sensations Become Routine
You leave your quiet country home and visit the city for the first time. The sound of traffic, the sight of crowds, the smell of pollution, and the motion of escalators bombard your senses. Billions of neurons are firing messages; zillions of neurotransmitters are activating neuronal responses. Your nervous system is operating on overtime; that's why you're so "nervous"!

---

*If a person doesn't engage in a wide range of sensory experiences, it becomes more difficult to use certain synaptic connections. For instance, when astronauts return to Earth after a few days, they have trouble reestablishing their sense of balance, because their gravity receptors were not stimulated in space.

After a few days, you begin to grow accustomed to city sensations. You no longer jump each time you hear screeching brakes or get jostled on the subway. Neurotransmitters now have less of an excitatory effect and more of an inhibitory effect. As your nervous system adapts to repeated stimuli, you can pay less attention to every sensation—and still survive.

Painkillers Become Less Effective

You have chronic back pain, so you take a painkiller. At first, the medicine helps as the neurotransmitters activate a response. After a while, the medicinal effect wears off because postsynaptic neurons have raised their threshold. Instead of just one painkiller to make you comfortable, you now require two or three.

B) The Spinal Cord

Extending below the brain is the spinal cord, a long, thick structure of nervous tissue. It receives all sensations from peripheral nerves in our skin and muscles and relays these messages up to the brain. The brain then interprets the sensory messages and sends motor messages back down to the spinal cord, which sends messages out to peripheral nerves in specific body parts.

C) The Brain

The human brain evolved over the course of 500 million years. Dr. Paul D. MacLean, brain researcher at the National Institute of Mental Health, has proposed that each human is born with a "triune brain." (This model of brain development is one of many. For our purposes, it is the simplest.)

As we evolved, we added layers of brain material, each one improving earlier parts. The first layer is the reptilian complex: the "primitive brain." It is responsible for reflexive, instinctive behavior, such as self-preservation, reproduction, hunting, and fighting to establish territory.

The Triune Brain

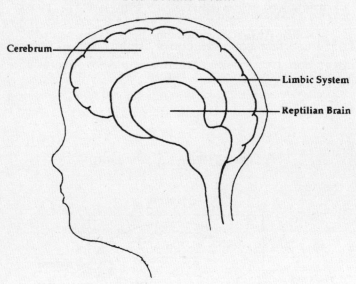

The second layer is the limbic system (Latin for "border"). It is the "seat of emotions," controlling hormones that enable us to feel angry, lustful, and jealous, as well as pleased and happy. Sometimes called the "smell brain," this system processes smell and taste, which have a powerful effect on our emotions.

The limbic system adds feelings to otherwise instinctive behavior. Thus, when we feel threatened, we fight or flee—or shut down. When we feel safe, we can play—and when we play, we can learn.

The third layer is the cerebrum: the "thinking brain." It is responsible for the organization of the most complex sensory intake. Detailed processing of sensations occurs here, so we can think, remember, make decisions, solve problems, plan and execute our actions, and communicate through language.

FOUR BRAIN PARTS USED IN SENSORY INTEGRATION

Four important brain structures are involved in sensory integration. Let's glance at them and see how they fit into the triune brain.

A Cross-Section of the Brain

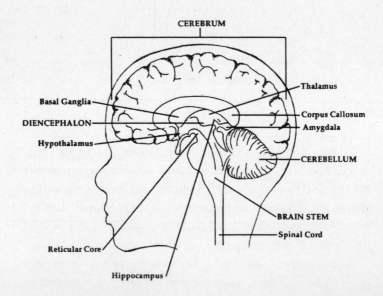

CEREBRUM

Basal Ganglia

DIENCEPHALON

Hypothalamus

Thalamus

Corpus Callosum

Amygdala

CEREBELLUM

BRAIN STEM

Spinal Cord

Reticular Core

Hippocampus

1. The Brain Stem

The brain stem, part of the "primitive brain," is an extension of the spinal cord. The brain stem performs four key functions.

• *A crossroads*, it receives sensory messages, particularly from skin and muscles in the head and neck, and relays this information to the cerebrum. In turn, the cerebrum sends out messages for motor coordination.

• *A switching gate*, it is the location where sensations from the left side of the body cross over to the right cerebral hemisphere, and vice versa. It is here that outgoing responses from the left hemisphere instruct the right side of the body what to do, and vice versa.

• *A clearinghouse*, it processes vestibular sensations necessary for hearing, maintaining our balance, seeing moving objects, and focusing our attention on one thing or another.

• *A regulator*, it processes sensations from internal organs and controls breathing, heartbeat, and digestion. It is the seat of the reticular core, a neuronal network that exchanges data with the vestibular system to guide our sense of timing for waking up, falling asleep, getting excited, and calming down.

2. The Cerebellum

Another part of the primitive brain is the cerebellum (Latin for "little brain"). Processing proprioceptive and vestibular sensations, it coordinates muscle tone, balance, and all our body movements. It controls fine motor skills, especially repetitive movements, such as touch-typing and practicing scales. It lets us move easily, precisely, and with good timing. An Olympic diver has a finely tuned cerebellum that allows him to execute a seemingly effortless dive.

3. *The Diencephalon*

The diencephalon (Greek for "divided brain"), sometimes called the "tweenbrain," nestles in the center of the brain. A part of the limbic system, the diencephalon is associated with several important structures.

The basal ganglia are clusters of nerves that coordinate vestibular sensations necessary for balance and voluntary movement. The basal ganglia relay messages among the inner ear, the cerebellum, and the cerebrum.

The hippocampus (Greek for "sea horse," which it resembles) compares old and new stimuli. If it remembers a sensation, like the feel of comfortable shoes, it sends out inhibitory neurons to tell the cortex not to get aroused. If the sensation is new, like too-tight boots, it alerts the cortex with excitatory neurons.

The amygdala (Greek for "almond") connects impulses from the olfactory system and the cortex. It processes emotional memories, such as the smell of an old boyfriend's cologne, and influences emotional behavior, especially anger.

The hypothalamus controls the autonomic nervous system, regulating temperature, water metabolism, reproduction, hunger and thirst, and our state of alertness. It also has centers for emotions: anger, fear, pain, and pleasure.

The thalamus is the key relay station for processing all sensory data except smell. "Thalamus" means "couch" in Greek; it is where the cerebral hemispheres sit. Most sensations pass through it en route to our great gift, the cerebrum.

4. The Cerebrum

The most recently developed layer of the triune brain is the cerebrum (Latin for "brain"). Its wrinkled surface is the cerebral cortex (Latin for "bark"), often referred to as the neocortex because it is new, in evolutionary terms. The cerebrum is composed of two cerebral hemispheres.

Why do we need two hemispheres? One theory is that the right and left hemispheres developed when early humanoids lived in trees and learned to use one hand independently from the other. This was a useful survival skill: one hand could gather fruit while the other clung to a branch. Asymmetric use of the hands and asymmetric hemispheres in the brain developed together in a process called lateralization (from Latin for "side").

With lateralization came specialization. Specialization describes the different jobs of the two hemispheres. With discrete duties, the right and left hemispheres must work together for us to function at a high level.

In general, the left hemisphere is the cognitive side. It directs analytical, logical, and verbal tasks, such as doing math and using language. It controls the right side of the body, which is usually the action-oriented side.

In general, the right hemisphere is the sensory, intuitive side. It directs nonverbal activities, such as recognizing faces, visualizing the shape of a pyramid, and responding to music. It controls the left side of the body.

The corpus callosum (Latin for "hard-skinned body"), a bundle of billions of nerve fibers, connects the hemispheres. This neural highway carries messages back and forth, and integrates the memories, perceptions, and responses that each hemisphere processes separately. Thus, our right hemisphere creates an original thought or tune, and our left lets us write it down. Our right and left eyes look at someone and see a whole person, not two separate halves. Our right hand knows what our left hand is doing.

Four Major Cortical Lobes

Each hemisphere has its own set of four major cortical lobes. Each lobe has a right side and a left side, both of which must work together, relaying neural messages back and forth, in order for the complex task of specialization to occur. The lobes have many administrative duties.

The occipital lobes are for vision. They begin to process visual images before sending them to the parietal and temporal lobes for further interpretation.

The parietal lobes are for body sense. They process proprioceptive messages, so we sense the position of our body in space, and tactile messages such as pain, temperature, and touch discrimination. These lobes interact with

The Left Hemisphere, Showing the Cortical Lobes, Sensory Cortex, and Motor Cortex

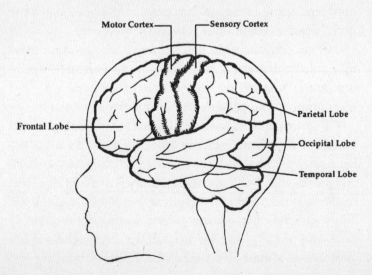

other brain parts to give the "whole picture." For instance, they receive visual messages from the occipital lobes and integrate them with auditory and tactile messages, thus aiding vision and spatial awareness.

The temporal lobes are for hearing, for interpreting music and language, for refining vestibular sensations, and for memory.

The frontal lobes are for executive thinking. They have a motor area for organizing voluntary body movement, and a prefrontal area concerned with aspects of personality—speech, reasoning, remembering, self-control, problem solving, and planning ahead.

The Sensory Cortex and the Motor Cortex

Lying on the top are strips called the sensory cortex and motor cortex. The sensory cortex receives tactile and proprioceptive sensations from the body. The motor cortex sends messages through peripheral nerves to the muscles.

In the early twentieth century, a Canadian neurosurgeon, Wilder Penfield, studied these cortical areas to learn about neural functions. The "maps" below, based on his research, seem comically out of proportion. Their purpose is serious, however: to illustrate the relative importance of our body parts.

Considerable portions of the sensory cortex are dedicated to receiving messages from the head and the hands—more than from the torso or arm, for instance. The reason is that body function is more important than body size; the head and hands have the most complex functions and thus produce the most sensations. Similarly large portions of the motor cortex are devoted to sending messages to direct the functions of the fingers, hands, tongue, and throat.

Penfield's Maps

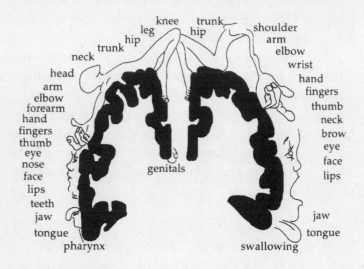

The Sensory Cortex   The Motor Cortex

Illustrating how the sensory cortex and motor cortex assign specific areas to different body parts, according to their relative importance.

<u>Cerebral Hemispheres Make Us Human</u>

Our cerebral hemispheres permit us to learn human skills, such as the ability to stand upright, thereby freeing our hands for manipulating and carrying objects. They enable us to speak, to reason, and to use symbols, thus enabling humankind to develop culture. They allow us to remember the past and to plan for the future, thereby increasing our chances for survival. They give us the mental tools not only to react but also to pro-act, that is, to anticipate what will happen next and to prepare an appropriate response. The locus of our finest movements and loftiest thoughts, they make us human.

Three Examples of How the Central Nervous System Processes Sensations

The Paper Cut

Working at the copy machine, you get a paper cut on your finger. Tactile receptors in your skin send the message via myelinated sensory neurons through your peripheral nervous system to your brain: up your arm, through your spinal cord to your brain stem to your thalamus to the sensory cortex. The sensory cortex analyzes the message and tells neurotransmitters to fire excitatory impulses.

First you become aware of the sense of light touch pressure; a millisecond later, you are conscious of the tissue-damaging pain. Meanwhile, motor neurons send impulses to your finger. You say "Ouch!" and pull your finger away from the paper.

The Fall from the Ladder

Perched on a ladder, you stretch to paint the ceiling. Your triune brain is totally involved: cerebrum, as you plan the next stroke; limbic system, as you smell the paint and remember your first painting experience with Dad; and reptilian complex, as you improve your "nest."

You tilt your chin up a little higher, and your inner ear sends messages to your brain stem about this change of neck and head position. The brain stem relays the vestibular information to your cerebellum, basal ganglia, thalamus, and cerebrum.

Suddenly you feel dizzy, because your head is far off-center. You lose your balance, drop the paint can, and tumble to the floor.

Your hypothalamus registers that you are hurt, afraid, and angry. It alerts your autonomic nervous system to increase your heart rate and to sweat.

You lie in a heap. You can't think about the spilling paint; when you feel endangered, your cerebrum shuts down and the reptilian brain takes over. Your instinct is self-preservation, so you wait until your reticular core calms you down. Regaining control, you realize that you are bruised but not broken. You arise and get busy.

The Car Door Maneuver

Your arms are full of packages and you must close the car door. Your parietal and occipital lobes exchange information to help you gauge your spatial relationship to the car and to plan and execute the maneuver.

Motor neurons send messages through your cerebellum and spinal cord to muscles in your right leg. Excitatory neurons activate muscles on the back of your thigh, instructing them to flex. Inhibitory neurons activate muscles on the front of your thigh, instructing them to extend. Motor planning enables you to bend your knee and lift your right leg.

Meanwhile, the opposite happens in your left leg, which straightens. You stabilize your body and keep your balance.

Proprioceptors in your legs tell your brain what's happening. You push your right foot against the car door and slam it shut.

THE SENSORY PROCESSING
MACHINE: SUMMARY

This discussion of the "sensory processing machine" demonstrates the crucial interrelationship of the central nervous system and the senses. It also shows that all parts of the central nervous system must communicate in order to integrate senses.

It is critical to understand that no matter how much advanced brain power a child has, intelligence alone is not sufficient for organized, daily functioning if the underlying senses are not integrated. Sensory integration depends on a sensory processing machine that is in good working order.

GLOSSARY

Academic learning: the development of conceptual skills, such as learning to read words and multiply numbers, and to apply what one learns today to what one learned yesterday.

Active touch: using one's hands, feet, and mouth to gather tactile information about objects in the environment.

Activity level: the degree of one's mental, emotional, or physical arousal. Activity level can be high, low, or in between.

Adaptive behavior: the ability to respond actively and purposefully to changing circumstances. An action or thought, an adaptive response promotes sensory integration as one meets new challenges and thus learns something new.

Allied health professional: a specialist trained in biological, physical, medical, and behavioral sciences, e.g., an occupational therapist.

Amygdala: the brain structure that processes smell sensations and produces memories with an emotional component.

Articulation: the production of speech sounds.

Attention deficit disorder (ADD): a neurological syndrome characterized by serious and persistent inattention and impulsivity. When constant, fidgety movement (hyperactivity) is an additional characteristic, the syndrome is called **Attention deficit disorder with hyperactivity (ADHD).**

Audition: the ability to receive and apprehend sounds; hearing.

Auditory integration training: a method of sound stimulation designed to improve a person's listening and communicative skills, learning capabilities, motor coordination, body awareness, and self-esteem.

Auditory perception: the ability to receive, identify, discriminate, understand, and respond to sounds.

Auditory-language processing skills: the abilities of listening and verbally communicating, acquired as one hears and perceives sounds and interacts with the environment.

Auditory discrimination—differentiating among sounds.

Auditory figure-ground—the ability to discriminate between sounds in the foreground and background, so that one can focus on a particular sound or voice without being distracted by other sounds.

Auditory sequencing—the ability to recall and repeat in logical order what has been heard.

Language—the organized use of words and phrases to interpret what one hears or reads and to communicate one's thoughts and feelings.

Autism: a lifelong neurological disability, usually appearing during the first three years of life, which severely impairs the person's sensory processing, communication, social interaction, and development.

Autonomic nervous system: one of the three components of the nervous system; controls automatic, unconscious bodily functions, such as breathing, sweating, shivering, and digesting.

Aversive response: a feeling of revulsion and repugnance toward a sensation, accompanied by an intense desire to avoid or turn away from it.

Axon: a long fiber extending from the cell body of a neuron that carries impulses away from it to other neurons.

Balzer-Martin Preschool Screening Program: an SI-based program for occupational therapists to use in school settings to identify risk factors for learning and behavior problems in three- to five-year-olds.

Basal ganglia: the cluster of nerves in the brain that helps coordinate and modulate body movement.

Behavior: whatever one does, through actions, feelings, perceptions, thoughts, words, or movements, in response to stimulation.

Bilateral coordination: the ability to use both sides of the body together in a smooth, simultaneous, and coordinated manner.

Bilateral integration: the neurological process of integrating sensations from both body sides; the foundation for bilateral coordination.

Binocularity (see **Eye-motor skills**).

Body awareness, body image, body percept, or **body scheme:** the mental picture of one's own body parts, where they are, how they interrelate, and how they move.

Body position: the placement of one's head, limbs, and trunk. Proprioception is the sense of body position.

Brain: the portion of the central nervous system that receives sensory messages; interprets, integrates, and organizes them; and sends out messages to produce motor, language, or emotional responses.

Brain-behavior: pertaining to the relationship of incoming sensory messages and outgoing motor, language, or emotional responses.

Brain stem: a primitive brain part, which regulates elementary sensorimotor processes, such as breathing, swallowing, becoming aroused, and calming down.

Central nervous system (CNS): the part of the nervous system, consisting of the brain and spinal cord, that coordinates the activity of the entire nervous system.

Cerebellum: the brain part that directs accurate body movements and balance, and that processes all other types of sensation.

Cerebral cortex: the outer layer of the cerebrum that coordinates higher nervous activity; **neocortex.**

Cerebral hemispheres: The two lateral halves of the cerebrum, which continue sensory processing begun at lower levels of the central nervous system, and which direct voluntary behavior.

Cerebrum: the front part of the brain, composed of two cerebral hemispheres, where detailed processing of sensations occurs; the "thinking brain."

Cortical lobes: the four sections of the cerebral hemispheres devoted to processing vision (occipital); touch and proprioception (parietal); memory and hearing (temporal); and speech, problem solving, voluntary movement, and emotions (frontal).

Deep pressure (see **Touch pressure**).

Defensive (or **protective**) **system:** the component of a sensory system that alerts one to real or potential danger and causes a self-protective response. This system is innate.

Developmental delay: the acquisition of specific skills after the expected age.

Diencephalon: the brain portion serving as a relay station for incoming sensory information and outgoing motor responses.

Discriminative system: the component of a sensory system that allows one to distinguish differences among stimuli. This system is not innate but develops with time and practice.

Distractibility: the inability to fix one's attention on any one stimulus.

Dyslexia: severe difficulty in using or understanding language while listening, speaking, reading, writing, or spelling.

Dyspraxia: difficulty in planning, sequencing, and carrying out unfamiliar actions in a skillful manner. Poor motor planning is a result of dyspraxia. (See **Praxis**.)

Early intervention: treatment or therapy to prevent problems or to improve a young child's health and development, such as eyeglasses or ear tubes for medical problems, and speech/language therapy or occupational therapy for developmental problems.

Emotional security: the sense that one is lovable and loved, that other people are trustworthy, and that one has the competence to function effectively in everyday life.

Evaluation: the use of assessment tools, such as tests and observations, to measure a person's developmental level and individual skills, or to identify a possible difficulty.

Expressive language: the spoken or written words and phrases that one produces to communicate feelings and thoughts to others.

Extension: the pull of the muscles away from the front of the body; straightening or stretching.

Eye-hand coordination: the efficient teamwork of the eyes and hands, necessary for activities such as playing with toys, dressing, and writing.

Eye-motor skills: movements of muscles in the eyes; **ocular-motor skills.**

Binocularity (binocular vision; eye teaming)—forming a single visual image from two images that the eyes separately record.

Fixation—aiming one's eye at an object or shifting one's gaze from one object to another.

Focusing—accommodating one's vision smoothly between near and distant objects.

Tracking—following a moving object or a line of print with the eyes.

Facilitation: the neurological process that promotes connections between sensory intake and behavioral output.

Far senses: the senses of hearing, vision, taste, smell, and protective touch, which respond to external stimuli coming from the environment.

Fetal alcohol syndrome: a set of symptoms, including growth retardation, facial abnormalities, mental retardation and developmental delays, caused by the mother's chronic alcoholism during pregnancy.

Fight-or-flight response: the instinctive reaction to defend oneself from real or perceived danger by becoming aggressive or by withdrawing.

Fine motor: referring to movement of the small muscles in the fingers, toes, eyes, and tongue.

Flexion: movement of the muscles around a joint to pull a body part toward its front or center; bending.

Four Levels: the smooth, sequential development of sensory integration, from infancy through elementary school age.

Fragile X syndrome: a set of symptoms, including mental retardation, facial anomalies, and deficits in communicative, behavioral, social, and motor skills; caused by an abnormality of the X chromosome.

Grading of movement: the ability to flex and extend muscles according to how much pressure is necessary to exert; a function of proprioception.

Gravitational insecurity: extreme fear and anxiety that one will fall when one's head position changes. **Gravitational security** is the sense that one is stable on earth and not endangered by ordinary movements or changes in head position.

Gravity receptors: organs in the inner ear that respond to changes in gravitational pull.

Gross motor: referring to movement of large muscles in the arms, legs, and trunk.

Gustatory sense: the sense of perceiving flavor; taste.

Habituation: the neurological process of tuning out familiar sensations.

Hand preference: right- or lefthandedness, which becomes established in a child as lateralization of the cerebral hemispheres develops.

Hidden senses (see **Near senses**).

Hippocampus: the brain structure that compares familiar and novel sensory stimuli and is involved with memory.

Hyperactivity: excessive mobility, motor function, or activity, such as fingertapping, jumping from one's seat, or constantly moving some part of the body; "fidgetiness."

Hypersensitivity (also **Hyper-reactivity** or **Hyper-responsiveness**): oversensitivity to sensory stimuli, characterized by a tendency to be either fearful and cautious, or negative and defiant.

Hyposensitivity (also **Hyporeactivity** or **Hyporesponsiveness**): undersensitivity to sensory stimuli, characterized by a tendency either to crave intense sensations or to withdraw and be difficult to engage.

Hypothalamus: the brain structure that regulates unconscious bodily processes such as body temperature and metabolic functions.

Increased tolerance for movement: under-reactivity to typical amounts of movement stimulation; often characterized by craving for intense movement experiences such as rocking and spinning.

IDEA: the Individuals with Disabilities Education Act, P.L. 99–457, and amendments. This legislation requires school districts to provide occupational therapy as a related service to children who need it in order to benefit from education.

IEP: Individualized Education Program, a legal document specifying the needs of a child identified as having a disability and providing for special education and related services.

Inhibition: the useful neurological process that reduces unnecessary synaptic connections and checks one's overreaction to sensations.

Inner drive: every person's self-motivation to participate actively in experiences that promote sensory integration.

Inner ear: the organ that receives sensations of the pull of gravity and of changes in balance and head position.

Integration: the combination of many parts into a unified, harmonious whole.

Interoception: the near sense involving both the conscious awareness and the unconscious regulation of bodily processes of the heart, liver, stomach, and other internal organs.

Intolerance to movement: overreactivity to moving or being moved rapidly, often characterized by extreme distress when spinning or by avoidance of movement through space.

Kinesthesia: the conscious awareness of joint position and body movement in space, such as knowing where to place one's feet when climbing stairs, without visual cues.

Lateralization: the process of establishing preference of one side of the brain for directing skilled motor function on the opposite side of the body, while the opposite side is used for stabilization. Lateralization is necessary for establishing hand preference and crossing the body midline.

Learned helplessness: the tendency to depend on others for guidance and decisions, to lack self-help skills, and to be a passive learner; often related to poor self-esteem.

Learning disability: an identified difficulty with reading, writing, spelling, computing, and communicating. (SI Dysfunction may cause significant learning problems that are often neither recognized nor identified as learning disabilities.)

Light touch (see **Touch pressure**).

Limbic system: the section of the brain that processes messages from all the senses and is involved primarily with one's emotions and inner drive; the "seat of emotions"; the "smell brain."

Linear movement: a motion in which one moves in a line, from front to back, side to side, or up and down.

Low tone (see **Muscle tone**).

Mental retardation: significantly subaverage intellectual functioning and impairments in adaptive behavior; caused by injury, disease, or abnormality before age eighteen.

Midline: a median line dividing the two halves of the body. **Crossing the midline** is the ability to use one side or part of the body (hand, foot, or eye) in the space of the other side or part.

Modulation: the brain's regulation of its own activity.

Motor control: the ability to regulate and monitor the motions of one's muscles for coordinated movement.

Motor coordination: the ability of several muscles or muscle groups to work together harmoniously to perform movements.

Motor cortex: the portion of the cerebrum that sends out messages to direct the movement and coordination of muscles; **motor strip**.

Motor learning: the process of mastering simple movement skills essential for developing more complex movement skills.

Motor planning: the ability to conceive of, organize, sequence, and carry out an unfamiliar and complex body movement in a coordinated manner; a piece of **praxis.**

Muscle tone: the degree of tension normally present when one's muscles are relaxed, or in a resting state.

Low tone is the lack of supportive muscle tone, usually with increased mobility at the joints; the person with low tone seems "loose and floppy."

Myelination: the gradual insulation of a neural axon with a fatty substance called myelin; a process that protects the axon and accelerates synaptic connections.

Near senses: internal senses that regulate bodily functions, such as heart rate, hunger, and arousal. Among the near senses are the tactile, vestibular, and proprioceptive senses, which are subconscious, which one cannot control, and which are the primary building blocks of sensory integration. Also called the **hidden senses**.

Neocortex (see **Cerebral cortex**).

Neurology: the science of the nerves and the nervous system. A **neurologist** is a physician who diagnoses and treats diseases of the brain and central nervous system.

Neuromuscular: relating to the relationship of nerves and muscles.

Neuron: the nerve cell, which is the functional and structural unit of the nervous system and the fundamental building block of the brain. **Sensory neurons** receive messages from receptors in the eyes, ears, skin, muscles, joints, and organs; and **motor neurons** send out messages to the body for appropriate responses.

Occupational therapy (O.T.): a health profession that helps people improve the functioning of their nervous system in order to develop skills leading to independence in personal, social, academic, and vocational pursuits. An **occupational therapist** (also **O.T.**) is an allied health professional trained in the biological, physical, medical, and behavioral sciences, including

neurology, anatomy, development, kinesiology, orthopedics, psychiatry, and psychology.

Ocular-motor (see **Eye-motor skills**).

Olfactory sense: the far sense that perceives odor; smell.

Optometrist: a specialist who examines eyes, prescribes
lenses, and provides vision therapy to prevent or eliminate visual problems and enhance a person's visual
performance.

Oscillation: up-and-down or to-and-fro linear movement, such as swinging, bouncing, and jumping.

Passive movement: the act of being moved by something or someone.

Passive touch: the act of being touched by something or
someone without initiating it.

Peripheral nervous system: one of the three components of the nervous system. Through the spinal cord,
peripheral nerves in one's skin, eyes, ears, muscles, and
organs send sensory impulses to the brain and receive
motor impulses from the brain.

Pervasive developmental disorder: severe, overall
impairment in the ability to regulate sensory experiences, affecting the child's affect and behavior, interaction with others, and communication skills; similar to,
but milder than, **autism**.

Physical therapy: a health profession devoted to improving one's physical abilities through activities that
strengthen muscular control and motor coordination.

Plasticity: the ability of the brain to change or to be
changed as a result of activity, especially as one
responds to sensations.

Postural background adjustments: automatic movements in one's trunk and limbs, allowing a person to use
only the muscles necessary for a particular motion.

Postural stability: the feeling of security and self-confidence when moving in space, based on one's body awareness. SI Dysfunction may cause **postural insecurity**, the feeling that one's body is not stable.

Praxis: the ability to interact successfully with the physical environment; to plan, organize, and carry out a sequence of unfamiliar actions; and to do what one needs and wants to do. **Praxis** (Greek for "doing, action, practice") is a broad term denoting voluntary and coordinated action. **Motor planning** is often used as a synonym.

Prefrontal cortex: the cortical lobe in the cerebral hemispheres that coordinates speech, reasoning, remembering, problem solving, self-control, and planning ahead.

Proprioception/Proprioceptive sense: the unconscious awareness of sensations coming from one's joints, muscles, tendons, and ligaments; the "position sense."

Protective system (see **Defensive system**).

Psychotherapy: treatment by psychological means of mental, emotional, or behavior problems.

Receptive language: the ability to understand how words express ideas and feelings; language that one takes in by listening and reading.

Receptors: special cells, located throughout one's body, that receive specific sensory messages and send them for processing to the central nervous system.

Reflex: an automatic, innate response to sensory stimulation.

Reptilian brain: in evolutionary terms, the oldest part of the brain, controlling reflexive, instinctive behavior; also called **R-complex** or **reptilian complex**; the "primitive brain."

Reticular core: a network of neurons in the brain stem that receives impulses from every sensory system and that is the center for arousal and for calming down.

Rotary movement: turning or spinning in circles.

Screening: a quick, informal procedure for the early identification of children's health or developmental problems.

Self-help skills: competence in taking care of one's personal needs, such as bathing, dressing, eating, grooming, and studying.

Self-regulation: the ability to control one's activity level and state of alertness, as well as one's emotional, mental, or physical responses to sensations; self-organization.

Self-therapy: active, voluntary participation in experiences that promote self-regulation, such as spinning in circles to stimulate one's vestibular system.

Sensorimotor: pertaining to the brain-behavior process of taking in sensory messages and reacting with a physical response.

Sensory cortex: the portion of the cerebrum that receives sensations from the body; **sensory strip**.

Sensory defensiveness: the tendency to have a high level of sensitivity to harmless sensations.

Sensory diet: the multisensory experiences that one normally seeks on a daily basis to satisfy one's sensory appetite; a planned and scheduled activity program that an occupational therapist develops to help a person become more self-regulated.

Sensory integration (SI): the normal neurological process of taking in information from one's body and environment through the senses, of organizing and unifying this information, and of using it to plan and execute adaptive responses to different challenges in order to learn and function smoothly in daily life.

Sensory Integration Dysfunction (SI Dysfunction): the inefficient neurological processing of information received through the senses, causing problems with learning, development, and behavior. Also called **sensory integration disorder** and **sensory integrative dysfunction**.

Sensory integration theory: a concept based on neurology, research, and behavior that explains the brain-behavior relationship.

Sensory integration treatment: a technique of occupational therapy, which provides playful, meaningful activities that enhance an individual's sensory intake and lead to more adaptive functioning in daily life.

"Sensory processing machine": Dr. A. Jean Ayres's term for the brain.

Sequencing: putting movements, sounds, sights, objects, thoughts, letters, and numbers in consecutive order, according to time and space.

Sleep regulation problem: an irregular pattern of sleeping, such as difficulty falling asleep or sleeping through the night, or the need for an unusual amount of sleep.

Social skills: effective interaction and communication with others, necessary for developing and keeping friendships.

Somatosensory: referring to tactile-proprioceptive perception of touch sensations and body position; body-sensing.

Special education: individualized instruction for the child who has difficulty learning at school.

Specialization: the process whereby one part of the brain becomes most efficient at a particular function.

Speech: the physical actions of communicating a verbal message.

Speech-and-language therapy: treatment to help a person develop or improve articulation, communication skills, and oral-motor skills.

Spinal cord: the long, thick cord of nervous tissue that receives tactile and proprioceptive messages from skin, joints, and muscles, and that sends out motor messages for movement.

Splinter skill: an isolated ability that one develops with much effort, but that one cannot generalize for other purposes.

State: the degree of one's attentiveness, mood, or motor response to sensory stimulation.

Stimulus (pl., stimuli): something that activates a sensory receptor and produces a response.

Synapse: the junction of two neurons where an impulse is transmitted from one neuron to another.

Tactile defensiveness: the tendency to react negatively and emotionally to unexpected, light touch sensations.

Tactile discrimination: the awareness of touching or of being touched by something; the ability to distinguish differences in touch sensations.

Tactile perception: awareness of the physical attributes of an object, such as its size, shape, temperature, density, and texture.

Tactile-proprioceptive: referring to simultaneous sensations of touch and body position.

Tactile sense: the sensory system that receives sensations of pressure, vibration, movement, temperature and pain, primarily through receptors in the skin; the sense of **touch**.

Thalamus: the brain part that processes all sensations except smell.

Touch pressure: the tactile stimulus that causes receptors in the skin to respond. **Deep pressure**, such as a hug, activates receptors in the discriminative system. **Light touch**, such as a kiss, activates receptors in the protective system.

Triune brain: Paul MacLean's theory that the brain is composed of three systems (the reptilian complex, the limbic system, and the cerebrum).

Vestibular sense: the sensory system that responds to changes in head position and to body movement through space, and that coordinates movements of the eyes, head, and body. Receptors are in the inner ear.

Vestibular-proprioceptive: referring to simultaneous sensations of head and body position when one moves.

Vision: the process of identifying sights, understanding what the eyes see, and preparing for a response.

Vision therapy: treatment to help a person improve visual skills and to prevent learning-related visual problems; optometric visual training.

Visualization: the act of forming mental images of objects, people, or scenarios.

Visual-motor: referring to one's movements based on the perception of visual information.

Visual perception: the ability to perceive and interpret what the eyes see.

Visual-spatial processing skills: perceptions based on sensory information received through the eyes and body as one interacts with the environment and moves one's body through space.

Depth perception—the ability to see objects in three dimensions and to judge relative distances between objects, or between oneself and objects.

Directionality—the awareness of right/left, forward/back, and up/down, and the ability to move oneself in those directions.

Form constancy—recognition of a shape regardless of its size, position, or texture.

Position in space—awareness of the spatial orientation of letters, words, numbers, or drawings on a page, or of an object in the environment.

Spatial awareness—the perception of one's proximity to, or distance from, an object, as well as the perception of the relationship of one's body parts.

Visual discrimination—differentiating among symbols and forms, such as matching or separating colors, shapes, numbers, letters, and words.

Visual figure-ground—differentiation between objects in the foreground and in the background.

RESOURCES

The catalog companies, clinics, and organizations listed below provide a variety of services for children, parents, educators, occupational therapists, and professionals.

CATALOGS

Abilitations
One Sportime Way, Atlanta, GA 30340
Telephone: (770) 449-5700 or 1-800-850-8602
   Fax: 1-800-845-1535
Website: http://www.abilitations.com
   Sensorimotor equipment for development and restoration of physical and mental ability through movement.

Achievers Unlimited, Inc.
104 South Main Street, Suite 417, Fond du Lac, WI 54935
Telephone: (920) 924-9898 or 1-800-924-9897
   Fax: (920) 924-9885
E-mail: achieverkd@excel.net
Website: http://www.achieverswisconsin.com
   Activity kits and workbooks to improve children's motor and visual development.

Belle Curve Records, Inc.
P.O. Box 18387, Boulder, CO 80308
Telephone: (303) 546-6211 or 1-888-357-5867
   Fax: (303) 546-6360
Website: http://www.bellecurve.com
   Musical medicine for body, mind, and spirit. Workshops for parents and professionals. Audiotapes for children, including *Songames for Sensory Integration, Danceland,* and *The Alert Program.* Informational audiotapes: *Making Sense of Sensory Integration* and *Teachers Ask About Sensory Integration.*

Exceptional Parent Resource Guide
555 Kinderkamack Road, Oradell, NJ 07649-1517
Telephone: (201) 634-6550   Fax: (201) 634-6599
E-mail: vieprnt@concentric.net
Website: http://www.eparent.com

A guide to national organizations, associations, products, and services to support parenting your child or young adult with a disability or special healthcare needs. Published by *Exceptional Parent* magazine.

Kaplan Concepts for Exceptional Children
P.O. Box 609, 1310 Lewisville-Clemmons Road, Lewisville, NC 27023-0609
Customer service: 1-800-334-2014   Fax: 1-800-452-7526
E-mail: info@kaplanco.com
Website: http://kaplanco.com

Products for evaluation, motor skills, cognitive development, and self-help skills; adaptive equipment; and other resources.

OT Ideas, Inc.
124 Morris Turnpike, Randolph, NJ 07869
Telephone: (973) 895-3622   Fax: (973) 895-4204
E-mail: otideas@nac.net
Website: http://www.otideas.com

Therapeutic products, specializing in scissors, tools, and toys to develop hand coordination, for use in schools and clinics.

PDP Products & Professional Development Programs
14398 North 59th Street, Oak Park Heights, MN 55082
Telephone: (651) 439-8865   Fax: (651) 439-0421
E-mail: prodevprg@aol.com
Website: http://members.aol.com/prodevprg

Toys and equipment that promote sensory processing, postural control, attention, self-regulation, and skills. Materials for working with clients with developmental and neurobehavioral problems. Workshops and continuing education seminars.

Playful Puppets, Inc.
9002 Stoneleigh Court, Fairfax, VA 22031
Telephone: (703) 280-5070   Fax: (703) 280-0918
E-mail: fann@tidalwave.net
Website: http://www.playfulpuppets.com

Puppets That Swallow, useful for therapeutic and educational purposes, including feeding, oral-motor, and sensorimotor activities, speech and language activities, and signing.

Pocket Full of Therapy, Inc.
P.O. Box 174, Morganville, NJ 07751
Telephone and Fax: (732) 441-0404, or 1-800-PFOT-124
E-mail: pfot@pfot.com
Website: http://www.pfot.com
    Therapeutic, fun materials and toys for therapists, teachers, and
parents to use to motivate children.

Rifton Equipment
P.O. Box 901, Route 213, Rifton, NY 12471
Telephone: 1-800-777-4244   Fax: 1-800-336-5948
    Equipment for mobility, standing, sitting, play, and hygiene.

Sammons Preston
An AbilityOne Company
P.O. Box 5071, Bolingbrook, IL 60440-5071
Telephone: 1-800-323-5547 (Canada: 800-665-9200)
    Fax: 1-800-547-4333
E-mail: sp@sammonspreston.com
Website: http://www.sammonspreston.com
    Pediatric therapeutic products (*Tumble Forms*) for bathing, feeding
and dressing, positioning, mobility, motor development, and sensory
integration, to use in homes, schools, or clinics.

Sensory Comfort
Jeremiah Hart House, The Hill, Portsmouth, NH 03801
Telephone: (603) 436-8797 or 1-888-436-2622
    Fax: (603) 436-8422
E-mail: ja@sensorycomfort.com
Website: http://www.sensorycomfort.com
    Books, cassettes, videos, school and household products, toys, "fid-
gets," clothing—and seamless socks—to make life more comfortable
for children and adults with sensory processing differences.

Southpaw Enterprises
P.O. Box 1047, Dayton, OH 45401
Telephone: 1-800-228-1698   Fax: (937) 252-8502
E-mail: therapy@erinet.com
Website: http://www.southpawenterprises.com
    Sensory integration and developmental products, including swings,
bolsters, weighted vests, and inflatable equipment, for therapeutic pro-
fessionals to use with children with special needs.

Therapro
225 Arlington, Framingham, MA 01702
Telephone: 1-800-257-5376   Fax: 1-888-860-6254
E-mail: karenc and/or paulw@theraproducts.com
Website: http://www.theraproducts.com

Therapeutic equipment and toys, including unique kits and samplers for developing fine motor, visual motor, and oral motor skills.

Therapy Skill Builders
555 Academic Court, San Antonio, TX 78204-2498
Telephone: (210) 299-1061 or 1-800-211-8378
  Fax: (210) 949-4452
Website: http://www.hbtpc.com
  Complete line of resources for the occupational therapist, ranging from some of the most widely used assessments to innovative therapy products.

TherapyWorks, Inc.
4901 Butte Place NW, Albuquerque, NM 87120
Telephone: (505) 897-3478   Fax: (505) 899-4071
Website: http://www.alertprogram.com
  Training, publications, and products related to *How Does Your Engine Run? The Alert Program for Self-Regulation.* Products include leader's guide for professionals, introductory booklet for parents and teachers, and audiotape with songs for children having SI and attention challenges.

Clinics

The Abilities Center, Inc.
Therapeutic Center for Children and Adults
5600 West Maple Road, Suite A-100, West Bloomfield, MI 48322
Telephone: (248) 855-0030   Fax: (248) 737-9620
E-mail: actherapy@aol.com
Website: www.abilitiescenter.com
  Therapeutic center for children and adults, providing occupational, physical, and speech-language therapy, with specialties in sensory integration, therapeutic listening, and neurodevelopmental treatment. Newsletter, educational conferences, and therapeutic products for use in homes, schools, and clinics.

Children's Center for Neurodevelopmental Studies, Inc.
5430 West Glenn Drive, Glendale, AZ 85301-2628
Telephone: (602) 915-0345   Fax: (602) 937-5425
  Education, SI therapy, speech, and music for children with developmental delays. Conferences, books, research articles, and videotapes for parents.

Developmental Therapy Associates, Inc.
3514 University Drive, Office #8, Durham, NC 27707
Telephone: (919) 493-7002
E-mail: dtaot@aol.com
Website: http://www.developmentaltherapy.com

O.T. and speech therapy using a sensory integrative approach. Auditory integration therapy. Programs to help at-risk babies and to improve social skills, fine motor skills, and bike-riding. Workshops, lectures, and newsletter.

Henry Occupational Therapy Services, Inc. (HOTS)
P.O. Box 145, Youngtown, AZ 85363-0145
Telephone: (602) 938-5813 or 1-888-371-1204
    Fax: (602) 504-8788
E-mail: hotsinc@amug.org
Website: http://www.gtcs.com/sponsors/henry
    Workshops for parents, educators, and professionals; consultations and training; and two videos: *Tools for Teachers* and *Tools for Students,* to help regular education teachers incorporate O.T. strategies into the classroom. Also a handbook to facilitate self-regulation, *Tool Chest for Teachers, Parents & Students.*

Lynne C. Israel and Associates, Inc.
1700 Kalaroma Road, NW, Suite 106, Washington, DC 20009
Telephone: (292) 986-9896   Fax: (202) 986-9893
E-mail: lciotassoc.@aol.com
    Inquiries welcomed to discuss your particular needs. OT and PT evaluation and treatment for infants through maturity. Experts in NDT, SI, and early intervention. Training for parents, educators, and professionals. Handwriting, social skills groups, and summer camp offered. International clientele. French and Spanish spoken.

Christy Kennedy, OTR/L
234 East Parkwood Road, Decatur, GA 30030-2813
Telephone: (404) 378-5734   Fax: (404) 377-7878
E-mail: ckennedy@mindspring.com
    SI services, including Samonas Sound Therapy. Sponsor of Atlanta Pediatric Conferences on topics related to sensory integration, for professionals, parents, and teachers.

Occupational Therapy Associates (OTA) - Watertown, P.C.
124 Watertown Street, Watertown, MA 02472
Telephone: (617) 923-4410   Fax: (617) 923-0468
E-mail: otawater@aol.com
    Boston area clinic providing evaluation of and treatment for children and adults with SI Dysfunction. Consultation and mentoring; teaching and research.

Pediatric Therapy Network
1815 West 213th Street, Suite 140, Torrance, CA 90501
Telephone: (310) 328-0276   Fax: (310) 328-7058
    Sensory integration services.

SABB Development Center
6509 Democracy Boulevard, Bethesda, MD 20817
Telephone: (301) 897-8484   Fax: (301) 897-8486
E-mail: drstrab@erols.com
Websites: http://www.lifeEnrichment.com/vision.htm and
   www.visionhelp.com
   Integration of O.T. and optometric vision therapy in the same office.
Information for parents and teachers about developmental delays and
the benefits of an integrative approach to therapy. Referrals to therapists
in your area.

Sound Listening and Learning Center
2701 East Camelback Road, Suite 205, Phoenix, AZ 85016
Telephone: (602) 381-0086   Fax: (602) 957-6741
E-mail: info@soundlistening.com
Website: http://www.soundlistening.com
   Auditory integration training, using the Tomatis Method, a program of sound stimulation and audio-vocal practice with patented
equipment. Consultations, information, and referrals to Tomatis centers in your area.

The Spectrum Center
4715 Cordell Avenue, Bethesda, MD 20814
Telephone: (301) 657-0988   Fax: (301) 657-0989
E-mail: spectrum@his.com
Website: http://www.tomatis.net
   Auditory integration training, using the Tomatis Method, for children with varying disabilities, including autism, developmental delays,
learning disabilities, and SI Dysfunction. Informational brochures and
consultations.

ORGANIZATIONS

Administration on Developmental Disabilities (ADD)
Administration for Children and Families
U.S. Department of Health and Human Services
370 L'Enfant Promenade, SW, Washington, DC 20447
Telephone: (202) 690-6590   Fax: (202) 690-6904
E-mail: add@acf.dhhs.gov
Website: http://www.acf.dhhs.gov/programs/add
   Referrals to federally funded agencies that provide developmental
disabilities programs addressing issues such as prevention, diagnosis,
early intervention, therapy, and education.

American Occupational Therapy Association, Inc. (AOTA)
Location: 4720 Montgomery Lane, Bethesda, MD
Mailing Address: P.O. Box 31220, Bethesda, MD 20824-1220
Telephone: (301) 652-AOTA or 1-800-668-8255
   Fax: (301) 652-7711
Website, with E-mail addresses: http://www.aota.org

  Books, videos, continuing education workshops, and other resources
for occupational therapists, as well as products for parents, such as a
handbook, *Sensory Integration: A Foundation for Development.*

American Speech-Language-Hearing Association (ASHA)
10801 Rockville Pike, Rockville, MD 20852
Telephone: (301) 897-5700 or 1-800-638-TALK
   Fax: (301) 571-0457
E-mail: irc@asha.org

  Free brochures and other printed materials; and referrals to audiolo-
gists and speech-language therapists in your area.

The Council for Exceptional Children (CEC)
1920 Association Drive, Reston, VA 22091-1589
Telephone: 1-888-CEC-SPED   Fax: (703) 264-9494
E-mail: service@cec.sped.org
Website: http://www.cec.sped.org/ericec.htm

  Free dissemination, through a federally funded clearinghouse, of
publications and information on disabilities and/or gifted education.

Developmental Delay Resources (DDR)
4401 East-West Highway, Suite 207, Bethesda, MD 20814
Telephone: (301) 652-2263   Fax: (301) 652-9133
E-mail: devdelay@mindspring.com
Website: http://www.devdelay.org

  Information, conferences, and a quarterly newsletter, *New Develop-
ments,* to educate parents and professionals about healthy options for
treating the whole child. Extensive list of hard-to-find books and materials on SI, vision, immunizations, health, and nutrition.

Learning Disabilities Association (LDA)
4156 Library Road, Pittsburgh, PA 15234-1349
Telephone: (412) 341-1515   Fax: (412) 344-0224
E-mail: ldanatl@usaor.net
Website: http://www.ldanatl.org

  National membership organization of professionals and parents that
provides a bibliography of resources and free listings of state learning
disabilities associations.

The Mozart Effect Resource Center
3526 Washington Avenue, Saint Louis, MO 63103-1019
Telephone: (314) 531-4756 or 1-800-721-2177   Fax: (314) 531-8384
E-mail: music@mozarteffect.com
Website: http://www.mozarteffect.com
   Workshops and programs about the effect of music on learning, health, and behavior—at home, school, or in therapy. Also, *The Mozart Effect* recordings, and books about auditory processing and auditory integration training.

National Information Center for Children and Youth with Disabilities
   (NICHCY)
P.O. Box 1492, Washington, DC 20013-1492
Telephone: (202) 884-8200 V/TTY or 1-800-695-0285 V/TTY
   Fax: (202) 884-8441
E-mail: nichcy@aed.org
Website: http://www.nichcy.org
   Information and referral clearinghouse for families, professionals, educators, and others working with children with disability-related issues. Information includes fact sheets on IDEA and the legal aspects of education; referrals include resource lists of supportive organizations in your state.

National Institute of Child Health and Human Development
   (NICHD)
Center for Research for Mothers and Children
Child Development and Behavior Branch, Executive Building, Room
   4B05
6100 Executive Boulevard, MSC 7510, Bethesda, MD 20892-7510
Telephone: (301) 496-9849   Fax: (301) 480-7773
Website: http://www.nih.gov/nichd/
   Free copies of latest research on learning disabilities.

Optometric Extension Program Foundation, Inc.
1921 East Carnegie Avenue, Suite 3-L, Santa Ana, CA 92705-5510
Telephone: (949) 250-8070   Fax: (949) 250-8157
E-mail: smc.oep@worldnet.att.net
Website: http://www.oep.org
   Books, pamphlets, and educational materials on vision development, vision therapy, and research in vision.

Parents Active for Vision Education (P.A.V.E.)
National Headquarters
4135 54th Place, San Diego, CA 92105-2303

Telephone: (619) 287-0081 or 1-800-PAVE-988
    Fax: (619) 287-0084
E-mail: vision@pave-eye.com
Website: http://www.electriciti.com/vision
    Information and support for parents, educators, and other profes-
sionals about the relationship between vision and academic achieve-
ment.

Parent Educational Advocacy Training Center (PEATC)
6320 Augusta Drive, Springfield, VA 22150
Telephone: (703) 923-0010 (voice), (703) 569-6200 (Latino Outreach),
    or 1-800-869-6782 (toll-free, VA only)   Fax: (703) 923-0030
E-mail: partners@peatc.org
Website: http://www.peatc.org
    Information, support, workshops, books and publications, the
newsletter *The PEATC Press,* and *Understanding Special Education:
The Video,* to assist parents, educators, and other professionals in comprehending the legal rights of children with disabilities. Also, referrals
to other federally funded parent centers in your area.

The Parent Network for the Post-Institutionalized Child (PNPIC)
P. O. Box 613, Meadow Lands, PA 15347
Telephone (voice mail only): (412) 222-1776
    Fax: (770) 979-3140
E-mail: pnpic@aol.com
Website: http://www.pnpic.org
    Quarterly newsletter, *The Post,* and support for adoptive families of
children primarily from Eastern Bloc orphanages.

Pediatric Therapy Network
1815 West 213th Street, Suite 140, Torrance, CA 90501
Telephone: (310) 328-0276   Fax: (310) 328-7058
Website: http://www.pediatric therapy.com
    Individual occupational, physical, and speech-language therapy and
assessments. Group programs such as Leaps and Bounds, for early
intervention, and Camp Escapades, a summer day camp. Clinical training site for USC's graduate-level course in SI theory and treatment.

Saint Columba's Nursery School
4201 Albemarle Street, NW, Washington, DC 20016
Telephone: (202) 363-4121   Fax: (202) 686-9774
    Manual for the Balzer-Martin Preschool Screening (BAPS), an SI-
based program for occupational therapists to use in school settings to
identify risk factors for learning and behavior problems in three- to
five-year-olds.

Sensory Integration International (SII)/The Ayres Clinic
1602 Cabrillo Avenue, Torrance, CA 90501-2817
Telephone: (310) 320-2335   Fax: (310) 320-9982
E-mail: sensoryint@earthlink.net
Website: http://home.earthlink.net/~sensoryint/
   SII membership, publications, educational courses, SIPT Certified Therapist Lists, and resources to help educate people regarding SI and several other dysfunctions.

ZERO to THREE
734 15th Street, NW, Suite 1000, Washington, DC 20005-1013
Telephone: (202) 638-1144; for customer service:
   1-800-899-4301   Fax: (202) 638-0851
E-mail: 0to3@zerotothree.org
Website: http://www.zerotothree.org
   Services, conferences, and publications to improve the healthy physical, cognitive, emotional, and social development of infants, toddlers, and families.

INTERNET RESOURCES

The World Wide Web has countless sites with valuable information. In addition to the sites listed above, these may also be helpful:

http://www.and.ca/sensory/sendys.html
http://www.bv.net/~john/bethsot1.html
http://www.autism.org/si.html
http://www.doverehab.com
http://www.fragilex.org
http://www.mindspring.com/%7emariep/si/sensory.
   integration.html
http://www.mondenet.com/~chrisck/sensory.html
http://www.out-of-sync-child.com
http://www.sinetwork.org
http://www.tsbvi.edu/outreach/seehear/fall97/sensory.htm

RECOMMENDED READING

Becoming educated about sensory integration and related topics will help you help your child. Here is a list of books that will help you see the big picture. (This list has been updated since the publication in March 1998 of *The Out-of-Sync Child*.)

Some of these may be hard to find in bookstores, but many are available through Developmental Delay Resources, which maintains an excellent booklist. If you see "(DDR)" after the listing of a book you want, you may obtain it by contacting:

Developmental Delay Resources
4401 East West Highway, Suite 207
Bethesda, Maryland 20814
Tel: (301) 652-2263   Fax: (301) 652-9133
E-mail: devdelay.mindspring.com
Website: http://www.devdelay.org

ACTIVITIES TO STRENGTHEN SENSORY INTEGRATION

Bissell, Julie, M.A., O.T.R.; Jean Fisher, M.A., O.T.R.; Carol Owens, O.T.R.; & Patricia Polcyn, O.T.R. (1988). *Sensory Motor Handbook: A Guide for Implementing and Modifying*

Activities in the Classroom. Torrance, CA: Sensory Integration International.

Hanson, Joanne, M.S., C.C.C.-S.L.P. (1998). *Progress with Puppets: Speech and Language Activities for Young Children.* Arlington, VA: Building Blocks Therapy. (DDR)

Henry, Diana, O.T.R., et al. *Tool Chest for Teachers, Parents & Students: A Handbook to Facilitate Self-Regulation* (accompanies two videos: *Tools for Teachers* and *Tools for Students*). Youngtown, AZ: Henry Occupational Therapy Services, 1-888-371-1204.

Kranowitz, Carol Stock, M.A. (1995). *101 Activities for Kids in Tight Spaces.* New York: St. Martin's Press. (DDR)

Krull, Sharron Werlin, and Norma Don (1986). *Play Power: Games and Activities for Young Children.* Concord, CA 94521: Play Power, 1365 St. Catherine Court.

Young, Susan B, O.T.R. (1988). *Movement Is Fun: A Preschool Movement Program.* Torrance, CA: Sensory Integration International.

Brain Development and Learning

Cherry, Clare, Douglas Godwin, & Jesse Staples (1989). *Is the Left Brain Always Right? A Guide to Whole Child Development.* Belmont, CA: David S. Lake Publishers.

Furth, Hans G., & Harry Wachs (1975). *Thinking Goes to School: Piaget's Theory in Practice.* New York: Oxford University Press.

Gardner, Howard (1993). *Frames of Mind: The Theory of Multiple Intelligences.* New York: Basic Books.

Goleman, Daniel (1995). *Emotional Intelligence.* New York: Bantam.

Hannaford, Carla, Ph.D. (1995). *Smart Moves: Why Learning Is Not All In Your Head.* Arlington, Virginia: Great Ocean Publishers. (DDR)

Healy, Jane M., Ph.D. (1998). *Failure to Connect: How Computers Affect Our Children's Minds—for Better and Worse.* New York: Simon & Schuster.

——— (1990). *Endangered Minds: Why Children Don't Think and What We Can Do About It.* New York: Simon & Schuster.

——— (1987). *Your Child's Growing Mind: A Guide to*

Learning and Brain Development from Birth to Adolescence.
New York: Doubleday.

Restak, Richard M., M.D. (1984). *The Brain.* New York:
Bantam.

NORMAL CHILD DEVELOPMENT

Ames, Louise Bates, Ph.D., & Frances L. Ilg, M.D. (1976).
Your Three-Year-Old: Friend or Enemy. New York: Delta.
———— (1976). *Your Four-Year-Old: Wild and Wonderful.* New
York: Delacorte.
———— (1979). *Your Five-Year-Old: Sunny and Serene.* New
York: Dell.

Brazelton, T. Berry, M.D. (1986). *Infants and Mothers:
Differences in Development.* New York: Delacorte.

Chess, Stella, M.D., & Alexander Thomas, M.D. (1989). *Know
Your Child: An Authoritative Guide for Today's Parents.* New
York: Basic Books.

Greenspan, Stanley I., M.D., & Nancy T. Greenspan (1985).
*First Feelings: Milestones in the Emotional Development of
Your Baby and Child from Birth to Age Four.* New York:
Viking Penguin.
———— & N. T. Greenspan (1989). *The Essential Partnership:
How Parents Can Meet the Emotional Challenges of Infancy
and Childhood.* New York: Viking Penguin.
———— with Jacqueline Salmon (1993). *Playground Politics:
Understanding the Emotional Life of Your School-Age Child.*
Reading, MA: Addison-Wesley.

UNDERSTANDING, RAISING, AND
EDUCATING THE OUT-OF-SYNC CHILD

Anderson, Winifred, Stephen Chitwood, & Diedre Hayden
(1997). *Negotiating the Special Educational Maze: A Guide
for Parents and Teachers* (3rd ed.). Bethesda, MD: Woodbine
House, 1-800-843-7323.

Armstrong, Thomas, Ph.D. (1995). *The Myth of the A.D.D.
Child: 50 Ways to Improve Your Child's Behavior and*

Attention Span Without Drugs, Labels, or Coercion. New York: Dutton. (DDR)

Callanan, Charles R. (1990). *Since Owen: A Parent-to-Parent Guide for Care of the Disabled Child.* Baltimore: Johns Hopkins University Press.

Greene, Ross W., Ph.D. (1998). *The Explosive Child: A New Approach for Understanding and Parenting Easily Frustrated, "Chronically Inflexible" Children.* New York: HarperCollins.

Greenspan, Stanley I., M.D. (1995). *The Challenging Child: Understanding, Raising, and Enjoying the Five "Difficult" Types of Children.* Reading, MA: Addison-Wesley.

————, and Serena Wieder, Ph.D., with Robin Simons (1998). *The Child with Special Needs: Encouraging Intellectual and Emotional Growth.* Reading, MA: Addison-Wesley.

Hallowell, Edward M., M.D., & John J. Ratey, M.D. (1994). *Driven to Distraction: Recognizing and Coping with Attention Deficit Disorder from Childhood through Adulthood.* New York: Simon & Schuster (Touchstone).

Kurcinka, Mary Sheedy, M.A. (1991). *Raising Your Spirited Child: A Guide for Parents Whose Child Is More Intense, Sensitive, Perceptive, Persistent, Energetic.* New York: Harper Perennial.

Levine, Melvin D., M.D. (1990). *Keeping A Head in School: A Student's Book about Learning Abilities and Learning Disorders.* Cambridge, MA: Educators Publishing Service, Inc.

Rosner, Jerome, Dr. (1993). *Helping Children Overcome Learning Difficulties.* New York: Walker & Co.

Silver, Larry B., M.D. (1993). *Dr. Larry Silver's Advice to Parents on Attention-Deficit Hyperactivity Disorder.* Washington, DC: American Psychiatric Press.

———— (1998). *The Misunderstood Child: Understanding and Coping with Your Child's Learning Disabilities* (3rd edition.). New York: Random House/Times Books.

Smith, Sally L. (1995). *No Easy Answers: The Learning Disabled Child at Home and at School.* New York: Bantam Books.

Stehli, Annabel, Ed. (1995). *Dancing in the Rain: Stories of Exceptional Progress by Parents of Children with Special Needs.* Westport, CT: Georgiana Organization. (DDR)

Turecki, Stanley, M.D., with Leslie Tonner (1989). *The Difficult Child*. New York: Bantam Books.

Vail, Priscilla L. (1989). *Smart Kids with School Problems: Things to Know and Ways to Help*. New York: Plume Books.

SENSORY INTEGRATION

A Parent's Guide to Understanding Sensory Integration (1991). Torrance, CA: Sensory Integration International. (DDR)

Ayres, A. Jean, Ph.D., O.T.R. (1979). *Sensory Integration and the Child*. Los Angeles: Western Psychological Services. (DDR)

Quirk, Norma J., M.S., O.T.R., & Marie E. DiMatties, M.S., O.T.R. (1990). *The Relationship of Learning Problems and Classroom Performance to Sensory Integration*. 131 Dumas Road, Cherry Hill, NJ 08003.

Sassé, Margaret (1990). *If Only We'd Known . . . Early Childhood—and Its Importance to Academic Learning*. Victoria, Australia: Toddler Kindy Gymbaroo Pty. Ltd., (03) 9899-1699. (DDR)

Trott, Maryann Colby, M.A., with Marci K. Laurel, M.A., C.C.C.-S.L.P., & Susan L. Windeck, M.S., O.T.R./L. (1993). *SenseAbilities: Understanding Sensory Integration*. Tucson: Therapy Skill Builders. (DDR)

Wilbarger, Patricia, M.Ed., O.T.R., F.A.O.T.A., & Julia Leigh Wilbarger, M.S., O.T.R. (1991). *Sensory Defensiveness in Children Aged 2-12: An Intervention Guide for Parents and Other Caretakers*. Santa Barbara, CA 93109: Avanti Educational Programs.

SPEECH, LANGUAGE, AND HEARING

deHirsch, Katrina (1984). *Language and the Developing Child*. Baltimore: The Orton Dyslexia Society.

Madaule, Paul (1994). *When Listening Comes Alive: A Guide to Effective Learning and Communication*. Norval, Ontario, Canada LOP 1KO: Moulin Publishing.

Tomatis, Alfred A., Dr. (1996). *The Ear and Language* (Ed.: Billie M. Thompson). Ontario, Canada: Moulin Publishing.

Available from Sound Listening and Learning Center, Inc., 2701 E. Camelback Road, Suite 205, Phoenix, AZ 85016.

Vail, Priscilla L. (1996). *"Words Fail Me": How Language Works and What Happens When It Doesn't.* Rosemont, NJ: Modern Learning Press.

VISION

Appelbaum, Stanley A., O.D. (1989). *Sensory Integration: Optometric and Occupational Therapy Perspectives.* Santa Ana, CA: Optometric Extension Program. (DDR)

Kavner, Richard S., O.D. (1985). *Your Child's Vision: A Parent's Guide to Seeing, Growing, and Developing.* New York: Simon & Schuster. (DDR)

Seiderman, Arthur S., O.D., & Steven E. Marcus, O.D. (1989). *20/20 Is Not Enough: The New World of Vision.* New York: Fawcett Crest. (DDR)

Selected Bibliography

Books

Ackerman, Diane (1990). *A Natural History of the Senses.* New York: Random House.

Ackerman, Sandra, for the Institute of Medicine, National Academy of Sciences (1992). *Discovering the Brain.* Washington, DC: National Academy Press.

Batshaw, Mark L., M.D., and Yvonne M. Perret, M.A., M.S.W., L.C.S.W. (1992). *Children with Disabilities: A Medical Primer* (3d. ed.). Baltimore: Paul H. Brookes.

Carey, Joseph, Ed., Society for Neuroscience (1993). *Brain Facts: A Primer on the Brain and Nervous System.* Woodlawn, Md.: Graphtech.

Fisher, Anne G., Sc.D., O.T.R., Elizabeth A. Murray, Sc.D., O.T.R., and Anita C. Bundy, Sc.D., O.T.R. (1991). *Sensory Integration: Theory and Practice.* Philadelphia: F. A. Davis.

Greenspan, Stanley I., M.D. (1989). *The Development of the Ego: Implications for Personality Theory, Psychopathology, and the Psychotherapeutic Process.* Madison, CT: International Universities Press.

——— Chair (1994). *Diagnostic Classification (of Mental Health and Developmental Disorders of Infancy and Early Childhood): 0–3.* Arlington, VA: Zero to Three, National Center for Clinical Infant Programs.

———— with Beryl Lieff Benderly (1997). *The Growth of the Mind and the Endangered Origins of Intelligence*. Reading, MA: Addison-Wesley.

Kittredge, Mary (1990). *The Senses*. (The Encyclopedia of Health: The Healthy Body. Dale C. Garell, M.D., general editor.) New York: Chelsea House.

MacLean, Paul D., Ph.D. (1973). *A Triune Concept of the Brain and Behavior*. Toronto, Canada: University of Toronto Press.

Noback, Charles R., Ph.D., and Robert J. Demarest (1972). *The Nervous System: Introduction and Review*. New York: McGraw-Hill.

Parker, Steve (1990). *The Brain and Nervous System*. New York: Franklin Watts.

Sagan, Carl, Ph.D. (1977). *The Dragons of Eden: Speculations on the Evolution of Human Intelligence*. New York: Random House.

Silverstein, Alvin, Dr., and Virginia and Alvin Silverstein (1994). *The Nervous System*. New York: Twenty-first Century Books.

Tomatis, Alfred A., Dr. (1991). *The Conscious Ear*. Rhinebeck, NY: Station Hill Press.

ARTICLES

Anzalone, Marie E., Sc.D., O.T.R./L. (October/November, 1993). "Sensory Contributions to Action: A Sensory Integrative Approach." *Zero to Three, 14*(2).

Ballinger, Beth, O.D., F.C.O.V.D. (Summer 1995). "Visual Influences in the Learning Process." *Sensory Integration Quarterly, XXIII*(1).

Brazelton, T. Berry, M.D. (1994). "Touchpoints: opportunities for preventing problems in the parent-child relationship." *Acta Paediatrica, suppl. 394*.

Cermak, Sharon, Ed.D., O.T.R./L., F.A.O.T.A. (Spring, 1994). "Romanian children demonstrate sensory defensiveness." *Attachments*.

Cool, Steven J., Ph.D. (Summer, 1995). "Does sensory integration work?" *Sensory Integration Quarterly, XXIII*(1).

DeGangi, Georgia, Ph.D., O.T.R. (1991). "Sensory, emotional, and attentional problems in regulatory disordered infants." Part 1: Assessment; Part 2: Treatment. *Infants and Young Children, 3*(1–19).

Fischbach, Gerald D., M.D. (1994). "Mind and Brain: A *Scientific American* Special Report."

Greenspan, Stanley I., M.D., and Serena Wieder, Ph.D. (April/May, 1997). "An integrated developmental approach to interventions for young children with severe difficulties in relating and communicating." *Zero to Three, 17*(5).

Healy, Jane M., Ph.D. (Spring, 1996). "Children's brains at work in the preschool and primary years." *Early Childhood Connections*.

Murphy, Lois Barclay, Ph.D., with Rachel Moon, M.D. (October/November 1993). "Sensory Experiences in Infancy." *Zero to Three, 14*(2).

Porges, Stephen W., Ph.D. (October/November 1993). "The Infant's Sixth Sense: Awareness and Regulation of Bodily Processes." *Zero to Three, 14*(2).

Sullivan, Therese, M.S., O.T.R. (December 1991). "Abstract of a Master's Thesis: Toward an Operational Definition of Gravitational Insecurity." *Sensory Integration Quarterly, XIX*(4). Torrance, CA: Sensory Integration International.

Williamson, G. Gordon, Ph.D., O.T.R., and Marie Anzalone, Sc.D., O.T.R. (April/May 1997). "Sensory integration: a key component of the evaluation and treatment of young children with severe difficulties in relating and communicating." *Zero to Three, 17*(5).

INDEX

About the Author

Carol Stock Kranowitz has been teaching music, movement, and drama to preschoolers since 1976. Over time, she has observed many out-of-sync children and began to study sensory integration theory in order to help identify their needs and steer them into early intervention.

In her workshops and writings, she explains to parents, educators, and other early childhood professionals how SI issues play out—and provides specific techniques for addressing dysfunction at home and school.

A graduate of Barnard College, she has an M.A. in Education & Human Development from The George Washington University. She and her husband have two sons and live in Bethesda, Maryland. She is also the author of *101 Activities for Kids in Tight Spaces* (St. Martin's Press).